THE COMPLETE

A**HOLE'S
GUIDE

TO HANDLING CHICKS

DAN INDANTE
AND
KARL MARKS

ST. MARTIN'S GRIFFIN 🐾 NEW YORK 〽

THE COMPLETE

A**HOLE'S GUIDE

TO HANDLING CHICKS

www.stmartins.com

Library of Congress Cataloging-in-Publication Data

Indante, Dan.
    The complete a**hole's guide to handling chicks / Dan Indante and Karl Marks.
      p.   cm.
    ISBN 0-312-31084-6
      1. Man-woman relationships. 2. Interpersonal relations.
    I. Title: Complete a**hole's guide to handling chicks. II. Marks, Karl.
    III. Title.
HQ801.M37135   2003
307—dc21   2002045213

10   9   8   7

CONTENTS

CHICKS,
WHAT THE FUCK?

So here you are, reading a book on how to become an asshole. Why is that? Chances are you're tired of being a "nice guy" while every chick on the planet walks all over you, spends your money, shatters your ego, and then leaves you with nothing but humiliation, depression, and a big bottle of Jergen's hand cream.

In this day and age, men are continuously flooded with how-to books, primers, and psychological treatises that supposedly give them insight into the female mind. Let's face it, they're all wrong! There's not a piece of advice in any of those supposedly respectable publications that gives you a real understanding of the sickness and disease that infects most women's heads.

Recognizing this absence of legitimate, reliable information, we felt the need to provide a low-cost solution to the eternal question: "How the hell did that asshole get *that* smoking hot chick?" It's a mystery that has confounded men throughout the years. No matter how many times you witness the event, it's still amazing to see the prick musician loudly berating his gorgeous model girlfriend as they walk down the street.

The fact is, nice guys finish last, and chicks like dicks. How many times have you been dumped by a girl who decided she wanted to get back together with the guy who used to cheat on her? We know that doesn't make sense to a logical and intelligent man like you, but, as you'll see, the chick mind operates with absolutely no rhyme or reason. Or, more simply put:

CHICKS ARE OUT OF THEIR FUCKIN' MINDS

If you don't believe in that basic theory, you're not ready to accept our advice, and in all likelihood you have a vagina. Accordingly, you should save this book for another time, because, right now, these words will simply be wasted on you. Once common sense kicks in and you accept this timeless truth, strap yourself down, grab a six-pack, and get ready for a trip through the highways and byways of sheer madness: the female brain.

That's right—we're going to take you deeper into the woman's psyche than you ever thought possible. Be forewarned, though. It will be more terrifying than bunking with Mike Tyson, more disgusting than going down on your own mother, and more disturbing than a hermaphrodite orgy. But in the end the journey will be worth it. For, once you become a fully indoctrinated asshole, you will be able to manipulate chicks' minds as if they were nothing more than Silly Putty.[1]

To reach the fugue state of complete, unadulterated, asshole nirvana will require much dedication. Many of the things we tell you will appear counterintuitive. For instance, to make a woman want you, you have to pretend that you don't want her at all? Does that make sense? In the sick, twisted mind of your average female, of course it does. The principles behind this and other apparent contradictions are not always

---

[1] We apologize to the manufacturers of Silly Putty. We mean no disrespect.

easy to understand, but fortunately for you, they're all right here in black and white.

You wanna know how to deal with your first sexual experience? We've got you covered. Trying to nail your receptionist? It couldn't be easier. How about handling a wife who's constantly hounding you for more cash? Yup, we've got that, too. It's all here for you to review, analyze, and apply to your own relationships.

If you're already an asshole, then welcome, brother! You're most likely knee-deep in trim, and as you read these pages, you're probably getting blown. However, that doesn't mean you won't need us down the line. There are literally thousands of chick confrontations that you will face during your lifetime, so you'll want to stay abreast of the subtle changes in rules and regulations. Consider us your free roadside assistance, as you encounter the blown-out tires and overheated radiators of the female mind.

So here it is, boys, 269 pages of meeting, cheating, dumping, dating, loving, hating, marrying, divorcing, fucking, tricking, deceiving, and manipulating the fairer sex. Good luck, and happy hunting!

FIFTY TIPS ON BEING A BETTER ASSHOLE

THE COMPLETE

A**HOLE'S
GUIDE

TO HANDLING CHICKS

Chapter One

FROM BIRTH TO BEATING OFF

THE BIRTH OF AN ASSHOLE

It all started one day when your parents were drunk and Dad attacked your nearly passed-out mom after she had finished her third glass of white zinfandel. From that auspicious debut, you began your life as a little bad-ass sperm attacking the ovum like it was day-old pizza. Spitting on all the other pansy sperm, you set up base camp on that egg and spent the next nine months like a goddamn king. You were in a warm haze the entire time, eating constantly, never worrying about blind dates, cheating girlfriends, or the female orgasm. In fact, it was so great there in the womb, when you finally got out, you knew you were going to spend the rest of your life trying to get right back in.

THE PUREST FORM OF ASSHOLE

Regardless of what kind of sympathetic "nice guy" disease you're currently trying to purge from your system, you need to remember that you were a complete asshole when you first shot out of Mom. Think about it: you shit when you wanted to and some chick would clean it off your diapers. You cried like hell and made sure that nobody could sleep until you got what you wanted. You even puked on people who didn't feed you correctly. You were master of your domain, so nobody was about to fuck with you.

And what was the result of your blatant selfishness and complete disregard for everybody else? Did women hate you? Of course not! They thought you were the cutest thing they'd ever seen. They played with you, constantly rubbed your butt, and two or three times a day, one of them would let you suck on a boob for twenty to thirty minutes at a time. This is why infants are the purest form of assholes. They understand that women are there to serve them, and they don't give a shit about anything but the next nipple they're going to suck on.

If given the opportunity, you would carry on like this for the rest of your life. After all, you let a guy crap, burp, fart, puke, and take afternoon naps whenever he wants, and there's pretty much no question that he's going to try to keep that deal going for as long as he can. So what happened to finally knock you off your pedestal? More chicks came along and screwed things up. Get used to it.

GIMME MY TOY, YOU BITCH!

Around age three or so, you begin spending time with girls your age and things start to change. Suddenly, you can't cry and get your way with them anymore. If you pee all over yourself, they're more apt to laugh at you than to help out, and, if you puke on them, you better be ready to get it right back in your face.

These challenges to your God-given right to be served by women are just the first of many dramatic differences you will start to notice. For example, the little girls are wearing pink, while your clothes are blue. Girls are playing with dolls, while your every attention is focused on smashing trucks or eating dirt. And you'll also start to notice that they cry a lot more than you do. They get frustrated, they cry. They get hungry, they cry. You cry, *they* cry. This is one of the few things from your early childhood that will continue throughout the rest of your life, so you should probably get used to it.

Not surprisingly, at this point in your development you begin to realize that women suck. The adults tend to fawn over the cute little girl in pigtails, while you gnaw on Fisher-Price racing cars and get no attention. Slights like these turn you off to girls and make you realize that you couldn't care less what they do, as long as they stay with their own kind and you get to hang out with your buddies and break stuff. Chicks play with chicks, little dudes play with little dudes, and everything in the world is right. Who'd have thought this would be the last time you'd ever have a healthy relationship with women?

CROSSING THE DANCE FLOOR

During the years between three and (about) eight, your life in the schoolyard stays relatively carefree. Testosterone is working its magic on little boys, turning them into hyper-competitive, out-of-control monsters, while estrogen is doing the same thing on the other side of the fence, making girls fashion-conscious and catty. However, with boys and girls streaming to opposite sides of the playground, they're each in their own little worlds, and the opposite sex doesn't bother the other much.

Then, one day it starts to happen. You're eight or nine years old, the school has set up a square dance, or something similarly retarded, and, while you're hanging out with your buddies next to the punch bowl (precursor to the keg), you stare across the floor and notice, for the first time, holy shit, that fourth-grade chick's got a great ass! You look to your left and you see one of your Little League teammates staring at a fifth-grader's suddenly developing boobs! To your right—oh my God!—one of your friends is actually walking across the dance floor to talk to . . . *girls*?! No boy has ever walked across the dance floor—certainly not to talk to some whiny little chick. You and your friends are not supposed to be interested in girls—you've got baseball cards to trade, comic books to read. What the hell is going on here?! What's happening inside your brain that suddenly makes girls interesting?

Well, we hate to tell you, but you've just begun a lifetime journey—a journey to hell and back, where you'll spend every waking moment desperately trying to get into the pants of one girl and out of the cross-hairs of another. You'll laugh, you'll cry, you'll dump, you'll be dumped. Where you look for companionship, you'll find loneliness. Where you seek passion, you'll find indifference. The things that occur around you will often leave you baffled; but, unfortunately, what seems like an answer one day turns into a question the next. This will be a tumultuous time, as you join the everlasting fraternity of guys who are embittered, frustrated, resentful, and downright pissed at the lunacy that characterizes the female existence. You're about to start dealing with chicks. You're only nine or ten years old and guess what? You're fucked.

HOW DO I GET HER?
THE BEGINNING OF THE END

At around eleven or twelve, your hormones are starting to kick in and the serious pain is about to commence. Realizing that you want women is not so bad; actually trying to get them is when it all goes to hell. Because you're too young to really know what's going on, you spend a lot of this time confused. Actually, you'll spend the rest of your life confused but, at age ten, you can't get blackout drunk, so you don't yet have the proper tools to deal with the whole woman thing.

Compounding this problem is the fact that chicks mature faster than dudes. They are already developing their sexual organs, and every one of them is about a foot taller than you. How are you supposed to treat a woman like dirt when she can probably kick your ass across the playground?

Grab your sack and start some shit, that's how! The only guys getting ass in middle school are the ones that antagonize the hell out of any girl within arms' reach. Even though the girls don't like being treated poorly, for some reason they're intrigued by surly behavior. Offer to carry a girl's books and she laughs in your face. Smack her in the back of the head and she'll be passing you notes during fifth period. This is a crucial fork in the road of your social development. "Assholes" are about to become distinct from "nice guys." Were you mature enough to realize that calling some girl a "bitch" would have her making out with you by lunchtime? Or were you too young to realize that being a nice guy means you spend the weekend playing Dungeons and Dragons?

Events start to move quickly as you pass through your teenage years. Right after your first growth spurt makes you realize that Pokemon cards don't hold a candle to a fifteen-year-old's sprouting boobs, you get thrown right into a freezing-cold ocean filled with chick sharks and chick barracudas, all looking to take a bite out of your tender, innocent ass. The next few years are going to be especially brutal. Your dick gets hard virtually every time you take a breath, girls' bodies are guaranteed to be firm, and, yet, you can't leave the house unless you're in the family SUV. How can you score some action if your mom's sitting in the front seat humming a disco song from 1974? The truth is, you can't, and that's why you're so frustrated. You've got enough testosterone coursing through your body to provide daily Viagra pills to half the North American senior-citizen population, but there's simply nothing you can do about it until. . . .

ROUGHING UP THE SUSPECT

Somewhere around twelve you realize that your penis has two very distinct states of mind: hard and soft. And it seems that the odometer is always stuck on hard. You wake up in the morning, you're hard. The wind blows, you're hard. You take a breath, you're hard. There comes a point that your dick is so hard, so often, that you finally decide to do something about it.

One day, when you can't take the pressure anymore, you pull it out of your pants and just start slapping it. Strangely, it feels good, so you keep going. You smack it, tug it, and work it around in circles. What starts off as innocent fun, however, soon turns into a much more serious affair. The more you rub, the better it feels. Your heart beats a little faster, you start to sweat, and then it happens for the first time: a chick sneaks into your mind. It could be any chick—your babysitter, the girl on TV, or that babe sitting next to you in social studies. Suddenly, you're wondering if this would feel better if she was doing all the tugging. Before you know it, you're having your first fantasy, and your seed is spilling all over the place.

At first, it shocks you. Where in the hell did all that stuff come from? Why are my legs weak? Why did it feel so fucking good? This, our young friend, is where the true pain begins. You'll spend the next four years sitting in a bedroom beating your meat like a butcher. You'll start naming your hand after every girl in school, and you'll subscribe to *Sports Illustrated* just to get The Swimsuit Issue. Chances are, you're jerking off so many times a day that you can lift an eighteen-wheeler with your right hand but can barely pick up a fork with your left. Unfortunately, none of it will ever be enough. The more you jerk it, the more you want some chick to lend you a helping hand. But how—how can you possibly get some girl to touch your penis? This is the make-or-break moment for every young man.

Unfortunately, most boys fall to the dark side of the force and start kissing chicks' asses in hopes of getting to grab one. These poor kids will eventually end up in the humiliating and lonely world of the "pussy-whipped"—a place where you could waste away for eternity if there wasn't a book like this to finally pull you out. The rest of the boys—the assholes—understand exactly how to get little girls to touch their little male penises. They simply pull it out and slap some chick in the face with it. Eventually, they'll catch some seventh grader with her mouth open, and it's all roses from there.

Okay, so the rewards may not be too substantial at this age, because you're probably not "dating" in the eighth grade. But, hey, you are playing a little grab-ass underneath the bleachers after a football game, or you're finding some other slut who will let you feel her up behind the Phys. Ed. trailers. That's pretty cool in junior high school, but, trust us, if you can further develop your asshole skills, it's just the prelude to bigger and better things. Get ready, you're going to high school.

Chapter Two

HIGH SCHOOL

WELCOME MAT

High school—a time of wonder, a time of discovery, a time to realize that chicks are going to fuck up your life beyond all recognition. High school is kind of like junior adulthood. You're standing at the precipice of maturity, but you're still too much of a kid to have any semblance of a clue as to what's going on. Girls spend most of their day crying because their hair is too stringy or their boobs aren't developing fast enough. Boys discover porn and try to establish the world land-speed record for jerking off. Now is the time when you'll most likely get your first taste of beer, your first car, your first date, your first job, and your first realization that running out to the playground for a game of hand-ball is not going to make all of your troubles go away. Welcome to the world. It's not going to get any easier.

FIRSTS

As we've described to you, high school is all about firsts. You may have difficulties adjusting the first time you have an unexpected experience, even if it's good, because you're not real sure how to handle the emotions that come with something new. Plus, you're in high school, so you're an idiot anyway. But, because you've had the foresight to pick up this book, we're going to let you in on some of the mystical secrets of high school and walk you through the magic and tragic moments that you'll be forced to deal with over the next four years. Don't screw it up.

THE FIRST . . .	WHAT IT MEANS	HOW MOST GUYS DEAL WITH IT	HOW THE ASSHOLE DEALS WITH IT
Kiss	Some chick finally likes you.	Their stomach will drop, their face will flush, their heart will race. They'll think they're about to get married, and then they'll run home to take care of the raging erection that just popped up.	You couldn't care less, and you're probably going to be pissed off that she wouldn't let you go any further. Kissing is for kids, not for assholes. While your friends are focused on this woman's kiss, your only concern is finding the next girl you'll be making out with.
Date	You're going to spend a bunch of money and not	They'll spend hours getting ready. They'll read	You'll show up an hour late wearing a t-shirt and jeans.

THE FIRST . . .	WHAT IT MEANS	HOW MOST GUYS DEAL WITH IT	HOW THE ASSHOLE DEALS WITH IT
Date *(cont.)*	know what the hell you're doing, i.e. you're going to waste a lot of money.	magazines to see where to go, wash their car, ask their mom fifty times how they look. By the time they get to the girl's house, they'll be a nervous wreck.	You won't have the first clue what you're going to do and the only thing you'll really care about is how long it's going to take until you've got her top off. If she doesn't like it, you'll drop her off early and go find your buddies so you can play video games.
Time picking up chicks	Welcome to the wonderful world of failure.	They don't know what to say. Their palms are sweaty. They don't know what to do with their hands. They'll be back at their own table in under five minutes.	You're shocked that the girl didn't come over to pick *you* up. You don't care if she thinks you're interesting, funny, or good-looking. If she's not falling all over herself trying to impress you, she's not worth the time.
Time getting turned down by chicks	You're now part of the asshole fraternity. The first time some chick turns you down is the first time you really start to understand why you'll spend the rest of your life hating	They cry. Their self-confidence disappears. They don't come out of their bedroom for two weeks, and they resolve to spend the next five months taking steroids, because they think	You figure the chick's got to be out of her mind. It doesn't faze you, because she's clearly stupid, her boobs sag, she smells bad, and you wouldn't put your worst enemy's dick in her.

THE FIRST . . .	WHAT IT MEANS	HOW MOST GUYS DEAL WITH IT	HOW THE ASSHOLE DEALS WITH IT
Time getting turned down by chicks *(cont.)*	women with all of your heart and soul.	women won't dump a big, bulky dude. They're wrong.	The only reason you spoke to her in the first place is because your buddies told you she was a sure thing, and if she's not you're too busy scamming on her friends to care.
Girlfriend	You're about to get laid.	They'll kiss her ass up and down Main Street. They'll worship her, adore her, slave over her and, eventually, they'll get their hearts broken.	She is your slave. If you're not having sex three or four times a day, she's out the door. She's good to have, but if she starts to give you shit there are ten more who are better-looking, better in the sack, and who better watch out because you just might be single.
Sex	You're a man . . . who can't hold off on dropping your load for more than forty seconds.	Three strokes, done.	You will have jerked off at least five times that day to make sure that you don't shoot too quickly. You'll have spent a couple of hours studying porno to figure out how it's really done and, when you're finished after a

THE FIRST . . .	WHAT IT MEANS	HOW MOST GUYS DEAL WITH IT	HOW THE ASSHOLE DEALS WITH IT
Sex *(cont.)*			couple of hours, you're going straight to sleep.
Time getting dumped	You'd better turn into an asshole real quick, or be prepared to go through this over and over and over again for the rest of your life.	Complete and total devastation. They don't think they'll ever find another girl again in their lives. They're convinced she was the one and that they're destined to be lonely for the rest of their lives.	Whatever, bitch.
Alcohol	You'll now have a way to deal with the pain that high school will inevitably cause you.	Slurring their speech, getting in fights, making general asses out of themselves, when they're not hunched over the porcelain God violently throwing up everything they've eaten in the last couple of days.	You'll probably do the same. Sorry, even assholes can't control themselves when they're drunk.
Drugs	You'll now have a way to deal with the pain that high school will inevitably cause you that alcohol can't get rid of.	They'll pass out. They'll lose their minds. They'll do stupid stuff, like jump out of trees. Drugs are not good.	Being an asshole doesn't mean you're stupid. Stay away from drugs until you're older and you can afford rehab.

THE FIRST . . .	WHAT IT MEANS	HOW MOST GUYS DEAL WITH IT	HOW THE ASSHOLE DEALS WITH IT
Job	You'll finally understand that, no matter how much you hate your parents, your boss is worse.	They'll screw it up. They won't show up on time, they won't do their work, they'll make a mess. They'll be unemployed next week.	A job equals money. Money equals chicks. Do your work, collect your paycheck, bang cheerleaders. Very simple equation.
Car	When you try to cop a feel on your girlfriend, you won't have to worry that your mom will see you in the rearview mirror.	They think a car's for transportation. What a bunch of dorks.	Your car represents independence, which, again, equals women. Also, your car has a back seat, which means you don't have to go home to get laid. In reality, getting your car will be the true first step towards being a real asshole. Before you have a car, you're pretty limited in what you can accomplish. Once you're behind the wheel, you are set to explode. Congratulations on this momentous occasion. It almost brings a tear to our eye.
Night you don't come home	The battle is pitched between you and your parents.	They'll apologize profusely. They'll beg for forgiveness. They'll get	Your mom will be pissed off, but when your dad realizes you stayed out because

THE FIRST . . .	WHAT IT MEANS	HOW MOST GUYS DEAL WITH IT	HOW THE ASSHOLE DEALS WITH IT
Night you don't come home *(cont.)*		grounded for two months.	you were schtupping some hot blonde, he should let you off easy.
Screw-up that directly affects your future	If you get bad grades now, you don't go to college. Try making $100,000 a year with nothing but a high school diploma. It ain't easy.	They think they're cool, but when they barely graduate and the only job they get is mopping up the jerk-off booth at the local porn shop, they'll cry themselves to sleep every night wishing they had spent a little time studying.	Again, you may be an asshole but you're no idiot. Of course you'll never let anybody know that you study, but you should be working your ass off to succeed. Getting into a good college is your best bet to make big cash when you get older, and big cash equals chicks. Don't let your screwed-up attitude destroy your chances to bang supermodels one day.
Pecking order	Social hierarchy. Your schoolmates are not just kids now, they're social strata and, if you don't watch out, you're consigned to whatever level you fall into.	They'll spend a lot of time bummed out that they're not hanging with a better group. They'll feel isolated, ashamed and lonely. They'll remain trapped there for the next four years unable to move, unable to breathe.	You are the pecking order. Basically, no matter where you land in the social hierarchy, once you start hooking up with chicks, people will think you're cool. Just follow these rules, do exactly what we say, and you'll rule the school in no time.

THE BACK-SEAT BOOGIE

Now that you're in high school, things start to change. Why? Because when you're in high school, you get a car. With a car comes a back seat. With a back seat comes what is most likely your first real opportunity to get a little lovin'. Moreover, the other guys get cars, too, and if their car is better than yours, they stand a much better chance of landing that blue-eyed piece of ass than you do. This will be the first time you come face-to-face with the bitter competition other guys will offer you. Just because his parents were willing to drop an extra ten grand to get him a convertible, he's banging the hottest blonde in the school. Sucks, huh? Get used to it.

Now that you're starting to understand what you'll be dealing with for the rest of your life, we're going to give you your first piece of advice:

TIP #1: GET A COOL CAR.

This is good advice, whether you're a fifteen-year-old sophomore or a forty-five-year-old accountant, but since we're only up to the high school section of the book, we're throwing it in here. Plus, we've been babbling for a couple of chapters, and we figured an "advice" book should eventually give out some advice. Page 15 is as good as any other spot. Pay attention. If you don't listen to us now, you could spend the rest of your life eating Doritos with a stack of *Playboys* in one hand and a raw penis in the other.

CHICKS ARE THE ENEMY

TIP #2: KNOW THAT CHICKS ARE THE ENEMY.

This is as true in high school as it will be for the rest of your life. You've probably heard the old adage: keep your friends close, but keep your enemies closer. To do that, you have to know what you're up against. Women are a formidable power, but knowing what to look for might help you gain a little tactical advantage. In reality, you probably have no chance of any advantage whatsoever at age sixteen; but, if you're in high school and actually reading this book, you're cool enough to have a shot. Here are the different kinds of chicks you're going to encounter.

TYPE OF CHICK	GUYS SHE DATES	COMMON CHARACTER- ISTICS	BEST OPENING LINE TO USE ON HER
Prom queen	Prom king, nobody else is good enough for her.	Fake tits; never has less than four people around her; won't give you a blowjob until you've dated for at least six months; thinks her shit smells like roses.	I'm going to be featured in *Teen People* next month.
Piece of ass	Guys who are thirty or older.	Hot face; hot ass; hot tits; hot clothes; you've got no shot.	Have you seen my Mercedes?

TYPE OF CHICK	GUYS SHE DATES	COMMON CHARACTER-ISTICS	BEST OPENING LINE TO USE ON HER
Cheerleader	Quarterbacks, student body president, her dad.	Bubbly; school spirited; obnoxious; big hair; squeaky voice.	Do you want to be my athletic supporter?
Nice girl	Not you.	We wouldn't know one if we saw her and, if we did, we'd get the hell away from her as soon as possible.	My friends call me an asshole, but they've never seen me taking care of my puppies.
Student body president	Claims she's too busy to date.	Always rushing somewhere; short hair; constantly in meetings; holding a two-liter water bottle at all times.	I have thirty freshman votes in my pocket for the right kind of girl.
Slut	Anybody, anytime, anywhere.	Very, very, very friendly; tight pants; ever-present cleavage; pretty good-looking, but has definitely been dragged around the block a couple of times.	I have a penis.
Valedictorian	Math teacher, Science teacher, Salutatorian.	Glasses; 85-lb. bookbag; always speaks in grammatically correct sentences; constantly filling out college applications.	What do you think you would *really* do for an "A"?

TYPE OF CHICK	GUYS SHE DATES	COMMON CHARACTER-ISTICS	BEST OPENING LINE TO USE ON HER
Volleyball player	Other women, any guy who's taller than her.	Tall; ponytail; massive calves; stoops constantly so she looks shorter than guys; floor burns; no make-up.	I'm a girl, too.
Math Club president	Computer geeks, dorks, social misfits.	Stringy hair; zits; can't find girls smart enough to be her friend; at least two cans of Diet Coke in her backpack.	Have you seen the latest version of Doom?
Druggie	Her dealer, guys with crack pipes.	Black jacket; black makeup; black hair; black boyfriend.	Wanna get high?
Unpopular girl	Nobody.	Big butt; no friends; generally seen eating and glaring at popular people.	If you're talking to her, it doesn't matter what you say.

Now that you know what the enemy looks like, you're going to have to start developing certain coping mechanisms. These are tricks of the trade that you must learn at an early age. Some of them may be a little advanced for your still-developing mind and body but the habits you form now will likely recur throughout the rest of your life. Since we're sure that you don't want to spend the next fifty years as some chick's "friend," you've got to start practicing now.

a. *Never, Ever, Ever Say "I'm Sorry"*—Golden Rule #1. In fact, this one's so big, we're even putting it on the list.

TIP #3: NEVER SAY "I'M SORRY."

If a woman catches you backtracking she's got you. Once she knows that you feel bad about something, she'll go off on an emotional feeding frenzy. She will attack everything you do, everything you've ever said, and everything that she feels she can rip on without getting you so upset that you slap her. Even if she's not the type to hammer you for doing something wrong, once you've said "I'm sorry" she'll never think of you as the strong, confident stud you once were. You'll just be another pantywaist buying her dinner until she finds somebody who's going to smack her ass the way she likes it. So remember, no matter what you do—whether it's sleeping with her best friend, puking on her prom dress, or smashing her dad's car—never, ever, ever, ever, ever say you're sorry.

b. *Cover Your Ass*—Be prepared for women to screw you over at the drop of a hat. If she knows that you like her, she's going to tell everybody in school and embarrass the hell out of you. If you try to grab her boobs at the wrong time, she'll claim you're a rapist. Make sure they never have any dirt on you and that everything you do is completely deniable.

TIP #4: DON'T PUT ANYTHING IN WRITING.

c. *Don't Put Anything in Writing*—One of the asshole's greatest allies is the ability to lie. No matter what you said or did, a properly trained asshole can lie, deny, weasel, sidestep, or connive his way out of it—unless it's in writing. Once you put it on paper, it immediately becomes undisputable fact. That means no love letters, poems, or other cheesy expressions of creativity. This is especially true with e-mail. One click of a mouse will have the entire school laughing at what a sissy you are.

d. *Spread Disinformation*—It's guaranteed that the women in your life are talking about you behind your back. Although that would be good if they're discussing your inhuman sexual prowess or your nine-inch schlong, the odds of that are pretty low. Therefore, you must get the jump on them. If you think she's going to say you're too aggressive, spread a rumor that she made you pull off the freeway so she could blow you. If you think she might talk about that little, uh, problem you had in bed, immediately tell everybody that she farts every time you go down on her. It's okay if the stories get back to her, because she won't have the self-confidence to provide any defense. Not to mention, once every guy in school realizes he'll get "brown chin" by mowing her box she'll be forced back onto your hog by a lack of any other alternative.

WATCH YOUR BACK—YOUR FRIENDS WON'T

Once women become a major factor in your life, your friendships with your male buddies become a whole lot different, too. Before you cared about girls, it was all about you and your boys. You played baseball together, you sat in front of video games for hours, you shot hoops all day. Now that women have entered the scene, all of that will change . . . drastically.

Why? When you were ten, you didn't have to worry that your best friend was going to get a blowjob from your girlfriend in the back seat of his car. In Little League, you weren't jealous when the women in the stands would cheer for your more talented teammate, because they were all moms. But, once you're in high school and your hormones are racing around like the Indy 500, every time something happens between you and your buddies that affects your ability to get laid (probably for the first time), you're going to be pissed, enormously pissed. Interestingly, this will probably not be a lifelong occurrence. Once you've reached your twenties, you'll have developed enough confidence that you couldn't care less what a chick does, whether it's with a stranger or your buddy. Sure, there will be times when your coworker sleeps with your wife—and that's a bummer—but there will be just as many times that you and some other guy laugh your asses off at the fact that you both banged the same chick and never called her again.

But that's way in the future. Now, when your brain has yet to catch up with a body that is literally sprinting into adulthood, the dynamics between your chick, your buddies, and you is an ever-changing, emotionally charged event. The biggest thing to remember is that, for all intents and purposes, *men are your enemies, too*! We're not saying that you can't have friends. It's critical that you have a bunch of buddies who can help you hit on cheerleaders or get a play-ground basketball game going if necessary. But when it comes to get-ting women, every man or boy that you know should be considered a mortal enemy to be defeated at any opportunity. We don't care if you've known him since you were two years old, if he's within a hun-dred yards of your girlfriend, he's Charles Manson, Adolf Hitler, Osama bin Laden, and Benito Mussolini all rolled into one. Attack first, ask questions later.

PECKING ORDER

When you get into high school, you become a kind of mini-adult. There are still playground rules that you have to deal with, but, in a lot of ways, you're much closer to being an adult than you are to being a grade-schooler. You've got a car, so you're independent. You can have a job, so you might have some money. You can now bang chicks, so you're going to have pain, misery, and torture.

However, high school's biggest blow to your system will be the establishment of the infamous "pecking order." This is the rigid social stratification that makes some kids popular beyond their wildest dreams and other kids so suicidally depressed that they bring firearms to school. Class warfare is something you probably never dealt with before. When you're in elementary or junior high school, everybody, more or less, is the same. Yeah, maybe some kids have rich families, or some are great athletes, but your ability to take advantage of those talents is pretty limited when you're twelve years old.

Think about it: if you're thirteen and your dad's rich, big deal, maybe you get a nicer pair of shoes than the next guy. In high school, a rich father means a BMW, and a BMW means you get chicks. Ask the kid with the 1987 Hyundai Galant how much tail he gets driving down the road, and then ask yourself whether money really makes a difference at this level.

Basically, it's a whole different world now and what you have means something. Unfortunately, in high school, it's difficult to be upwardly or downwardly mobile so chances are good that you're stuck where you are. Luckily, this will change when you get older, but for now you're just going to have to deal with it. Here are some of the more general classifications that you might fall into:

WHO YOU ARE— IN DESCENDING ORDER DOWN THE FOOD CHAIN	WHAT YOU CAN EXPECT	CHICKS YOU CAN GET	HOW TO MOVE UP IN THE WORLD
Star athlete	The world. All the chicks dig you, adults want to be around you, colleges beg you to visit their campuses—and they'll give you sorority girls if you do. You are king of the hill, top of the heap. Fuck you.	Take your pick. Cheerleaders, prom queens, blondes, redheads, college girls. They all know you might make a lot of money someday and you're in good enough shape that you can bang 'em for hours on end. It's all yours for the taking . . . unless you blow out a knee, at which point we'll spend the rest of the year laughing our asses off as you hobble around on crutches, you has-been.	You can't move up in the world unless you become a star college athlete where you literally rule the world, not just your school. Congratulations, you win. You prick.
Popular guy	This could be a cool position. Chicks want your action, guys want to be you, regular sex is yours for the taking. The only danger is that you're a popular "nice guy" and every woman wants to be your friend. If that's the case, knock	This really depends on your school. If you're in Texas, being popular doesn't mean jack if you don't play football. In California, though, you're banging all the hot blondes as long as you're a BMOC. If you're good looking and	You can't move up too far, unless you can jump forty-two inches or hit a baseball out of the county. In high school, being popular means you're better than 98 percent of the school population, so be happy where you are and don't

WHO YOU ARE— IN DESCENDING ORDER DOWN THE FOOD CHAIN	WHAT YOU CAN EXPECT	CHICKS YOU CAN GET	HOW TO MOVE UP IN THE WORLD
Popular guy *(cont.)*	yourself ten rungs down the ladder because you're a loser.	popular, you'd better be scooping up the hot chicks or you're just a waste of humanity.	pop off too much to the dorks, because you never know how many of them got hunting rifles for their birthdays.
Rich kid	A BMW, a big-ass house, and a credit card. Cash makes chicks want you, even in high school. Don't hide it—make sure they all know you have money. Use it to get them into bed with you and then dump 'em without spending a dime.	You can get most chicks, provided you're not a fat dope. Some are tougher, like cheerleaders, who are looking for pure status or muscles. Usually money is a good substitute, but you may have to be happy with hot chicks who'll blow you. Trust us, you could do a lot worse.	If you've got cash, your ability to move up or down is really a case of genetics. If your mom is actually your dad's second trophy wife, you may have gotten some solid genes. If your mom is his dumpy, fat first wife, you could be screwed.
Mediocre athlete	Simply being on a team gives you a modicum of status, even if you're not that good. Chicks like to wear your uniform, you're probably in decent shape, and you get to leave school at 1 p.m. on game days. Your life is okay, but you'll	You'll get laid, but not with the elite. Cheerleaders and prom queens are out of the question. You will probably hook up with some groupies and, once you're a senior, you can have your pick of freshmen. You're way ahead of the	Creatine, anabolics, testosterone, teramex, sudies, ephedrine, ribose, taurine, stanozolol, steranabol, sybolin, primobolan, anavar, furazabol. Or you could just work out once in a while, you fat, lazy fuck!

WHO YOU ARE— IN DESCENDING ORDER DOWN THE FOOD CHAIN	WHAT YOU CAN EXPECT	CHICKS YOU CAN GET	HOW TO MOVE UP IN THE WORLD
Mediocre athlete *(cont.)*	spend a lot of time wishing it were better. Sorry, "almost" at the top might be worse than being on the bottom.	game, so don't bitch.	
Drunk	High school introduces you to the concept of keg parties, which leads to the first sighting of the popular drunk. Being a drunk is cool because people think you know how to party. You should go to all the "in" events and chicks will want to hang out with you because you're fun. Just make sure you've got a sophomore skank who puts out after driving you home at the end of the night.	Party chicks. Girls who are out until the wee hours getting sloppy are your natural prey. Often, these girls are hot, and that's a definite plus. More often, they're passed out, which is even better. Just make sure you pace yourself until about 2 A.M. when the sheer volume of shit-faced girls makes getting laid as easy as punching out a freshman.	A lot of things you can do here but you're too drunk or hungover to do them. Buying booze for the "elite," getting people on lists at cool parties, being drunk-funny instead of drunk-aggressive are all ways to improve your social standing. Although these are simple tasks, they aren't easy to do when you're vomiting half the time. Don't lose your control.
Drama groupie	A niche position— not necessarily a bad one, either. A lot of people will think you're gay, but, on	Artsy chicks. The mainstream is probably out of your league, unless you look like Tom	Do you really want to move up? If you're a drama dude, you clearly don't have a

WHO YOU ARE—IN DESCENDING ORDER DOWN THE FOOD CHAIN	WHAT YOU CAN EXPECT	CHICKS YOU CAN GET	HOW TO MOVE UP IN THE WORLD
Drama groupie *(cont.)*	the flip side, a bunch of girls will think you're artistic, talented, and worth a backstage blowjob after a great performance. Stay away from the football players and you should be fine.	Cruise, but there's a whole bunch of funky little girls who get off on the creative aspects of your personality. Memorize some lines from a Brando film, pretend you're intensely into "your craft," and you should score pretty easily.	problem with being off the beaten path so fuck 'em, hang with your group, bang the production assistants, and pray that you land a sitcom when you'll get all the puss there is to get.
Pothead	Like the drama groupie, this is another niche position. A lot of kids do drugs in high school, and your reputation as a pothead will make you cool to a certain sector of the population. The only problem is you're gonna have to give up some of your stash to be accepted.	This could be an eclectic group. There are a lot of hot chicks, even some "elite" chicks, who are drugged out of their minds in high school. Sure, you can get the goth women and the ones who are stoned, but, if your stuff is top quality you might bag yourself a piece of ass in the process.	You should be too stoned to care where you stand in the hierarchy. Some tasty buds should be infinitely more preferable to any "social climbing" tendencies you might have.
Everyday joe	Not too cold, not too hot, sorry, not too popular. You'll go to an occasional party, maybe even	You're not getting the pick of the litter, that's for sure. Your best bet for some trim is to find some	You are one of the few guys who could really do some moving around. You can work out like a

WHO YOU ARE— IN DESCENDING ORDER DOWN THE FOOD CHAIN	WHAT YOU CAN EXPECT	CHICKS YOU CAN GET	HOW TO MOVE UP IN THE WORLD
Everyday joe (cont.)	make out with a girl who's drunk. But your high school experience will be pretty damn boring. Expect to spend a lot of time wishing you were somebody else.	other boring girl who you can screw for the entire four years. Beating the bushes for new chicks will be like beating your head against the wall for not much reward. Why put in the effort?	maniac and become an athlete. You can become a drunk party guy, or a pothead dealer without too much trouble. Or you can continue to have guys kick your ass and chicks avoid you. Which sounds better?
New kid	Although this is generally a tough spot to be in, you can also turn it into a positive. People's perceptions of you are totally clean— the rumors about "the gay thing" from your past are now gone. You can create a new you and build a decent life. Unfortunately, everybody in school has already known each other for twelve years, so it's not going to be easy. You know all those high school movies where the new kid gets the hot chick?	This could go either way. If you work the new program right, you could end up with hot chicks. If you're too shy to just go up and say "hi" to new people, you're screwed and you'll watch a lot of TV. Some girls will be sympathetic to your plight, and that's always good for a hummer or two. Be aggressive and you might be okay.	Like the everyday joe, you can move up, but you don't have the "boring" stigma that he's got. Yours might be a little tougher, though, because every advantage you'll get you'll have to work for. It's going to be arduous, but, would you rather grab your sack and introduce yourself to a new girl, or sit at home on Saturday tugging away to the new issue of *Maxim*?

WHO YOU ARE— IN DESCENDING ORDER DOWN THE FOOD CHAIN	WHAT YOU CAN EXPECT	CHICKS YOU CAN GET	HOW TO MOVE UP IN THE WORLD
New kid *(cont.)*	Forget about it, they're fiction. Settle for a fat girl who puts out.		
Band member	Unless you're Wynton Marsalis or Harry Connick, Jr., you're a loser. You might be fat, too. The only way out of this predicament you've gotten yourself into is if you start a rock band. If you can accomplish that, you'll bang every hot chick within 150 miles of you. If you don't, blank this four years out of your memory and pray that things change in college.	If you're not in a rock band, none. If you're in a rock band, everybody. Which way do you want to go?	This is easy—drop the saxophone and pick up a guitar. Rock musicians can be fat, ugly, stupid, bald, morally reprehensible, and have a nonexistent dick—and they still get laid more than any human being since Hugh Hefner. (Look at any member of Def Leppard, for example.) Schedule some lessons right now.
Homosexual	Assuming you can avoid hate crimes, in the twenty-first century being a homo in high school's probably not so bad. Most people don't care whose dick you suck, and you'll	Drag queens, dudes in public bathrooms, forty-year-old gay men who want a young trophy, NAMBLA veterans.	You're gay, face it, and you're not going anywhere in high school. You might rock the house in the underground gay scene, but you should get the hell away from school as soon as possible to

WHO YOU ARE— IN DESCENDING ORDER DOWN THE FOOD CHAIN	WHAT YOU CAN EXPECT	CHICKS YOU CAN GET	HOW TO MOVE UP IN THE WORLD
Homosexual *(cont.)*	have a built-in group of people who'll help you design clothes, pick out new drapes, and watch *Queer as Folk*.		avoid the taunting of football players and other assorted Neanderthals.
Computer geek	Snickers bars, Diet Cokes, and *Star Trek* every single Friday and Saturday night for four long, arduous years.	You'll be banging the hottest chicks in *Maxim, FHM, Playboy*, and *Stuff* magazines. Too bad you'll be alone when you're doing it.	For the next few years, you're screwed. But, look at the bright side, Bill Gates was a complete friggin' loser in high school, and he's worth fifty billion dollars now. Of course, he still married an ugly chick, so maybe you really are screwed forever.

YOUR FIRST PINCUSHION

For most people, high school is one damn, depressing place. Regardless of the pain that you will inevitably endure, there is one thing that will brighten everything up for you: a nymphomaniac girlfriend who would rather play "hide the salami" than breathe.

TIP #5: FIND A HIGH SCHOOL GIRLFRIEND WHO PUTS OUT.

A girlfriend in high school is an absolute must. Let's face it, even if you're God's gift to women, while you're a high school student, you're not going to have that many chances to score. When you finally do have one, most likely you'll lack the resources to make it happen. You don't have money, so chicks are automatically going to be hesitant to put out. You don't have your own place, so you've got to do it someplace awkward, like a baseball dugout or a crack house. And let's be real, you don't have much experience, so you're probably going to say something stupid 90 percent of the time.

The point to all of this is that you need a girlfriend so you don't have to run after puss that much. Of course, we expect you to try to find other trim when you have a girlfriend, but when you fail miserably you must always have somebody to come back to, both figuratively and literally. Plus, don't spend too much time worried about whether she's the hottest piece of ass in school or if her father drives a Porsche. Think of yourself as a fighter. You've got to slam the punching bag a thousand times before you actually climb into the ring. Your sixteen-year-old girlfriend is nothing more than a speed bag on the express route to the championship fight.

You'll have plenty of time to go after the "elite" chicks when you're in college and after. Right now, all you need is sex practice. The only criteria necessary for a high school girlfriend is that she puts out . . . all the friggin' time. You're young, and you have so much energy you could be having sex three or four times a day, every day, for four years straight. That's between 4,380 and 5,840 sexual encounters by the end of high school! With those kinds of numbers, you are going to be a sexual superstar when you show up at college and, if you don't think being outstanding in bed is a turn-on to a sorority girl, let us show you the parade of guys whose premature ejaculations spelled the end to their collegiate social life.

SO YOU'RE LOOKING TO GET LAID

Okay, you've taken our advice and gotten yourself a girlfriend. Statistics say that over half of high school students today are having sex. However, if you take a closer look at the statistics, you'll notice that only 20 percent of the girls claim to have sex in high school, while 54 percent of the boys are allegedly schtupping themselves silly. Somewhere the math doesn't add up. Ya wanna know why? Because guys lie all the goddamn time. At sixteen, your ability to get laid will count for about 85 percent of your popularity quotient in school, so you've got even more motivation to fabricate a sexual history for the statisticians. The point we want to make, though, is that, if you're a high school boy who hasn't had sex yet, don't sweat it, you're nowhere near alone. And, according to the statistics, only 20 percent of women are banging the headpost against the wall so it's pretty likely that not only are you a newbie, but your chick doesn't know the first thing about good lovin' either.

But understand, you must get some tail, somewhere, before you graduate. When you land your first chick in high school, don't pretend to be a savvy veteran of the bedroom either, no matter how much of a cocky prick you are. Hell, if you can identify the G-spot on a vaginal wall map, you're probably ahead of most of your buddies. Just remember, regardless of your looks, social status, or personality deficiencies, you've got to figure out how to get laid now so you don't end up in a sorority bedroom not knowing what the hell you're doing. Don't stress-out, though, because we're here to help. We've put together an Appendix to guide you through the various stages of fucking—how to get through them without embarrassing yourself, making a mess, or otherwise turning into a blubbering idiot. Please turn to page 251 for all the information you need to know, and, for God's sake, try not to get the pages sticky, you neophyte.

HIGH SCHOOL FINAL EXAMINATION

1. *When you were two years old, you didn't mind hanging out with chicks your age because:*
    a. They enjoyed eating dirt, just like you
    b. You could wear their blue clothes
    c. They rarely cried
    d. They didn't act like chicks just yet

2. *When you were nine, your buddy crossed the dance floor to:*
    a. Scam on some fifth-grader with a solid butt
    b. Teach the principal how to do The Funky Chicken
    c. Spike the punch bowl with grain alcohol
    d. Get to the chicken on the other side

3. *A hot car in high school equals:*
    a. A guaranteed DUI
    b. A Grand Theft Auto conviction
    c. Hot chicks
    d. A moped

4. *You need a girlfriend in high school in order to:*
    a. Get plenty of sex practice for college
    b. Prove to your father that you're not gay
    c. Get half of her paycheck
    d. Ensure that you'll get married

5. *If you're a star athlete in high school, you are:*
    a. Totally unpopular
    b. Incapable of getting chicks
    c. Shunned by colleges
    d. Despised by the authors of this book

6. *If some high school kid tells you he's had a hundred different women, he's:*
    a. Really Brad Pitt in disguise
    b. Lying his ass off
    c. The world's youngest serial rapist
    d. Talking about his one hundred prior lives

7. *You should only say you're sorry when:*
    a. You grab some chick's boob and she objects
    b. You're drunk and being obnoxious
    c. You've beaned your buddy in a Little League game
    d. Pigs fly out of your ass

8. *If you see your high school best friend talking to your girlfriend, you should treat him like:*
    a. Benito Mussolini
    b. Adolf Hitler
    c. Osama bin Laden
    d. All of the above

9. *If you're rich in high school:*
    a. It doesn't matter, because you can't buy a house
    b. You get a BMW and chicks
    c. You're not happy unless you're a good person, too
    d. You wish you could afford a Hyundai Galant

10. *Chicks are:*
    a. Your friends
    b. Great basketball teammates
    c. The enemy
    d. Everything that's good in the world

ANSWERS
1-d, 2-a, 3-c, 4-a, 5-d, 6-b, 7-d, 8-d, 9-b, 10-c.

Chapter Three

COLLEGE

WELCOME MAT

You've made it to college, thank God. College is without a doubt the longest vacation you will ever take. Even if you screwed around in high school and smoked too much dope to graduate, you should still spend as much time as possible on the local campus to check out the action. During this time in your life pretty much anything goes—the beer is plentiful, the women are experimental, and responsibility is nothing more than another word you don't know how to spell. You should have one focus for these four, or five, or six years:

FUCK AS MANY CHICKS AS YOU POSSIBLY CAN

Any night that doesn't end with a sub-twenty-one-year-old girl passed out on your floor is an outright disaster. As Andrew "Dice" Clay once said, "two tits, a hole, and a heartbeat" is all you really need to get started. In college, that line is 100 percent correct, except for the part about the heartbeat. You should be attacking chicks as if they're the last diuretic at a sorority dinner party. And don't forget the most important tool you'll have to get laid: beer! If you have beer, the girls will eventually follow. Beer will also be the catalyst that allows you to pack more parties, more sex, and more unbridled hedonism into these next few years than you or your parents ever thought humanly possible. We hope you enjoy it. Why? Because it's all downhill from here.

YOUR HIGH SCHOOL GIRLFRIEND

Your first major decision as a college student is "what should I do with my high school girlfriend?" As we explained to you in the last chapter, you need a girlfriend in high school so you can spend a few years learning how to trigger your partner's second, third, and fourth orgasms. Some of you may have gone overboard and actually developed feelings for the girl. This is entirely unacceptable but, due to your youth and inexperience, we'll give you a pass this time. However, no matter how much you love her (yeah, right!), once you're in college your girlfriend is just another pair of tits in a much, much larger world of nipples. But remember, since college is all about fucking, your high school girlfriend can be a great place to start and pick up momentum. The key to working these relationships to your advantage is learning how to effectively manage "distance," i.e., the mileage between you and your chick. Here's what we mean:

a. *If She Lives Far, Far Away from You*—This is a no-brainer: continue banging her while you hit on every girl within a hundred yards of your dorm room. The key to making this relationship work, though, is to demand her loyalty while you jump on any girl who's had more than two drinks. As you're impersonating the

Happy Hooker, your girlfriend will be pining away at home while storing up enough vaginal fluid to fill the community pool. Also, think of the psychological toll it'll take on her: she's locked up in a sexless cage, thousands of miles away from her Man. She's drunk, guys are hitting on her; hell, she's damn near about to burst. By the time she does see you, she'll be so primed and wet that you could literally shove a football inside of her.

But that's not all; it gets better. Here are some of the other fringe benefits you get when visiting the wonderful world of the out-of-state girlfriend:

1. *Conjugal visits*—A weekend with your out-of-state girlfriend will be forty-eight hours of vicious, teeth-grinding, headboard-smashing, back-shredding sexual insanity. Not only will she be insatiable, but experimentation with whips, chains, small animals, and all sorts of ceramic products will be entirely acceptable.

2. *Guaranteed sex*—If you're going through a temporary drought, you're only a plane ride away from Old Faithful.

3. *Jealousy*—If she's a piece of ass, when you walk around campus, other women will be jealous. Chicks who see the two of you together will be intensely curious about what it is in your pants that allowed you to land her. Better than that, on Monday she'll be gone and the other women will have no obstacle to finding out.

4. *Image*—Chicks dig dudes with chicks. Plus, your public display of commitment will seem to indicate that you're "boyfriend material," an extremely desirable quality to sorority tramps who get dissed on a weekly basis. Add the fact that nothing pumps up a college girl's fragile little ego like stealing a man from his girlfriend, and you can expect to be knee-deep in trim for the next couple of months.

The only real problem with the long-distance girlfriend is the surreal phone bill you're going to receive every month. She still thinks you're her boyfriend—even though she's been reduced to little more than a tri-yearly sexual pinch hitter—so she needs to continuously call and talk to you about her day, her life, her job, her school, and all the other bullshit that you couldn't care less about. This will cost you. Other than that, these relationships are the ideal collegiate situation.

> ## TIP #6: DUMP YOUR HIGH SCHOOL GIRLFRIEND IF SHE GOES TO YOUR COLLEGE.

b. *If She Goes to the Same School*—Dump the bitch before your first class. If you don't lose her immediately, you will never meet another chick in college. You'll no longer be "Mike and Suzy"; you'll be "that couple." Every guy will think you're a fag because you can't pick up any chicks. Every girl will think you're a wimp because you chose to stay with Suzy Homemaker. Try to break up in a friendly manner, though, so she doesn't start banging all your friends or floating rumors about your thumb-sized penis. If, despite your efforts, she does something nasty anyway, have a buddy videotape her taking it from behind and barking like a dog. Then, send a copy to her mom. That always seems to shut them up for a while.

c. *If She Lives Within Driving Distance*—Keep her, but use extreme caution. Driving relationships only work when they are treated like long-distance relationships. Here are some warning signs that will let you know when to dump her:

1. *You're spending every weekend together*—Remember, your goal is to screw many chicks, not to screw one chick many times. If you guys are together this much, why don't you just buy her a ring, donate your penis to science, and get it over with already?

2. *She's a big fan of the surprise visit*—Nothing is worse than getting caught in the act. Unless she wants to join in which, oddly enough, never seems to happen. Remember, chicks are crazy, demented, and lack the most elementary reasoning skills. Lorena Bobbitt, for example, cut off her husband's penis because he didn't like the salad dressing she used. Would you cut off your chick's boob if she used thousand-island instead of ranch dressing? Of course not, but you're a guy so you're not stupid. Anyway, the point is since women are so unpredictable, there is no telling how your girlfriend will react if she walks in while you're doing the tube steak boogie with some random dorm chick. Best-case scenario, you're chasing her down the hall with a rock-hard dick trying to explain yourself. That's one of the few times in your life when having a raging hard-on will actually be a problem for you.

YOU'RE NOT IN KANSAS ANYMORE

> ### TIP #7: COLLEGE IS NOT IN KANSAS ANYMORE (UNLESS YOU GO TO COLLEGE IN KANSAS).

When it comes to chicks and dating, high school and college are about as similar as Kenny Loggins and Eminem. Sure, they may both play music, but if you use the same dance moves at their concerts, you're probably going to get your ass kicked. Here are a couple of lessons on how chicks will differ now that you've moved into "higher" education:

SUBJECT	HIGH SCHOOL	COLLEGE	HOW TO TAKE ADVANTAGE
Drinking	Very few high school girls drink on a regular basis. If they do, they are either the rich or the cool kids, which means you probably couldn't score with them. Or they are complete fall-down drunks, which means you probably don't want to score with them.	Every college chick drinks— no exceptions. If you're in college, you're drinking. Case closed. Any woman you meet that says she doesn't drink is either lying or Mormon. Either way, she should be shot. (If you bought this book in Utah, you're now entitled to a full refund).	Get them drunk and fuck them. It's that simple. Always have vodka, orange juice, and ice cubes in your room. Any occasion is worth a couple of drinks, even if you're partying because it's, say, a Wednesday. God gave us beer so that ugly guys can always get laid. Don't disrespect his wishes.
Drugs	There is no real drug scene in high school. Sure, you've got the stoners and the occasional dabblers, but the vast majority of high school chicks will not do drugs.	The drug scene is everywhere. College is practically a drug supermarket: shrooms, ecstasy, and all the real hard stuff is there for the taking. Pot is so commonplace it might be offered in the dorm cafeteria. Virtually all college girls will, at the minimum, experiment with drugs in college and, at the maximum, become strung-out, hollow-eyed prostitutes.	Always be present during a chick's experimentation phase. Mind-expanding drugs lead to leg-spreading sex. The same girl that's never smoked pot has probably never kissed her best friend or had a ménage à trois either. Include as many of these acts as possible into one evening so that it's easier for the chick to write it off as one of those "crazy

SUBJECT	HIGH SCHOOL	COLLEGE	HOW TO TAKE ADVANTAGE
Drinking *(cont.)*			nights." If a girl is a regular user, find her the good stuff. Normally, she would pay a pretty penny for it, so chances are she'll barter with sex.
Living	At the end of the night, everyone goes home.	Suddenly, your best friend lives right next to you and there are a hundred hot sluts living down the hall. Everybody is drunk, and there is not a parent in sight! It's almost too easy.	Cruise your dorm late at night with a six-pack under your arm. Most bars close around 2 A.M., but you can always find some chicks still looking to party. If you can get the party girls in your dorm room until about 3 to 4 A.M., and you *can't* hook up with them, then you should return this book and pick up *A Man's Guide to Dating Men*.
Sex	Not many chicks put out in high school. We should just be thankful that the ones that do are usually such whores they'll take on six or seven guys by the time they graduate.	*No* chick will leave college a virgin, unless she attends BYU or Bob Jones University. Every girl will bang somebody, and, as an asshole, it's your job to make sure	Flirt constantly. Become a flirting machine. Do not ever talk to a chick without having sex somehow enter into her mind during the conversation. After enough flirting, she

SUBJECT	HIGH SCHOOL	COLLEGE	HOW TO TAKE ADVANTAGE
Sex *(cont.)*		that somebody is *you.*	will start to associate the very mention of your name with sex. Pump enough drinks into her and she may think that she's already had sex with you, which, of course, will eliminate any inhibitions about doing it again.
Social status	The pecking order is firmly established in high school. Women use their social status as a club to beat over the head of any guy who's one or more strata below her.	She was prom queen? Who gives a shit? So were six other chicks in your freshman writing seminar. She is nobody in college. She's starting from scratch, so she can't pull any attitude. And she's probably scared as hell that she won't make any friends, so you've got her right where you want her.	Play on these insecurities, take her to parties, introduce her to people. Become her ticket to popularity. More than likely, she'll start sleeping with you out of sheer relief that somebody's taking care of her. If she doesn't, threaten to take it all away. If you can't, then start spreading nasty rumors, because that always makes you feel better.
Limits	High school chicks are usually pretty good about setting their limits and sticking to them.	College chicks are all about going past their limits. They want to expand their minds, their	Take advantage of this quickly before they develop any sense of self-control. Give them

SUBJECT	HIGH SCHOOL	COLLEGE	HOW TO TAKE ADVANTAGE
Limits *(cont.)*	That's mainly because they haven't yet discovered the joys of drugs and alcohol. The point is, if she doesn't want you getting to third base chances are you're not going to.	experiences, and their worlds in general. They don't know how much alcohol is too much, they don't know when to stop partying, and they sure as hell don't know the line between a whole lotta sex and life as a dime-store prostitute.	that extra shot of liquor or one more bong hit. Remind her that gang bangs and girl-on-girl action are both a healthy part of every coed's college experience. Become the one that expands their universe, gains their trust, and screws them seven different ways to Sunday.
You	Every chick in high school knows you, probably since you were a little kid. If you're Billy Freeman—the guy who puked in gym class—you're never getting laid, no matter how hard you try.	Nobody knows you.	Reinvent yourself. Suddenly, you can become Billy Freeman—the only guy in high school to ever bag the entire cheerleading squad. The possibilities are endless.

THE CHICK ROSTER—
UNDERSTANDING THE ENEMY

College chicks, whoa. The single biggest change between high school and college is the diversity and variety of chicks that you'll find once you've reached this magical age. In high school, the only girls you came into contact with were ones from your own neighborhood. That means that they had roughly the same amount of money as you, they lived in roughly the same environment, and they were roughly the same type of people.

However, now that you've matriculated (you're in college so you should be using big words like that), the variety is astounding. Old girls, ethnic girls, foreign girls, brainiacs, fat, short, poor, rich, fair-skinned, dark-skinned. There are more chicks in your "Intro to Macroeconomics" lecture than existed in your entire high school. And what does that mean? It means that you don't have the first friggin' clue how to relate to any of them. Thank God we're here to help:

TYPE OF CHICK	COMMON CHARACTER-ISTICS	HOW TO NAIL THEM	WHAT TO AVOID
Garden-variety sorority girl (sorority chicks can be broken down into two distinct groups, which will be shown below)	Follow-the-herd mentality. These posers will do anything—anything!—that their friends tell them to do or that they think they're supposed to do, including stuff that could lead to jail time for you, if not done properly.	Be a fraternity guy, athlete, any type that puts them at the center of attention (guys who are famous, or attend parties that everybody wants to get into). Give them anything that will make their friends jealous—jewelry, hot cars, nightly orgasms.	Substance—these chicks couldn't care less if you're smart, attentive, caring, thoughtful, or anything else that might mean something in the real world. Flash them a sweatshirt with the Greek letters of the most popular frat house on campus though, and they'll spread their legs wider than a football goalpost.
Gung-ho sorority chick	Gung-ho sorority chicks will only date guys that are also involved with the Greek system (or	Join the right fraternity. Ask her what her favorite house is, and then rush it the following	Any semblance of independence—if she thinks you don't hang out with fraternity boys at

TYPE OF CHICK	COMMON CHARACTER- ISTICS	HOW TO NAIL THEM	WHAT TO AVOID
Gung-ho sorority chick *(cont.)*	athletes). These girls specialize in Greek politics and care about little more than the popularity of their house. They use men as a means of social status and carefully pick boys based on the fraternities they belong to. Most of them freely abuse alcohol and dabble with drugs on a regular basis.	semester. Even if you don't get a bid, you can lie about it until you get her in the sack.	fraternity events, then she couldn't care less about you. If you have a mind of your own, hide it as if it's a crazy uncle locked up in the attic.
Disenchanted sorority chick	The disenchanted sorority sisters were generally pressured into joining a sorority, or just did it for the wrong reasons. Once they saw how catty and bulimic all of those bitches are, they lost interest.	These girls will mostly date any guy that matches their interests, regardless of social status or fraternity membership. Make sure to bag on all the stereo-typical qualities of the gung-ho sorority sisters. This will generally trick her into thinking you understand where she's coming from, which is always a good way to get laid.	Greek letters—take that fraternity sweatshirt off! Don't invite her to your next social with the Tri-Delts, and, for the love of God, don't expect to bang her when you've got five of your fraternity brothers hiding in your closet.

TYPE OF CHICK	COMMON CHARACTER- ISTICS	HOW TO NAIL THEM	WHAT TO AVOID
Female athlete	Lesbianism, height, sweats. Heterosexual female athletes are embarrassed by their athletic prowess, and they're terrified guys will think they're man-hating dykes. Unfortunately, most of them *are* man-hating dykes, so be careful to stay away from those. Conversely, the heteros will try extra-hard to be a "girly girl" away from the court to avoid the stereo-type. Therefore, they may not go for the typical asshole stuff. What makes it more difficult is that athletes generally don't party because alcohol is horrible for performance. Accordingly, you need to catch her out drinking after a big win. It may be your only chance to bang her before she realizes what the hell she's doing.	If she's a lesbian, she'll respond to chicks. If she's not, you've got to treat her as if she's the most feminine creature since Scarlett O'Hara. Due to her dyke-related fears, she needs to be treated like a petite flower, even if she's an overgrown pituitary monster. This is one of the many instances when you have to shelve your instinctual asshole tendencies in order to bag some trippy chick. It's probably worth it if she's still going down on you at 3 A.M.	Sports—playing sports, discussing sports, reading about sports, watching sports on TV, knowing about sports, thinking about sports, telling stories about sports, remembering sports, clothes that have the word "sport" in them.

TYPE OF CHICK	COMMON CHARACTER-ISTICS	HOW TO NAIL THEM	WHAT TO AVOID
Granola chick	Hairy armpits, unwashed hair, do-rag, insanely liberal politics, Birkenstocks, a face unsullied by makeup. These bleeding-heart liberals are among the most strident hypocrites in the world. A college girl is clueless as it is; but give her a strong political leaning and you can barely talk to the bitch. Somebody is always trying to ruin the world, and these chicks are trying to stop that from happening. Any coed more concerned with the ethical treatment of science lab hamsters than getting drunk deserves our deepest sympathies.	Don't. It's hardly worth it. Half of these causes don't require their female members to shave their legs. Not to mention, if she gets so worked up about things that don't even affect her, imagine what you're in for if she doesn't like the way you munch her rug. Still, if she's just so hot that you have to have her, the only way is to bite the bullet and join the cause. Our hopes and prayers are with you.	Granola chicks—unless you're a Grateful-Dead-head, too, in which case the two of you will have a wonderful ten years, driving a VW bus with peace stickers all over it. At that point, of course, you'll realize you need a job to feed your kids, and then you'll become just another conservative, establishment, fascist pig like the rest of us, but, hey, right now you guys are saving the world, right? Whatever.
Student government	Power trips, long speeches, rabid school spirit. These women are especially tough because they think their political	Full-throated, heated, radical arguments followed immediately by out-of-control screwing. These girls are passionate and	A dismissive, uncaring attitude. She will immediately leave if you don't show enough interest in her passion. Yes,

TYPE OF CHICK	COMMON CHARACTER-ISTICS	HOW TO NAIL THEM	WHAT TO AVOID
Student government (cont.)	prowess makes them the equal of men. They have forgotten that evolution blessed them with inferior strength, emotional instability, and a monthly bleeding period. Her battles will leave you exhausted, so she'd better make up for it by swinging from the chandeliers when you guys are having sex.	driven and you have to match their intensity in life and in the sack. Keep them challenged intellectually and engaged in conversation, with breaks only for blowjobs and pepperoni pizza.	even though the lack of any concern for human beings is a critical asshole trait, you're growing up and you need to know when to hold 'em and know when to fold 'em. If blowing her off is just going to send her into your roommate's bed, how much good have you done?
Library queen	Long nights in the study rooms, sheer panic when exams roll around, an ever-present excuse when you want to go out on a weekday. These chicks don't even consider your school a college, it's more like a gateway to graduate school. They simply live to study. She's fun to have around when you need to borrow somebody's notes; otherwise, you'd probably be better	All-night study sessions. Unfortunately, you must offer your support. These chicks are strictly academics-oriented and, if you really want to poke her, you're going to have to play along. Dates will be in a coffee-house so she can study, long weekends will consist of paper-writing. Everywhere she turns, people are telling her to lighten up and enjoy	Life, fun, friends. Did you really go to college to study? What, are you kidding me? You went to college to drink beers, bang sorority chicks, and vomit on a regular basis. Instead, are you going to go out with this girl and spend the next four years huddled in a library with a chick so stressed out about her finals that she stops menstruating? Get a grip, blow this

TYPE OF CHICK	COMMON CHARACTER-ISTICS	HOW TO NAIL THEM	WHAT TO AVOID
Library queen *(cont.)*	off hanging out with your mom. At least she'll pay for dinner.	herself and have a drink. You go the opposite way and tell her how much you respect her diligence. Bring her coffee late at night when she's studying. Eventually, she'll pass a big test and get frisky. When you bang her, do it *hard.* God knows, she needs it.	whore off, and go find yourself a dime-beer night at a local pub. Even if you strike out, it's better than being forced to actually read something.
Freshman	Innocence, naivete, complete inability to get a clue. Freshmen should not even be considered human beings. They are little headless, shaved pussies running around looking for a dick. For the first time in their lives, they are exposed to alcohol, boys, and bedrooms within the same one block radius. They are completely overwhelmed and impressionable in every way. Freshman girls will go way too far, way too fast,	It's important to jump on them early, and the first two weeks are critical. This is when they are most likely to run around with reckless abandon, acting like complete sluts. Once people start to talk badly of them, or once the silly bitches wise up a little, it becomes more difficult to put the handcuffs on them. Therefore, you should constantly pressure them to test their limits by upping the ante each time. These are by	Any self-doubt or lack of authority—a freshman chick is too scared to think on her own, and she needs the security of a man who will tell her what her thoughts are. If you can't get her into a party or show her the way around campus, she'd be just as well off with the fat, acne-ridden dork at the end of her dorm room floor. Know what you're doing, or fake it very, very well.

TYPE OF CHICK	COMMON CHARACTER-JSTICS	HOW TO NAIL THEM	WHAT TO AVOID
Freshman *(cont.)*	with regards to drinking, drug use, and sex.	the far the easiest targets you will ever encounter!	
Sophomore	**Dan's view**—Party machines. They've lost their "freshman fifteen" (pounds, that is). They know their way around campus, and they're not the timid, scared bunnies they were last year. They're getting used to independence and drinking themselves into a coma on a regular basis. Once they know their way around the bars, watch out!—because sophomore year is for sucking down as many beers as is humanly possible.	**Dan's view**—Give them a beer or a bong load. They don't want to hear about your classes, unless you're majoring in mixology. Find her a party, get her to a fraternity social, or just pour a gallon of booze down her throat before she walks out the door. Tomorrow morning, when you tell her what a great time she had, she'll be too hungover to know any different.	**Agreed**—Any discussion of school, your major, or your future. She's not concerned about any of that shit; not when there's dollar-beer night at the campus pub. She's too far away from graduation to be worried about a job, and she just got a fake i.d. from her sorority sister. Keep it at a level she can understand, right above the foam.
	Karl's view—After an entire freshman year of getting drunk and sucking dick, sophomore chicks need a good year to recover and wash the taste out of their mouth. They don't want to rage as much as they did	**Karl's view**—Appeal to their feminine side. Flowers, cards, candles—this is what they want. Last year was vodka shots and beer, this year is red wine and chocolates. If you style her even in the	

TYPE OF CHICK	COMMON CHARACTER-ISTICS	HOW TO NAIL THEM	WHAT TO AVOID
Sophomore *(cont.)*	last year, and they are jealous of all the younger and cuter girls that are garnering so much attention from the guys. They are looking for a little more stability.	slightest bit, she'll stick to you like a maternity suit and do anything to keep you around.	
Junior	Juniors are like middle children—the Jan Bradys of the college scene. She's not so young that she believes every line thrown at her by a fraternity guy; but she's not old enough to be a pissed-off, cynical senior. She wants to do well in school so she can get a good job, but she still likes to suck down five or ten wine coolers a night. Basically, she's a mess. Which should be easy pickings for an asshole like you.	Appeal to their intellect. Talk about the future, let them know that you share their concerns. Stage some fake study sessions that turn into social get-togethers. After you've both crammed all week for that brutal exam, she'll want to celebrate with you. Get her hammered, tell her to forget all of her worries, and then start cramming your way right up her ass.	Who the hell knows? A junior chick doesn't know what she wants, what she's doing, where she's going or anything else for that matter. Try to get her drunk because you know that always works. Otherwise, we don't have a clue.
Senior	Cynicism, bitterness, chip on the shoulder. They are all about their girlfriends and their	Grab them at the bars. Senior chicks can drink like champions. They go out constantly with	An aggressive bull-rush to their panties—these chicks need to be played a little, worn

TYPE OF CHICK	COMMON CHARACTER-ISTICS	HOW TO NAIL THEM	WHAT TO AVOID
Senior *(cont.)*	boyfriends. If she's single, then she's probably bitter. As a senior, she's tacked on some weight and can't possibly compete with the younger girls, which really pisses her off. They mostly want to spend time with their girlfriends, because they know there's not much time left. However, they also know that it is their last year of college, so when they party, they party hard.	their friends and get completely obliterated. Most of them are looking for older men, so they won't want to date you, but they will fuck you under the right circumstances. If all of her friends have boyfriends, they will be encouraging her to take home a new boy and bone him silly just for the sport of it.	down by compliments and any other lie that you can come up with. Seniors think they have the whole game figured out, and, if you try to bypass their emotional defense system with your standard rap, they'll be overjoyed to shut you down. Unless they're shit-faced, in which case you can do just about anything and get away with it.

THE MALE PECKING ORDER

Right now you might be asking, "Where is the guys' chart?" That's the beauty of college—for guys *there is no pecking order!* Anybody can and does get laid. Goofy, suave, funny, stupid, smart, athletic—it doesn't matter what your physical or mental impediments are, provided that you can come up with something—anything—that at least one chick thinks is worthy of a little lovin'. There are so many women, from so many different backgrounds, that, regardless of who you are or what you're into, you can still get laid! Why else do you think college is going to be the best time of your life?!

TIP #8: ANYBODY—WE REPEAT, *ANYBODY*—CAN GET LAID IN COLLEGE.

WHITHER THE CHICKS?

College is a huge departure from high school, in that you now have the ability to run in vastly different circles of people. In high school, how far could you really go? You either hung out in the quad with the popular people or a hundred yards away at the lunch tables with the stoners, or another hundred yards away at the gym with the jocks. In college, you've got a self-contained city, with hundreds of social groups spread out all over the place. Where and with whom does the asshole hang to ensure himself the maximum exposure to sorority girls and other tasty treats? Let's find out.

TIP #9: YOU *WILL* JOIN A FRATERNITY.

a. *Fraternities*—Asshole central. Fraternities are to assholes what the NBA is to six-foot-eleven black guys who can jump through the roof. (Don't ever call it a frat—do you call your country a "cunt"?) Every step of your development should be funneling you towards this one central universe. If you think that fraternities are a relic of a bygone era, or represent an element of college life that is too base or Neanderthal for you to handle, please run down to Nordstrom's, buy a pretty new scarf, and hang yourself with it, because we've got nothing else to say to you. If you've got your head on straight, though, let's think about the things you do as a fraternity dude:

- You drink beer
- You bang chicks
- You play bloody basketball games
- You drink more beer
- You haze pledges

It's almost too good to be true. The only bad part about the fraternity is that, at some point, they're going to make you leave. Since it is firmly established that you will join a house and spend the next four years doing everything in your power to entirely pollute your mind, body, and soul, we're just going to skip the "should you/shouldn't you join" question and move right on to what type of house is good for you. Here are your choices:

1. *Popular house*—While this would seem to be the obvious choice for you to join, remember that virtually every guy in the place is going to be an egomaniacal, bronzed, bulked-up prick. Although we imagine that accurately describes you, too, be careful that you don't end up one of many Indians trying to scalp the same pair of nipples. Before you join a house, make sure that you stack up well against the rest of the bros, because, no matter what kind of a stud you think you are, if a whole gaggle of sorority dunces show up for a party, and you're only the seventeenth-best-looking guy in the room, you might be looking at the mother of all bitch-getting battles.

2. *Athletic house*—Surprisingly, the athlete's house is not generally the best known or the most happening fraternity on campus. There are a bunch of reasons for this: athletes practice all the time, so they can't drink as much, they have to be careful to keep their names out of the school paper, and the whole place always smells like sweat. However, being involved with the athletes, especially in a big football school, will allow you to get leftover groupies on a fairly regular basis. You may not have the

most beer in the fridge, but you definitely have a whole boatload of freshmen begging to come to your BBQ after the next football game.

3. *Party house*—Another mixed blessing. Party houses *party*—hence, the name. You'll have a ton of beer bashes, endless dorm chicks running around, and a keg room unmatched on campus. But the raging party house is going to take a lot out of you. Constant binge drinking, ever-present drugs, and a propensity to watch the sun come up four mornings a week is going to wreak havoc on your body and put you in danger of flunking out before midterms. You must not get too carried away in the party house, or you'll put yourself in imminent danger of being carried away, right back to Mom's house while you dry out for a semester or two.

4. *Nice guy house*—You might as well wear a chastity belt. The positive: there will be tons of sorority girls running over to your place. The negative: every one of them will be looking for a shoulder to cry on after getting dumped by their asshole boyfriends. This, of course, will be three days before they go back to him. Hanging out in this house may allow you to lead the league in emotional assists, but you know that the only thing that really matters is how much you score. The one way you might be able to salvage your life as a member of a "nice guy" house is if you are truly a "wolf in sheep's clothing," i.e., if you are merely playing the chicks for a fool and making them think you care, when, in reality, you're pulling a Dennis Rodman, grabbing her on the rebound, and slamming it home.

5. *Dork house*—We mention the dork house only because it's going to be around the block and you'll have to deal with it. There are ways to make these houses work in your favor. When you schedule a social with the two smoking-hot chick houses on campus, invite the dork house and require them to buy all the beer. Plan a road trip and have the dorks take turns as

designated driver. Tell them that they can come to your post-football game BBQ if they save seats for you in the stadium's student section. Don't ever forget that you're an asshole, and, if it means that you have to take advantage of a bunch of skeevy dudes every once in a while, that's just part of the game.

b. *Dorms*—Most freshmen spend at least some time in the dorms, so you, the asshole, will probably end up there, too. There's nothing to be ashamed of as long as you do your duty by sleeping with at least two women on your floor. If you get screwed over and end up in an all-male dorm, you can always transfer to a different school.

c. *Clubs*—Joining clubs in college is an extremely dangerous activity. Yeah, there are cool clubs like the "Skull and Keys" at Yale, or the "Lords of Discipline" in the movie of the same name, but mostly clubs in college are for the unpopular and unloved to find someplace to hang out. You've got a fraternity. You've got sorority chicks. How is a club going to get you any more tail? You'd be better off blowing your hundred-dollar initiation fee on a hooker.

d. *Libraries*—In college, libraries are such unbelievable meat markets, the chicks might as well be hanging from hooks. This puts you in another serious asshole quagmire: you're an asshole, so you don't let people see you study. But then again, there are hundreds, if not thousands, of sorority girls at the library going into brain cramp as they try to understand big words. The solution? Sit down and crack open your biology book. Of course, you'll be a reading a *Playboy* sandwiched in between the chapters on human sexuality and STDs, but she doesn't need to know that.

e. *The Track*—Chicks like to run outside. The primary reason? Chicks know that, if they're indoors, they can't wrap a sweatshirt, around their big, fat asses. If they're running, however, they can claim that it's cold and they need the added clothing. It might be ninety-five degrees outside, with a heat index of one-thirty-seven, but every Tri-Delt on the track is wrapped up like she just stepped off of the frozen tundra.

f. *Resident Advisers (RAs) and Teaching Assistants (TAs)*— These positions are tough to call. Taking on responsibility is definitely not the way of the asshole. However, getting free stuff for doing virtually nothing does have its merits. The basic rule of thumb is this: only take the job if you are determined to use and abuse it for your own personal gratification. This includes taking advantage of young and insecure freshman girls in the dorms, as well as flunking the hot chicks in class and forcing them to blow you for a passing grade.

g. *Where Can You <u>Not</u> Find Assholes?*—Just think, *"If I were a nice, intelligent, pussy-whipped guy, which club would I join?"* You should come up with about 90 percent of the anti-asshole organizations.

BUILDING YOUR REP

Most college chicks don't care who you are, they simply care how you are perceived by others. You can be dumb as a stump, but if you have a 4.0 GPA chicks will think you're smart. You could be ugly, but if a chick's friends want to get a piece of your action, you immediately become desirable. The theory is pretty simple—chicks' complete lack of security makes them more concerned with other people's impressions of them than their own impressions of themselves. Accordingly, your reputation could be the key to getting college chicks. If you play your cards right, you can get laid on reputation alone. Here's a look at a variety of different tools that you have and how they can help you, or hurt you, when bird-dogging chicks:

a. *Sexual Rep*—Sure, size matters to some degree. If your chick is constantly asking, "are you in yet?", then there isn't much advice we can give you. But equally important to size are things like your stamina, creativity, and the ability to part your hair with your tongue. Do you know how you and your buddies sit around talking about the sluts you hooked up with the other night and describing everything that you did to them? Chicks do it as much as you! And they're about fifty times more graphic! A group of drunk chicks sitting in front of a half-eaten veggie pizza can discuss the clitoris for days on end. Because most guys they screw are drunk, passed out, or worse, women don't normally get the good stuff. When they do, they can't wait to run home and make their friends jealous by recounting the third and fourth orgasms they had the night before. Once you're a sexual dynamo in the sack, your stock will be soaring like a pre-IPO Internet company, circa 1999.

b. *Lies*—Lie, lie, lie, lie, lie, lie, lie, lie, lie. A chick wants a guy who's into art? You *love* art! She wants a guy who's smart? You've got a 4.0! She wants a guy with a ten-inch schlong? You've got a ten—wait a sec, you can't lie about the things that she'll eventually find out. But you can lie about damn near everything else.

c. *Alcohol, the Great Equalizer*—To a certain extent, it doesn't matter what the hell you do in college, because you always have booze to smooth things over. Nothing will help you get laid more than a healthy tolerance for alcohol. If you're the last one to pass out at parties, you get the final pick of women. Pissed off some girl at a party? Buy her a couple of shots and she'll be dancing with you before midnight. Grab some unwilling chick's boob? Blame it on the eighteen beers you drank right before. If the most gorgeous woman you've ever seen walks through the door, down a couple belts of grain alcohol and you'll be chatting her up in no time. Here are some of the finer points you'll need to know when dealing with booze:

1. *Build tolerance*—Buy a case of beer and sit at home alone with a deck of cards. Build yourself a pyramid of cards, and then

knock it down and drink a beer. Build the pyramid again, then knock it down and drink a beer. Repeat this process until you can no longer build the pyramid. This will let you know your tolerance. Acceptable college tolerance is fifteen beers, although you'll want to hit twenty before you graduate. If you get stuck on ten or so, join a sorority.

2. *If you have no tolerance, fake it*—If you can't build a pyramid after two beers, you're genetically inferior and you might want to consider a sex change. If you don't have enough money to get that done, here are some sure-fire ways to look like an alcoholic but remain stone sober.

   i. *Spilling beer*—With canned beer this is a piece of cake. Simply dump most of it from the get-go and carry around the empty can. Nobody will realize if it's full or not, especially the drunk-ass sorority girl who keeps following you around.

   ii. *Filling bottles*—If you're drinking from a bottle, it's trickier because people can see the level of beer. In this case, fill it with water, because nobody can tell the difference. When you've got a good crowd of people, pound the whole thing. If you do this six or seven times, people will think you're a God.

   iii. *Order virgin drinks*—Grab an orange juice and tell people you're drinking a screwdriver. Make sure you only do this with vodka drinks, because they won't be able to smell it. If you tell someone you're drinking a Jack and Coke, and they can't smell the Jack, you're busted. If someone grabs a taste of your drink and says there isn't any alcohol in it, the standard response is "Yeah, I could barely taste it either. I think they water down the vodka here, I'm gonna go grab a beer."

   iv. *Buy people Jager shots*—In a dark bar, a shot of Jagermeister is indistinguishable from Coke. Order one of each, and then give the Jager to your buddy while you shoot the Coca-Cola. After you do this four or five times, your

buddies will be stumbling around like idiots while you
automatically become The Man.

3. *Drinking challenges*—Part of being a supreme asshole is
occasionally throwing down the gauntlet and challenging your
fellow asshole brethren. In your collegiate career, you will
inevitably challenge or be challenged to numerous drinking
competitions. Fear not, for it won't be as bad as you think—
provided you abide by the following rule:

> ## TIP #10: NEVER BACK DOWN
> ## FROM A DRINKING CHALLENGE.

Pussing out on a chug contest will immediately catapult you
right down to "bitch." Even if you know the guy can out-drink
you, go for it anyway. It's not important to win, it's just
important to compete. Here's why:

  i. *They rarely finish*—Generally speaking, when a chick
     shows up or somebody delivers a pizza, you'll both be too
     distracted to continue. Plus, after three or four beers in a
     fifteen-minute time period, you're both too hammered to
     care much about winning the competition.
 ii. *Nobody wins*—In nine out of ten drinking competitions, both
     people end up so obliterated that there is no clear winner.
iii. *Both people lose in the morning*—No matter who won the
     night before, when you and your competitor wake up the
     next morning your heads will feel as if they had tire irons
     shoved through them. Who's the winner now?
 iv. *Both reputations win*—People love to talk about drinking
     competitions. Just partaking in one puts you above the rest
     of the crowd.

d. *Drugs*—If booze doesn't get you laid, drugs certainly will. You shouldn't do them to the point that you become a total burnout; but, if it's something you can handle, or you can afford rehab, it will definitely help you pull wool. Drugs separate the men from the boys. Everybody in college drinks, but fewer are willing to engage in illegal activities for their own sexual gratification. What's important is that you realize that certain chicks do drugs, and certain chicks don't. By doing drugs, you immediately have access to a larger pool of snatch than the non-drug users. Now, before we're hit with a lawsuit about contributing to the delinquency of a minor, understand that we're not promoting the use of drugs. All we're saying is that, if you buy boatloads of cocaine for a chick, you're guaranteed to get forty-eight straight hours of sex. With a couple bowls of dope, you'll only get about seven hours of sex, but she'll buy you a ton of Twinkles at the local Chevron Food Mart. Whatever you do with that information, it's on your conscience. Nevertheless, here are some things you'll need to know about mixing drugs and chicks:

1. *The chick is staunchly anti-drug*—Tell her you've done them before, but you don't anymore. Make up some horrible stories about being arrested, or almost dying. You'll be a bad, mysterious man that has experienced much more than she. This type of history will be mistaken for sexual prowess as well, leading you immediately into the bedroom.
2. *The chick is a drug abuser*—Get her the good shit so she's high as a kite. If possible, introduce her to a new drug and take it together. As the drugs expand her mind, use your cock to expand her rectum.
3. *She's never tried (freshman)*—Get her to use them and take advantage. Throw every cliché in the book at her. "It's college—you should experiment—it will help you fit it in—it makes you thinner." Try anything and everything, because

once she trusts you to get her high you're not more than thirty minutes away from getting her hymen, too.

e. *Cigarettes*—If you want to get laid, you need to be a bad boy. Smoking may kill you when you're eighty years old, but it is just plain sexy. Why else would we suck on those cancer sticks? It shows that you don't give a fuck about anything, which is always attractive to college females.

f. *Never Go to Class*—Assholes couldn't care less about teachers, or grades, or anything else. At least that's what they want people to think. It's important for you to give off this vibe, even though you want a decent GPA in order to get a better job, which gets your more money, which gets you more chicks. However, don't believe the hype that you actually have to attend school to get solid marks. Most college classes are taught from a book, and you can do just fine by reading it on your own time. If you absolutely must go to some classes, though, here is how to still be cool while doing it:

1. *Chronically show up late*—It shows that you don't care.
2. *Fall asleep*—Girls will think that you were partying all night.
3. *Reek of alcohol*—Soak your shirt in Jack Daniels and tell everyone that you're hammered.
4. *Drink in class*—Fill a forty-two-ounce souvenir Taco Bell drink with a vodka-tonic. Tell the hot chicks that you have it, and let them have a sip. Hopefully, they'll get so ripped that they end up at a bar with you afterwards.
5. *Hide*—Sit way in the back and leave early. Make sure nobody sees you, and pretend you didn't even go.
6. *Be quiet*—Never raise your hand to answer a question. When called upon, make a joke specifically designed to insult the professor or elicit a laugh. Other people will unquestionably talk about this later, and it is great for building an image. Your final exam is anonymous, so don't worry.

TIP #11: NEVER GET CAUGHT STUDYING.

g. *Never Get Caught Studying*—Assholes do not study, ever. There are plenty of times during the day that you can study without anyone ever finding out, though. Most people study at night, which is when the real assholes are out partying. Get up in the morning, take some time over the weekend, or study in the middle of the day. Just never get caught doing it, and never turn down a chance to party because you have work to do. If you do this right, you can still pull good grades. This makes women either think you're secretly brilliant or that you're the luckiest bastard on the planet. Both of these are attractive options.

h. *Fight*—Nothing will help you build your bad-boy, asshole image better than kicking a little ass. It gives you instant respect among your peers and it turns chicks to no end. However, getting *your* ass kicked can propel you to pussydom faster than anything else, so follow these rules carefully before you start duking it out with somebody.

   1. *Always fight bigger dudes*—Picking on smaller guys makes you a pussy. Not to mention, God forbid, one of them kicks your ass. You've got nothing to gain and everything to lose if you brawl with a midget.
   2. *Make sure you have him outnumbered*—If he has three friends, you'd better have four. Nothing is worse than kicking some guy's ass, only to have two of his friends pull you off and beat the shit out of you.
   3. *Be more sober*—Again, the great equalizer.
   4. *Hit him in the face*—Body shots may win a WBC championship, but most college fights only last two or three punches. Not to mention, even if you open up on his rib cage like Sugar Ray Leonard, nobody can tell the following morning.

You need to connect with the nose, eyes, or mouth. We strongly recommend the nose. First of all, it will bleed like a mofo, which makes you look like a total ass-kicker. Also, if you break his nose, he will have to walk around with two black eyes for the next month, a reminder to everyone of how cool you are.

5. *Protect your face at all costs*—Even if you lose the fight, make sure you're not taking away any souvenirs on your pretty face. Again, it's better to *look like* you have won than to *actually* have won.

DATING (I.E., GETTING BLACKOUT-DRUNK AND HAVING SEX)

TIP #12: IN COLLEGE, GROUP DATING IS GOOD.

In college, dating is all about groups. Sure, once in a while you'll take some tramp out to dinner and a movie, but that's definitely the exception to the rule. Almost all college dating starts with a lot of people and ends with individual couples pairing off to go home and have sex. Don't confuse this with a double date, or a group of several couples who are out on a date. Actually, the whole scenario doesn't really constitute a date at all, it's more like a mini-party. It is an event that is either organized by, or attended by, one of the datees. For example: "Me and my buddies are going to the campus bar later, you should stop by." The girl will then round up her friends and say "That guy I like is going to the campus bar tonight, we should go there." Although no formal date has been set, as soon as both groups arrive at the bar, the date has officially begun. Why do college kids go through this mass mating ritual, rather than just stepping up to the plate for a night alone with each other? We're glad you asked:

WHY?	GOOD FOR CHICKS?	GOOD FOR GUYS?	WATCH OUT FOR . . .
Perception	Remember that a chick is more concerned with what her friends think than what she thinks. In a group, her friends can go to the bathroom and give her the quick analysis. You'll need their approval before you get the girl.	Every other chick in the group is going to see you there with a woman. This is a major status symbol and makes you desirable to every jealous, single, and lonely chick at the gathering.	Looking like a dipshit. Even if the date is going horribly, you have to salvage it somehow. Even if your chick ends up being a man-hating dyke, bite your tongue and take the abuse. Every other chick in attendance will consider the way you treat your chick as a preview of what it would be like to date you.
Transportation	Because she arrives at the party with her own transportation, she can leave whenever she wants. She won't need to wait around for you to give her a ride.	This is not so good for you, because you'd rather have her trapped and completely dependent. But, hell, at least you can hang with buddies during the time it would've taken to pick her up.	Friends leaving early. Make sure you have your own transportation on any group date. Nothing is worse than getting dragged home early because your friend is a pussy.
Excuses	If she's not into you, one of her friends can fake an illness so that she can haul ass out of there without looking like she's running for cover.	You can do the exact same thing.	Mixed signals. There is a good chance that her friend might really be sick. Offer to help take her home. If the chick refuses, immediately start hitting on her friends.

WHY?	GOOD FOR CHICKS?	GOOD FOR GUYS?	WATCH OUT FOR . . .
It's less intimidating	With so many other people for you to talk to, she knows that she won't be scrutinized all night long.	You don't have to listen to her crap for five hours. You can take a break and pound a few beers to numb the sound of her voice.	Other assholes. If it's a bigger party, other guys will shamelessly scam on your chick. The best way to combat that situation is to have some of your buddies drag the scammer outside and kick the shit out of him.
Hooking up friends	If a girl is going to date you, she wants your mutual friends to date, too. That way, she has somebody else to keep tabs on you.	This is an awesome opportunity for you. If you manage to set up one of your buddies, you immediately open the door to chick-swapping and foursomes. Not to mention, if things aren't clicking with your date, it's perfectly acceptable to go after one of her friends.	Cock blockers. Some girls just love to make sure that nobody sleeps with any of their friends. If some chick is trying to cock block, you need to recognize it early on and get your buddies to run interference. Have them all hit on her, or get her drunk, or both. Unless you knock out the cock blocker, you're going home alone, so whatever you have to do is perfectly acceptable.

WHY?	GOOD FOR CHICKS?	GOOD FOR GUYS?	WATCH OUT FOR . . .
Security	College chicks like to get completely drunk and out of control—it's part of the fun. If a chick ends up puking and passing out in the bathroom, she'll want her friends to cover for her so she doesn't look bad in front of you.	She will drink way more with a group than she will with you alone. This gives you an opportunity to get her totally plastered and take her home willingly at the end of night.	Pushing her too hard. You want to get her trashed, but if she pukes even once, or doesn't look like she can stand, her friends will drag her out of there before you can even cop a cheap feel.

As you can see, group dating is a bit of a double-edged sword. Here are the ways in which to work each scenario so that you end up stabbing her with your penis:

a. *Meeting at a Bar*—If possible, have her get to the bar before you. She'll have loosened up with a couple of drinks, and you won't have to spend as much money on the leech if she's already semi-drunk. Regardless, try to keep yourself at no more than a light buzz, because you're going to need your wits about you. When you first see her, immediately gauge how drunk she is and pretend to be at the exact same level. Drunk chicks are afraid that sober guys will take advantage of them (which, of course, you will), so, if she's trashed, you're trashed. If she's sober, you're sober, but not for long. By the end of the night, you should both be hammered, which is virtually a money-back guarantee on getting laid.

b. *Meeting at a House Party*—Again, you will fake your level of intoxication to match hers exactly. Once you've got that down, house parties provide a great playing field for a little game of cat and mouse. At the beginning of the evening, shower her with attention, occupy all of her time, spend a couple of hours just having a conversation. Chicks love that garbage.

Meanwhile, you're feeding her a continuous flow of drinks and waiting for her defenses to crumble and her emotions to take over. When she's starting to really get into you, wander off and start talking to other people. Scout other chicks to make her jealous and hang out with your buddies so she knows you're popular. The key is to make sure that, while you are working the room, you make continuous and deliberate eye contact with her. Raise your eyebrows, wink, or do something funny when you know she's watching. The anticipation will very nearly kill her as she waits, growing more and more uncomfortable with the fact that you have other competing chicks and interests. Once she's about to burst, make your way back, corner her, whisper in her ear that she's the "hottest, sexiest thing in this place," and then get her the hell out of there. After all that teasing, you'll be lucky to get to your car before she's pulling your pants down.

c. *Dinner Parties, Dinners, and Eating*—Chicks often throw these little get-togethers in order to test a college boy. Until now, she's probably only seen you backpacking around campus or slogging down beers at the bar. Going out to dinner gives her a chance to test your manners and see how you clean up. Make sure to be on your best behavior, and don't get hammered, especially if she's throwing a party at her place. We know it's tough, because the manipulative little slut will have a warehouse full of booze for this event, but you have to restrain yourself. Again, don't get any drunker than she is which, unfortunately, will be stone sober. Make sure to sit next to her, as opposed to across from her. That way you can rub her leg, whisper in her ear, and not get caught checking out the other chicks at the table. Also, make sure that you feed her something. It could be anything, but a full cucumber or a dill pickle would be an excellent choice. She needs to get used to you shoving things into her mouth as soon as possible.

d. *Sporting Events*—This is your chance to shine. Previously, you couldn't get completely shit-faced, but at the game you can finally let it all out. Chicks love to see guys being guys when it comes to sports. Drink heavily, scream your lungs out, and head-butt every other guy within striking distance. If your team wins, go home and celebrate with a nice, sloppy fuck. If they lose, go home and take out your aggression with a nice, sloppy fuck.

e. *Organized Parties*—Whether these are school functions or fraternity/sorority mixers, they are the biggest pains in the ass you'll have to endure. There are so many other chicks at these events that it's nearly impossible to focus on your date (so she's going to be pissed), and you'd rather she not be there anyway. Your best bet is to talk to your date early on, pretend that you'd rather hang with her, but excuse yourself because your buddies are hammering you to be social. Proceed to get lost in the crowd immediately. Hit on chicks, get phone numbers, and try to bang anything that moves. During your prowl, periodically circle back to your date and tell her how miserable you are before leaving again in search of shaven pastures. Once you find a fresh womb, ditch the party and turn off your cell phone. The next morning, call the girl you came with and tell her that you're pissed off because she left the party without you. Ignore her detailed accounts of how she tried to find you all night long, and demand an immediate blowjob as retribution for her callous act.

f. *Study Groups*—No studying should take place. Assholes disrupt study groups, they don't participate in them. Show up late and make jokes while flirting. Bring a twelve-pack of beer and see if she'll have a few. Halfway through the study session, "accidentally" discover some drugs in your pocket and encourage using them with this line—"*Newsweek* said that this stuff increases your memory retention for at least a week after you use it." Who cares if you're lying, she's never going to try to look up the article anyway.

BUTTERING HER BISCUIT

In high school, your primary goal is to get at least one chick so you can develop a clue about how to shake your groove thing in the sack. College is for nonstop banging. Your singular goal as a college student is to bed down as many two-bit road whores as possible. If they're ugly, who cares, just don't let your friends see you. If they're fat, it's okay, as long as the lights are out and you're at least ten miles away from campus. If they're stupid—wait a sec, all chicks are stupid, who cares if they're stupid? Anyway, the point is that you should spend half your day in bed with somebody and the other half trying to find somebody else to get into bed with. And the best way to ensure a steady flow of trim is to turn yourself into a sexual kingpin. You want to leave women unable to speak, walk correctly, or form a sentence for at least two hours after you're done with them. Young man, you're going to have to learn how to lay pipe.

Now don't be alarmed if you're not Kama Sutra quite yet. You're still young and you've got all the time in the world to learn—unless, of course, you have a date *tonight*, in which case you've got about six hours. If you do it right you'll get to do it again, so go to the Appendix (page 251) to find out everything you need to know.

COLLEGE FINAL EXAMINATION

1. *You should always keep your out-of-state girlfriend because:*
    a. Phone sex is almost as good as real sex
    b. You won't spend that much money on your phone bill
    c. When she comes to visit you'll fuck her within an inch of her life
    d. Other girls at school will respect your commitment

2. *Which of the following statements is* false?
    a. Chicks will drink more in college than in high school
    b. Chicks will do more drugs in college than in high school
    c. Chicks will have more sex in college than in high school
    d. Chicks will become less neurotic and insecure in college than in high school

3. *Guys typically can't get laid in college because:*
    a. They don't play sports
    b. They dress poorly and have no class
    c. They don't know how to properly treat a woman
    d. Bullshit, every guy can get laid in college

4. *The best time to scam on a female collegiate athlete is when:*
    a. She's drunk out of her mind
    b. She's shooting free throws
    c. She's making out with her girlfriend
    d. You're five-foot-two

5. *When attending a dinner party at your chicks place, you should:*
    a. Make sure to finish every beer in the fridge
    b. Bring over a Barry Manilow CD to help set the mood

   c. Sit directly across from her

   d. Put something in her mouth, preferably a full cucumber or a polish sausage

6. *The most important rule for drinking like an asshole is:*
   a. Make sure you can drink everyone under the table
   b. Always fight when you're completely hammered
   c. Never show up to class sober
   d. Periodically back down from a drinking challenge

7. *Group dating is good for women because:*
   a. They all like to gang-bang
   b. By alternating words with their friends they can form coherent sentences
   c. If they pass out in the bathroom they won't wake up in your bedroom
   d. They are so bad with directions that they couldn't find the date alone

8. *Sporting events are great group dates because:*
   a. Women want you to get drunk and obnoxious
   b. Chicks are so into sports that they'll spend most of the time diagramming plays with you
   c. Being exposed to nachos and jalapeño poppers might make your chick really skinny
   d. You're allowed to head-butt her after a good play

9. *At a sporting event, you should:*
   a. Spend the first quarter making finger sandwiches
   b. Read the Bible
   c. Masturbate in front of the entire student section
   d. Get completely obliterated and head-butt anybody within ten feet of you

10. *If you're about to get in a fight at college you should:*
   a. Go over the Marquis of Queensberry Rules with your opponent
   b. Kneel down and pray with your opponent
   c. Hit him in the face before he gets his hands up
   d. Quickly drown nine shots of Goldschlager

ANSWERS
1-c, 2-d, 3-d, 4-a, 5-d, 6-a, 7-c, 8-a, 9-d, 10-c.

Chapter Four

AGES 21–27

WELCOME MAT

You are out of college! This is horrible! Why? Because once you're out of school everything goes to shit. School organized your life, set up defined rules and regulations, even gave you help when you needed it. You lived off your parents, partied yourself into a near-coma virtually every weekend, and accepted responsibility about as often as you accepted the check at the end of dinner. Boy, are those days over. There are no more freshmen in the dorm, and suddenly chicks don't think it's cool to get blackout drunk every night. While your education consisted of a series of quick, stressful examinations that were followed shortly thereafter by heavy consumption of alcohol, now your every waking minute is filled with paralyzing stress, as you try to stave off creditors while maintaining a high enough Visa card limit to fake the girls into thinking you have a little cash. Success that used to be measured by your GPA is now quantified by the size of your 401(k). Get used to it, get on with it, get a friggin' job.

YOU'RE NOT IN COLLEGE ANYMORE

TIP #13: YOU WILL MISS SCHOOL . . . A LOT.

The party is over. Put down that red cup of keg beer and turn in your black lights for good. Here's a list of disappointments that you can expect to deal with for the rest of your life.

CHANGE	COLLEGE	NOW
Chicks	You had access to tons of chicks, more than you could ever hope to get into bed. For every stuck-up bitch, there were at least two sluts that would blow you. And all of them were drunk or high, i.e., easy pickings.	The women are gone. It's unexplainable, but 90 percent of the women on Earth mysteriously disappear after you graduate from college. The only ones left are money-hungry bitches that only care about the size of your wallet.
Living	Everything you needed was within walking distance. Chicks to the left, your buddies to the right, and the campus pub right down the street.	You live alone or with a roommate. Your next-door neighbor is at least ten years older than you and calls security when the TV is turned up too high. There isn't a single hot chick in your entire complex, and even the average ones somehow got themselves a boyfriend before you arrived.

CHANGE	COLLEGE	NOW
Meeting people	"What's your major?" "What year are you?" "Do you know anything about this class?"	"Why did you choose to be an astrophysicist?" "Do you come here often?" "Why are you laughing at me and walking away?"
Not giving a shit	It was the pinnacle of cool. You could walk around in dirty jeans and a baseball cap while showing up to class hungover.	Unless you have a career path, goals, and some semblance of a life, you might as well be invisible. (Note: This does not apply to people in bands. As a matter of fact, nothing does. If you are in a band, you will get laid. Period.)
Dating	Group dating, tag teams, keg parties.	Expensive dinners, flowers, candles.
Money	Money was practically useless in college. Even if you were poor, you could still go to a party, get drunk for free, and bang a cheerleader.	It is the only thing that matters. Even if your penis is the size of a chick pea, as long as your wallet is the thickest thing in your pants, you are going to get laid.
Job	Flipping burgers was fine and bartending practically gave you the keys to the castle.	The only thing that pulls as much wool as money is power. Power comes from a job—a good job with a lofty title. Without it, you'd better have enough money to retire at twenty-five.

CHANGE	COLLEGE	NOW
Décor	Bean-bag chairs and futons were the only acceptable furniture.	Your black-light posters and the four-chamber bong you so lovingly refer to as "Python" are no longer appropriate decorations for your apartment. You'd better get some couches and scrub that black shit off the bottom of your shower if you ever expect a chick to spend the night.
Fighting	Beating somebody senseless was a sign of status and entirely necessary if you wanted to build a good reputation.	If you get into a fight now, people think you're retarded. Not to mention, college kids generally don't carry weapons. If you're fighting a total stranger in the real world, you'll be lucky to get no more than an ass whupping. Whether you're conscious or not at the end of the fracas, everyone will still look at you as a loser.

Don't worry about the above, though, it gets worse. We've got three words for the life you will lead once you're out of college: *this . . . ain't . . . school.* As a student, you had an idealized version of the world, since your parents or the government took care of most of your needs. Okay, okay, maybe you had a job working for the student administration where they paid you ten bucks an hour. At the time, that was enough to buy you beer, condoms, Red Bull, and your other basic necessities. And we're sure that you spent a majority of your time bitching about how hard you worked and how much you hated waking up before 10:30 A.M. every morning. Trust us, you'll never see "10:30" on your home alarm clock again.

Instead, now that you've left your educational nirvana, you get to find out what it's really like to bleed for every penny. And that's your life *aside* from chicks! Women? That's going to be a whole new experience, too.

School provided you so many natural advantages when it came to scamming on chicks that it will most likely take you years to adjust to your new surroundings. Although we touched on many of the things that artificially propped up your ability to get laid while you were a student, there are a few that need a little more elaboration:

a. *Alcohol*—Chicks don't get incoherently drunk at least three nights a week once you're in the real world. Back in school, as long as you knew there was a keg around, a ditzy sorority girl could always get so liquored-up that she actually thought you were good-looking. You know the old saying, "She's a two at 10 P.M., but a ten at 2 A.M."? It works the same way for women, and that's probably the reason why, even if you couldn't pick up a napkin at the start of a party, by the wee hours of the morning you were peeling the women off of you. Unfortunately, those days are essentially over. Women work now. They have to get up in the morning and, even more unfortunately, so do you. Yes, they'll still drink on weekends, but remember, your liver is just like the rest of your muscles: when you work it out, it gets stronger; when you don't, it will atrophy. Now that neither you nor the chicks you hang out with will be drinking as much, you won't have the tolerance that you used to have. Women are shit-faced after two beers, which means that they're not drinking for three hours, they're drinking for thirty minutes, so you don't have as much time to score. Basically, you're screwed, and not in the way you had hoped to be when you showed up.

> **TIP #14: DON'T KID YOURSELF,
> IT'S ALL ABOUT CASH IN
> THE REAL WORLD.**

b. *Money*—Who genuinely cared about money during college? What could you buy? A few more pitchers of beer, a PlayStation 2? So what? Now, however, the size of your wallet counts even more than the size of your schlong. It doesn't matter who you are, what you look like, or how intelligent your conversation, if you can jet off to Tahiti for the weekend without batting an eye, you're guaranteed to be banging Dallas Cowboys Cheerleaders as long as the bank roll holds out. Donald Trump? The most arrogant, self-obsessed, hideously ugly human being the world has ever known? We're sure there hasn't been a Miss America in the past twenty years that he hasn't screwed at least once while flying over Atlantic City in his helicopter. If you make a lot of money, you will be good-looking, funny, articulate, and inordinately desirable. Lose your money and you're an ugly, boring, stupid loser. Cool, huh?

c. *Responsibility*—You *thought* you had responsibility in college. You whined every day about how hard it was to study, go to class, prepare for exams, stay involved in campus activities, and get blind-drunk six nights a week. We hate to tell ya, but that's not responsibility. Responsibility is knowing that you've got to come up with eleven hundred bucks to pay for your shoe-box one-bedroom apartment or you're going to be out in the street. Responsibility is having a hard-assed boss who'll dock you a day's pay if you're not at your desk by 8 A.M. every morning. And don't forget, for these next few years, it's still easy! In a little while (about a hundred pages or so), you're going to be married, with kids screaming for their bottle every sixteen minutes. But don't think about that for now—we can't have you killing yourself before you finish reading this chapter. There's too much good stuff coming up.

d. *Your Image*—College is Birkenstocks, sweatpants, and long hair. The Working World is wingtips, business casual, and a tightly cropped 'do. When you were twenty it was cool to be an anti-authority, stoned-out, grungy mess. People thought you were hip, they thought you were cool, they thought you could get them good drugs. Now, though, if you walk into an interview with dreadlocks, the last person you shake hands with will be the security guards. You've got to clean yourself up, you dirty, disgusting pig. Shave the octagonal goatee. Wash your jeans. And for God's sake, cut your friggin' hair!

e. *Finding Chicks*—Whether or not you were actually banging a different chick every night during school, you undoubtedly had the *opportunity* to bang different chicks every night. You couldn't walk across the street without passing by fifteen new women who, if you played your cards right, you could've had. Other girls just showed up at your fraternity, your campus pub, or somebody's house party. That time in your life is over. If you want to meet women now, you've got to bust your ass.

DO NOT COMPROMISE YOUR MORALS

After reading the last section you're either (a) depressed, (b) terrified, or (c) both. There's really no need to worry. All other assholes before you have come through this transitional period with most of their faculties intact. Anyway, the point is that the biggest change you've got to make once you're out in the cold, cruel world is to learn how to modify your behavior without giving up your core asshole-ness. In school you could do pretty much anything you wanted. Now, you can't just be a blatant asshole in front of everybody. To carelessly move forward without altering the way you act towards people will result in unemployment, poverty, and extreme loneliness. Just remember that you are an asshole, and although you may compromise your previous asshole lifestyle, you will never compromise your asshole morals. The core tenet that you'll have to keep in mind as you read the remainder of this book, though, is that assholes do not simply charge forward blindly. When you find yourself in a situation where your asshole-ish behavior could ruin your life, or worse, make that chick sleep with somebody else, you've got to be mature enough to not do whatever stupid thing it was that you were thinking about doing.

PICKING UP CHICKS LIKE AN ASSHOLE

As we told you earlier, you're going to have to work your ass off to get women once you leave college. Whereas, you used to sit around and women just stumbled into you, now you've got to go out there, risk life, limb, and your ego, and pick up as many chicks as you possibly can. Most of them will be strangers who couldn't care less whether you lived, died, bought them a drink, or were completely humiliated in front of every guy you've ever known. This makes the act of picking up women fraught with danger. You have to be smarter than the women, which, of course, shouldn't be that tough.[1] Here are the different places you've got available to work your magic:

a. *Work*—Sleeping around at work is definitely not for the faint of heart. Maybe you've heard the pithy maxims, "Don't fish off the company pier," "Don't dip your pen in company ink," "Don't shit where you eat." There are entire books about workplace relationships. There are thousands of lawsuits about workplace relationships. It's tough enough to find a woman to sleep with you, but, if you're poking some coworker you've also got to worry

---

[1] The best and most sure-fire way to get laid by a total stranger is to have one of your friends convince the chick that you're somebody else. That's right, you need your buddies to lie their asses off for you. Once they've convinced some chick that you were England's biggest pop star before moving to America and completely losing your accent, she'll be stripping down before you get her back to the car.

about whether or not she's going to report it to the boss, if you're going to get fired for feeling her up at the water cooler, or if one night of premature ejaculation is going to lop fifteen grand off your salary.

Even if you do manage your way through those minefields, there's a serious question whether you would want to spend the entire day with the same chick you're nailing anyway. How are your other chicks going to call you if your primary girlfriend is two feet away from your desk? Another thing to think about is the fact that she's going to be with you all day . . . every day . . . all day. Do you think you can really stand the same chick twenty-four hours a day? What could you possibly have to say to her that you didn't say this morning or last night or yesterday afternoon? Unless your secretary has "D" cups and can suck a cantaloupe through a hundred feet of garden hose, we strongly recommend that you keep the pickle in your pants when you go to work every day.

Still, because we're dealing with assholes and we know you're going to do whatever the hell you want to do regardless of what we say, here is a guide to nailing the busy little beavers that make up the female working force:

TYPE	DESCRIPTION	HOW TO GET HER
The eager beaver	These are the Murphy Brown types that work extremely hard to get where they're going, and they usually have the brains to do it. They have educations from the nation's top schools and they understand office politics. You may think she's being friendly, but there's a good	Even though she's a hard-working chick, she's still a chick, which means she's insecure and needs a man's approval to feel like she's worth a damn. Don't let the business suit fool you; underneath is nothing but a garter belt. Motivated women know what they want in the workforce and

TYPE	DESCRIPTION	HOW TO GET HER
The eager beaver *(cont.)*	chance she's just using you as another stepping stone on her way to the top.	they know what they want in bed. Sex is a necessary release for these hyper-motivated sluts, so, if you can get them for a one-night stand, it will most likely resemble a four-hour bull ride. Hold on to her horns and pray that you don't get bucked right into unemployment.
The sharp-toothed beaver	These chicks are just like the eager beavers, only they are hot, and they're willing to bone their way up the corporate ladder. They dress like sluts and they disappear for hours on end in their boss's office. You will never actually catch them working, but they will generally make an appearance at the company Christmas party to accept their award for outstanding salesman or something similar.	DON'T! A night with the sharp-toothed beaver is similar to numbing your penis and shoving it in a pencil sharpener. Sure, it will feel good, but in the end you've got nothing but a useless bloody stump, which is exactly what she'll turn your career into. Ask yourself this question, "Would you put a fifty-year-old man's saggy balls in your mouth to get a promotion?" Hell no! But *she* would, which means she is stronger, tougher, and more ruthless than any other bitch you can imagine. The fact they are so damn hot makes them as tempting as mermaid sirens, but you must resist!
The shaved beaver	These are the hot chicks with no brains. As opposed to making a conscious decision to sleep their way to	Ask her out on a date and get her drunk. Keep in mind these chicks are stupid. They are routinely

TYPE	DESCRIPTION	HOW TO GET HER
The shaved beaver *(cont.)*	the top, they just get swept along the promotion trail as they bed down layers upon layers of management above them. They are as good-looking as they are stupid, and it is often a subject of discussion how she managed to become a vice president. Well, all you have to know to understand how she made it is that, underneath that skirt is a pair of kneepads and an ass like a ten-year-old boy.	taken advantage of, and when you do it, too, she won't object. Tell her she's smart, that you really enjoy working underneath her, and then see whether or not you can get dragged along in her sexual wake. Even if you don't get the promotion, you'll get a few hours of fun on top of her big-ass mahogany desk.
The support beaver	Secretaries, office administrators, executive assistants, and every other chick in a "going-nowhere" job fits into the category of support beavers. These chicks are just happy to have a place to go from nine to five, so that they don't have to sit on their asses, eating Oreos, and watching *All My Children* everyday. They are generally attractive women, picked because they are pleasing to the eyes and ears. They are such perfect targets for the trained asshole that they should literally come to work with a bullseye on their forehead.	Spend money on them and show them respect. We know what you're thinking: you never show a girl respect. But remember, you're just playing the game. Men in your company yell at these women, boss them around, and treat them like shit for eight hours a day. They are also underpaid and underappreciated, so, if you take them some place that they can't afford on their own salary, listen to them, and show even a modicum of respect, you are guaranteed to get some ass later on. Plus, when you get them drunk on that expensive wine, you will truly be able to act out all of your asshole fantasies. First, these women are used to

TYPE	DESCRIPTION	HOW TO GET HER
The support beaver *(cont.)*		taking orders, so by all means do horrible things to them. And second, they understand the value of a dollar, because they have very few. Therefore, the lure of cash will allow them to do things that normal people could not even imagine. These are unquestionably the most appealing chicks for any and every asshole.
Unemployed or lower-class beaver	These chicks are beaten down by the world and looking for anyone that has a couple of dollars in their pocket. Strippers, hookers, waitresses, out-of-work actresses (which is a Los Angeles slang term for strippers, hookers, and waitresses), all fall into this category.	These women have never even seen the finer things in life. If you can show them paradise, they will show you what it feels like to be dehydrated from sex. The only problem is because they are abused on a daily basis, the unemployed beaver has stronger-than-normal defense mechanisms. Imagine you're a waitress, and every asshole in the bar keeps hitting on you. What are you going to think of the next one who tries? The key to getting these chicks is repetition. Keep going to the bar, keep talking to them about things that they're interested in. Keep asking them out. Once they say yes, buy them a lobster and let them provide dessert.

b. *Weddings*—Going to your friend's wedding is a double-edged sword. On the one hand, you've lost a drinking buddy and a potential wingman, on the other hand, you get bridesmaids.

Weddings are a rare and sanctified event. Before women even know how to ask for money, they are brainwashed into thinking that their wedding will be the most perfect and romantic day of their life. When a single woman goes to a wedding, it is just a reminder of how pathetic her life has become and how far she's drifted from her eternal goal. As an asshole, it's your job to take advantage of this situation by turning into Prince Charming for at least one evening. If you talk a little, dance a little, and drink a lot, before the night is over, your tuxedo will be spread out all over the eighteenth green right outside the reception. And you won't be using your golf club for putting.

1. *Top five reasons why it's easy to get laid at a wedding*

   i. *It sucks to be a single chick*—A wedding is a reminder to every single woman that she hasn't found a decent man yet. By the end of the ceremony, she is so freaking lonely that she doesn't need Mr. Right, she just needs Mr. Right Now.

   ii. *Taking off the dress is more fun*—There's a simple formula to remember—for every hour of wedding time, chicks will spend four hours getting ready. After all of that ridiculous curling, ironing, shaving, painting, and buffing, they are dying to rip those clothes off and run around naked as the day they were born.

   iii. *Girls love to dance*—Nothing makes a chick hornier than dancing. If she's covered with sweat and shaking her ass, you can bet the bowling alley that she's not more than two Cosmopolitans away from getting nasty in the coat closet.

   iv. *Everyone is drunk*—If this isn't self-explanatory, please administer a paper cut to your scrotum.

v. *You look good*—You're wearing your finest suit and she's got beer goggles, isn't that great? Not that it really matters, though, because, by the end of the night, she'd sleep with a criminal just so that she wouldn't have to go home alone.

2. *Strike early and play marriage*—The best way to get laid at a wedding is to pick a chick early and work her all night. This is why bridesmaids and groomsmen are always in equal numbers. They are practically required to pair up at the end of the night. If you're a groomsman, it is your duty to tag the chick that you walk down the aisle with. By choosing somebody early on, she'll start to attribute her romantic feelings to you, and she will eat up virtually anything that you say.

c. *Funerals*—It's arguable, but a funeral may actually be a better place to pick up some ass than a wedding. If you're shaking your head and thinking that this section is in bad taste, then why did you read the rest of the book, you friggin' hypocrite? Facts are facts. When women mourn they feel vulnerable and need a strong man to latch onto. This is never more true than with a woman who has lost her breadwinner.

Widows, due to the depth of their pain, are undoubtedly the easiest targets you will find at any funeral. After all, they just lost their husband, which means they haven't gotten laid in at least a week. They also just inherited all of his money, which means they won't need so much of yours. On the flip side, you need to make sure that you check the husband's cause of death. Early heart attacks, alcoholism, and suicides are usually pretty strong signs that your luck won't be much better than his.

d. *Coffee Shops*—Ever since we started watching Jennifer Aniston's tits in that big, overstuffed chair every Thursday night, the concept of picking up tail in a coffee shop has been gaining steam.

You just know that somebody who has an ass like Courteney Cox is going to show up eventually. Coffee shops have become the pickup bars of the new millennium. You don't go there to have a cup of joe, you show up for the atmosphere. People are lounging around outside, playing chess, reading books about astrophysics, studying for final exams—all things that are about as fun for you as pulling out nose hairs. But the coffee shops do have chicks, and that's all that really counts. So, suck down another Sudanese Mango Coffee Bean and wait until after her fourth cup, when she's so wired she won't be able to do anything else but bang you.

e. *Bars*—God help you if you spend the majority of your time picking up chicks in bars. This is the most painful, thankless, and least-likely-to-work scenario for even the Zen Master of assholes. Bars are full of stuck-up, bitchy chicks that stand around all night looking for the coolest guy in the bar so they can blow him off and eventually go home alone. Half the chicks don't even drink, which means they're hazing us by not going to the coffee house in the first place.

TIP #15: THE BARS ARE BRUTAL.

Before you go down this road, make sure to check your ego at the door. You will be shot down, laughed at, and possibly embarrassed—but look at the bright side, at least you're not a chick. You are an asshole, and you need to remind yourself of that every night you hit the clubs. Before we get into the advice portion, though, you have to understand one concept: "periscope up."

"Periscope up" refers to submarines that are cruising along with their periscope out of the water. They are vulnerable at this point, because the enemy knows where the submarine is and they know that it's searching for something, probably the target for its next torpedo. When you are walking through a bar desperate for some action, your sexual periscope is up and chicks know who you are and what you're looking for. And they figure that, if you haven't been able to get it from anybody else, you sure as hell aren't worth their time. Your ability to hide your, uh, periscope, will generally be the deciding factor in determining whether you're going home with a person, or yet another video.

Now that we've got that out of the way, here are some of the most important points you'll need to know about hitting on women in bars:

1. *Act like you just don't care (periscope down)*—When a chick sees that you don't much care whether she talks to you or drowns in her Long Island Iced Tea, her female insecurity will jump into overdrive, as she desperately attempts to show you how good she is. Therefore, you must walk around the bar as if there isn't a single chick worthy of your pickle. None of these women mean anything, and they should consider themselves fortunate if you even talk to them. You must be convinced of this when you enter the bar. Women can smell it if you're not. Remember, any guy that looks eager never gets the beaver.

2. *Do not approach a chick unless you have something to say*—The bar is crawling with assholes that have absolutely nothing to offer. If you go up to a chick and say "Hi, my name is Fred," you're about as likely to get laid as a woman is to get smart. It doesn't matter what you say, as long as you are 100 percent sure that no other guy in the bar has said it to her. It may take a little work, but if you can come up with something original, she might even remember your name long enough to scream it out later.

3. *Lines don't work*—Even if you know one hundred of the funniest pickup lines ever made and you're using them as a mere comedic smoke screen—don't. Women do not think these

are funny, and if you tell her one that she's already heard, then you've already violated point number two. If you do have encyclopedic knowledge of pickup lines, you may bring them up later as an example of how lame "other" guys are. Most women will find them amusing, but only after they've gotten to know you a little bit.[2]

4. *Do not offer to buy her drinks until you are at least fifteen minutes into the conversation*—You are an asshole, not an ATM. This is the hardest rule for most guys to follow. It's as if the second you meet a chick in a bar, the words "Can I buy you a drink?" are ripped out of your mouth by some supernatural chick god. But you *must* control this impulse. Buying the drink too early screws you from the start. You must spend at least fifteen minutes in conversation, because if you offer a drink before she knows you, then:

   i. *She couldn't care less*—How many times have you bought some chick a drink, only to see her raise it up, say thanks, and then leave you there looking like a little bitch? You might as well have just offered her the money.

   ii. *She doesn't want to owe you*—Oftentimes, women think that if you buy them a drink, then they owe you something. Many of them will avoid this feeling of obligation by refusing the drink. Unfortunately, we take this as the world's greatest insult, when, in reality, we should thank them for not being the whore that takes the beer and walks off.

   iii. *They think you're getting them drunk*—Look, they know that you're eventually going to try and get them drunk, but don't be so obvious about it. Any guy that buys a drink for a total

[2] You're much better off doing something extremely original and creative: tear a napkin up so that it reads "Hi," send her an entire bottle of booze, or have the bartender hand her your coat with a message that says "What are you doing with my coat? I'm coming over to get it back." These types of tricks are universally considered "cute," and will, therefore, require the girl to give you, at the minimum, the time of day, and, at the maximum, the keys to her apartment.

stranger is obviously giving off signs of being "periscope up," which will consign him to a night of masturbation and watching the scrambled signal on the Spice Channel.

iv. *They expect it*—Every other guy in the bar is offering to buy them drinks, which gives you an excellent shot at being original. Not to mention, fuck every girl that thinks a pussy entitles them to free drinks. Only blowjobs should entitle a chick to discounts, and you shouldn't even consider a free one until she takes it in the ass.

v. *It makes you look boring*—You just met this chick and the only conversation you can generate is "Can I buy you a drink?" That's pathetic.

5. *Wait them out*—After fifteen minutes of conversation, both of your drinks will be empty. Because she is a chick and thinks that her genitalia entitle her to everything in the goddamn world, she will expect you to offer to buy her one more. Under no circumstances do you do this of your own accord. Wait until she says one of the following two things.

i. *"I'm gonna go grab a drink"*—This means it's been nice talking, but she's getting the hell out of there. Totally unacceptable. Your time is valuable, and she owes you money for wasting it. Before she can get up to go to the bar, sneak in a quick, "Great, could you grab me a beer?" The look on her face will be priceless. She will be caught entirely off guard. However, because she's a chick she's scared that if she says "no" it will somehow reflect poorly on her character. She'll go ahead and buy you the beer out of the sheer terror of not knowing what to do and not having a man around to explain it to her. When she returns, take the brew, say "thanks," and leave her there. She'll probably track you down later and beg for your children.

ii. *"I'm gonna grab a drink, do you want anything?"*—
Congratulations, this chick is into you so much that you
don't even have to spend your own money. Since it's clear
that she likes you, you should comment on both her
willingness to part with a few bucks and the sparks that
must have been flying between you two. She'll smile
appreciatively and you will be tempted to tell her that she
doesn't have to buy anything, you'll pick up the beers.
Don't! Only pussies crack at this point. Stand strong and
remember that you're an asshole. Since you're God's gift to
women, she *should* be buying you drinks, so just sit there,
wait for her to come back, and make sure that the condoms
in your wallet have not expired.

6. *Every drink you buy must be accompanied by a shot*—After she
   has bought you a drink, or you've spent so much time together
   without a drink that you're about to kill yourself, it's okay to
   start buying her booze. Just remember one thing: you're not
   buying drinks to be social or fit in, you're buying drinks to get
   this chick hammered. That's why you'll take her order and
   bring back two drinks and two shots. Make sure it's a girly shot,
   like a Lemon Drop or a Kamikaze, because then she'll have no
   excuse not to take it. Every time you return to the bar, bring
   back another shot with every drink. She'll eventually be so
   drunk, she'll start buying the shots, and then you're home free.

7. *Approach alone*—Although you always have a bunch of buddies
   with you at the bar, you must approach a girl by yourself. Even
   if she's sitting with other girls, you must not go in with
   reinforcements. One guy who walks up to a girl, or girls,
   appears to be innocent and nonthreatening. Two or more guys
   who swagger up to a bunch of women look like a pack of wild
   hyenas moving in for the kill. This is a clear indication that all
   of you are "periscope up," and you will be met by scorn,

derision and contempt, if the girls even acknowledge your presence in the first place.

8. *Be cordial to her friend, but focus on her*—When talking with a group of chicks, it is important to be cordial to all of them, but focus on the hottest one immediately. Her other friends will wonder why you are not talking to them, which means that *they* will start to like you. Once this happens, the hot chick will sense their interest and, in order to prove her dominance over the herd, will begin to monopolize the conversation with you just to keep them out of the loop, essentially doing the dirty work of blowing off the ugly chicks without you being blamed for it. As soon as you get an opening, separate her from the pack so she is helpless and alone. The bitter, abandoned friends won't care about her anymore, and you've got an open battlefield with a defenseless enemy.

9. *Bring a chick with you to the bar*—Again, think outside the box. Single guys go to bars with other guys. It's an immediate indication that their periscope is up, and you might as well paint the words "desperate and alone" on your forehead. If you show up with a chick, you are no longer considered a threat. Even if it's just a friend or your own sister, it gives off the following vibe to women:

   i. *You're not a dickhead*—If there is a woman that's willing to go out in public with you, other chicks will know that you're not a complete loser.

   ii. *Women find you desirable*—You're not holding a gun to her head, which means that this woman has made a conscious decision to spend time with you. If she's doing that, then surely you must have something to offer, even if it's just a twelve-foot speedboat or a penis that's one to one and a half inches longer than normal.

iii. You don't need another chick—If you've already got one, you're immediately seen as "periscope down," because other girls think you're taken. This gives you an excellent opportunity to sneak in the back door, so to speak.

iv. Jealousy—If we've said it once, we've said it a thousand times: chicks are catty, jealous bitches. They can't believe that any man in the bar wouldn't want them if they're holding a new Gucci bag that matches their fuck-me pumps. The fact you don't want her makes Gucci Girl blind with jealousy and rage, and she will resort to anything to make you like her. If you sense that some of the women in the room are in this state, tell your pseudo-date to go to the bathroom, and you will have a veritable tidal wave of female humanity attacking you the second she's gone.

10. *Bring a grenade-jumper*—Chicks travel in packs just like wolves. Grenades, or cock blockers, are women that will do anything to keep their friends from getting laid. They are usually short, fat, ugly, and generally unpleasant to be around. Since they couldn't get laid to save their own pathetic and miserable lives, they try to inflict their pain on everyone by making sure that nobody else gets any action either. These "grenades" can blow up an entire evening in your face, which is why you need a buddy there to smother them. This buddy, commonly referred to as a "wingman," will occupy the cock blocker, get her drunk, talk to her, distract her, and maybe even take her home and jump on her just to save your evening with the hot chick. These beloved wingmen are so important to you, that we've dedicated an entire section to them.

WINGMEN

The Lone Ranger had Tonto. Batman had Robin. Ellen DeGeneres had Anne Heche, until she became an alien, a heterosexual, and a complete friggin' lunatic, in that order. You will also need a wingman—somebody who'll talk to your chick's fat friend.

> ### TIP #16: GET YOURSELF
> ### A WINGMAN, MAV.

It will always bring a tear to the eye of an asshole to remember the scene in *Top Gun* where Maverick, under the gun from the Commie bastards and hearing his RIO's pleas to "get the hell out of here, Mav," refuses to leave his formation, stating: "I am not going to leave my wingman." The lump in your throat won't come from compassion, but from the memory of all those times that your wingman ended up making out with some 325-pound white-trash chick so you could get her cute, skinny, blonde friend.

Your wingman must have the same dedication as you. If there's a possibility that he's going to get spooked by some girl with an extra twenty pounds on her, you're going home broke, alone, and bitter. Pick your wingman with the same care that you'll use to pick your wife—he'll probably get you laid more often than she will, and, in all likelihood, you'll be with him way longer than she could ever hope to hold out. In short, he must be willing to die for you, but not expect the same commitment in return. After all, you're an asshole—you'll be damned if you're going to bang some pig while your buddy nails the prom queen. If, God forbid, this does happen, go fly yourself over to the next aircraft carrier and see if you can find some decent action. Hopefully, by the time you land yourself a hottie, his chick will have left with the cock blocker and he'll be able to swing over and lend you a hand.

You have to be careful when choosing a wingman. After all, you are inviting another dick to the party, and you want to make sure that it won't be bigger than yours. Here are some rules to live by when choosing your flying partner:

a. *He Should Never Be Better Looking than You Are*—This goes without saying. Imagine the humiliation when you call him over for help and he ends up banging your chick. You need to be the best-looking guy in the mix, or you're begging for trouble.

b. *He Must Be Different than You*—Your chick has a reason for wanting to sleep with you. Maybe you're funny, or rich, or you have tattoos. Whatever it is, she's obviously attracted to it, which means your wingman shouldn't have it. What if she thinks he's funnier, richer, or likes his tattoos better? It's not a risk worth taking.

c. *He Needs to Be Willing to Jump on the Grenade and Take One for the Team*—And we mean all the way. Plenty of wingmen will distract the girl or occupy her for a few minutes. Some will even go home with the girl and try to keep her busy while you get your groove on. These are decent co-pilots, but they sure as hell aren't going to Miramar. You need a sloppy bastard that's willing to lay pipe on Roseanne Barr, if that's what it takes. You might want to search out some guy who actually chooses to go hoggin', because this kind of brainless dedication to the cause is the only acceptable mentality for a true asshole's wingman.

d. *He Should Have Superior Beer Goggles*—At the end of the night, anything with tits is going to look like Pamela Anderson to you. But you have to be wary of ending up with an average-looking chick. If you keep bedding down nasty girls, eventually one of them will have a really cool personality and you'll end up marrying her and hating yourself forever. This is where your wingman needs to have a second set of eyes. Towards the end of the night, you will use his vision as your own. So, no matter how drunk he gets, a good wingman should still be able to discern between a hot chick and an ugly one, even if he's so drunk he's legally dead.

e. *He Needs to Be Supportive*—Part of being an asshole requires you to risk it all in going after some chick who, more likely than not, will shut you down just for the sport of it. You can't come back to the table and see your wingman laughing at you, everybody else will be doing that plenty. At this point, your buddy needs to be there to tell you what a filthy whore she was and keep you motivated enough to move on to the next one.

f. *He Needs to Be Responsible*—Even though you're trying to become more refined as you move through the adult world, a few beers inevitably sends you right back into college. You'll be grabbing a chick's ass and getting into fights with her boyfriend and the bouncer (in that order). Ultimately, you could be tossed out of the bar and end up wrapping your car around a tree on the drive home. A good wingman should be able to babysit you when you're out of control and not get pissed off in the morning after you called him a pussy and punched him in the face the night before.

g. *When You're with Him, You Get Laid*—You can disregard everything above, as long as your wingman brings home the bacon. Supportive? Responsible? Gay? Straight? Who really gives a shit, as long as you wake up next to some nameless piece of ass that's wearing your crusty man seed like a pair of diamond nipple rings?

ONE-NIGHT STANDS— THE ASSHOLE'S CORONATION

The one-night stand is a beautiful and sacred union that should be given its proper regard by every self-respecting asshole. It is not difficult to come by, but you need to target carefully, and lie accordingly.

> ### TIP #17: ONE-NIGHT STANDS ARE THE ASSHOLE'S GRADUATION.

For a twenty-two-year-old, a one-night stand can practically be considered a long-term relationship. In actuality, the one-night stand is a type of asshole coronation. When she leaves in the morning, it should be to the sound of a graduation march playing in the background. As an asshole, your primary mission in life is to use your screwed-up attitude to make chicks do things they claim they don't want to do—like sleeping with you, or giving you a blowjob in the backseat of your car—and then dump them like last week's garbage. The one-night stand personifies this quest.

Sleeping with them represents only half the battle, though. Sure, it's always exciting to bed down some new tramp, and the resulting orgasm also can be pretty cool, despite the fact that it only lasts about a second and a half. But the real enjoyment, the true victory, is when you send her on her way the next morning, *without* asking for her name, number or any other identifying information. There is almost nothing in the world better than slamming the door behind some semi-hooker after a night of stinky pinky, turning on the TV, eating a bowl of Honey Bunches of Oats, and falling immediately back to sleep. This is a triumphant feeling that usually occurs only after your country has beat the shit out of some pansy-ass Third World nation, like Iraq in 1991. In fact, if you'd like to refer to your one-night conquests as "Saddams," that is entirely acceptable.

So how do you go about getting yourself one? One-nighters come and go in spurts—sometimes you can't go to Burger King without ending up in a one-night stand; sometimes you could win the lottery and still not be able to pull a fat girl from a bar that's run out of nachos. Basically, you've just got to be on your toes at all times and in all situations, in case a one-night stand rears its gorgeous head. Here are some of the tricks of the trade:

a. *Where Do You Get Them?*

    1. *Illegal activities*—This includes underground raves, street racing, fights, etc. Chicks are much more likely to lose their inhibitions in the face of illegal activities, such as drug deals, riots, or other events of civil unrest. Plus, these types of gatherings personify the "bad boy" mentality that captivates virtually all women. The best course of action is to have sex *at* the event. Peg some little chick against the wall and hike her skirt up. Get some head in the back of the warehouse. You need to take advantage when they are still drugged-out and amped-up with adrenaline. If you wait to take them home, they might actually come to their senses before you have a chance to score.

    2. *Bars*—Chances are, since you're a working-class stiff, illegal events are going to come up about as often as a third consecutive hard-on. Therefore, you'll be left to look for one-night stands in the more typical venues, aka bars. However, certain bars are much more conducive to one-night stands than others. Here's where to find the drunk and horny:

        i. *General hotel bars*—The only chicks that hang out at hotel bars are chicks that are staying in the hotels. This means one of two things: they are either traveling on business, or traveling for leisure. If it's for leisure, they want a good fuck. If it's for business, they *need* a good fuck. Think of how lonely the road is for these women. They have no home, their boyfriend is miles away, and there they are, sitting in some pathetic hotel bar drowning their sorrows, waiting for an anonymous penis to come and relieve all of the pressure and pain.

ii. *Exclusive hotel bars*—Exclusive hotels offer something different from general hotel bars: very rich women whose husbands are cheating on them all the friggin' time. One of the advantages of being wealthy is that you have the means to poke virtually any chick you want, regardless of whether you have a wife at home. If you're rich enough that you send your wife to expensive hotels by herself, guess what? You're sleeping with every woman at your office, your health club, and your local PTA. The wife knows and accepts it because she gets to stay at exclusive hotels. But this makes her doubly excited about sleeping with some random guy, because it gives her some sort of psychic retribution over her husband.

iii. *Hole-in-the-wall bars*—If you go to a hole-in-the-wall bar, you get a pretty limited crowd: losers, social misfits, unemployables, and the just plain weird. Anybody who has a clue or a couple bucks in their pocket will go to a more popular bar, because that's where most of the hot chicks are. The mere fact that these people are resigned to sitting in a dark hole with one black-and-white TV flickering above the torn-up pool table indicates that nobody's going to have to pay Mensa dues this year. Anyway, the point is that the women you meet here just don't give a shit anymore. They've probably been beaten up a couple of times, their husbands are long gone, and the only guys who talk to them rarely have teeth. They look at a young, strong, handsome man like you buying beers with a hundred dollar bill, and you might as well be Brad Pitt, George Clooney, and Ron Jeremy's penis all rolled into one.

iv. *Out-of-town bars*—If you meet another traveling chick, then it's on. If, however, you meet a local, make sure to tell her you're leaving tomorrow. Even if you're on a project that will keep you there for months, she needs to think that tonight is now or never. Clearly, being out of town offers a few key advantages. First, you're never going to see any of these women again, so you can pretty much go for broke. Introduce the idea of having sex within the first three to five minutes, who cares? A few of them might smack you, but you only need one girl to take the bait. Second, there is no chance that she will ever run into your girlfriend, so whatever ambivalence you might have over getting caught should be eliminated. Third, the fact that you're staying in a hotel not only makes it logistically easy to get her back to wherever you're staying, but also will be mildly reassuring to the girl, who knows that she, too, has no real chance of being caught.

3. *Concerts*—Concerts are great because they're so loud that the chick has no idea what you're talking about and probably can't hear it when you say something stupid. Plus, she's most likely shit-faced, which will make you infinitely more attractive. The musical environment is also a plus, because women instinctively equate music with sex. So, while she's listening to a favorite band, her thoughts will be on getting a little loving. This, hopefully, is where you come in.

b. *How You Get Them*—Clearly, to get one-night stands, you have to do the same things you do to get other women, i.e., lie your freakin' ass off. The best part about the one-nighter, though, is that you shouldn't care how many lies you tell, because there's virtually no chance that you will ever be caught. Just make sure that the lie inspires immediate sexual longing. The woman must be so taken by what you say that she will sleep with you right there at the table if you'd move the salt shakers out of the way. Long-term stuff like "my parents are rich and are going to leave me money" doesn't cut it, because she doesn't care if you'll have cash in thirty years—what'll that do for her now? But, if you're a rock star, tomorrow she can run off and tell her friends she slept with the drummer from Mötley Crüe. Now that's a one-night stand! Here are some tips on what to say:

1. *Be on a business trip*—Like you, chicks don't want to get caught cheating by their boyfriends, and they sure don't want to get a slutty reputation. Trying to hit on a local chick is scary for them, because they know that they'll see you again and you're likely to spread rumors about her to every other guy within a hundred miles. Unless she's a professional whore, this will be an obstacle. However, if you claim to be on a business trip and she believes that you'll be on the next flight out of there, she can engage in all sorts of kinky fantasies without worrying about repercussions. Her loss of inhibitions is extremely valuable so you should continuously drop hints about how far you actually live from her, e.g., "God, I can't believe I have a six-hour flight tomorrow," "I sure hope my neighbors have learned some English while I've been gone," and "Would you ever consider moving to the Arctic Circle?" are all excellent conversation starters.

2. *Be discreet*—Again, chicks are just as nervous about getting caught in a one-night tryst as you are. If it appears as if she's going to come home with you, it's probably not a good idea to loudly proclaim that you've "got another one!" Also, winking at the guy sitting next to her and giving him a high five after she's asked you over for a drink is similarly frowned upon. Speak in hushed tones, and for God's sake don't ask the waiter where the best place is "to get a secret blowjob."

3. *Always be celebrating*—Even if you have nothing to celebrate, even if your cat just died, make up a reason to pop the cork on the bubbly. It gives chicks a reason to break away from their normal hum-drum local bar lives and really whoop it up with you. It also lets you act like a complete madman because you're so deliriously happy. For some reason, women find it okay to be obnoxious in these situations. Tell her you just closed a multi-million-dollar deal, or that your best friend just got married. The most important thing to remember is that the celebration only lasts one night. You're hightailing out of town the next day, and she'd better jump on quick if she wants a piece of the adrenaline rush. Because you've duped her into thinking that she'll never see you again, the chances of her going down on you increase tenfold.

c. *Repeat One-Night Stands*—Chicks have this stupid anti-slut mentally that says, "it doesn't really matter how many times I have sex, it just matters how many guys." This is why the truly experienced assholes are able to string out a particularly attractive one-night stand several times. The key to making this happen is to get her phone number in the morning. This will be entirely contradictory to the age-old ritual that usually culminates with the asshole crumpling it up and tossing it in the trash. While you would never think about calling some slut who slept with you the night she met you in a bar, occasionally, certain attributes like "D" cups, a propensity to bring other girls into bed, or double jointedness, may inspire you to give her another call. Don't feel bad if you want to give this a shot, just please remember not to tell any of your friends that you're screwing some disgusting, skanky whore more than once.

1. *Girl in every port*—Repeat one-night stands are acceptable if the girl lives in a different city, because none of your friends will find out, and she's not going to bother you and your girlfriend. Accordingly, you are entirely justified to seek out a

girl in every American town that you visit on a regular basis. As an asshole, it is your job to try and bang a chick every time you are in a new city, as well as re-banging one in a city that you go to frequently. The key to maintaining a nationwide contingent of women is to ensure that you never lose touch with them. E-mail is an excellent tool that can be used to flirt with chicks from thousands of miles, and an occasional message or funny gift will keep her just interested enough to bang you again when you come back to town. If you play this right, you can have women waiting for you all over the country, or even the world.

2. *When to boot the repeater*—The first time that your evening does not end in sex, run like hell and don't look back. Typically, the repeat one-night stand has a shelf life of two to four additional "dates"—"date" being defined as you meeting her somewhere, having sex, and then leaving immediately thereafter. If you let it drag on too long you'll get yourself into trouble, because another retarded chick rule will take over: "I can't keep screwing some random guy that doesn't really care about me." With you "swinging into town" so often, she'll start to feel guilty, and might want a more committed distance relationship, or she might want to just be friends. The second any of these issues come up, sidestep them and head straight for the bedroom. If she doesn't give it up, lose her number and get a new cell phone.

DATING (LOBSTER = BLOWJOB)

Group dates? Gone. Bumping into ten hot sorority chicks at the bar before ending up in the bathroom making out with one of them? Gone. *Felicity* night at the dorms? Gone.

With all of these standard dating rituals over and done with, what the hell are you going to do? The new and not-so-improved world of dating is another tough thing to adjust to. First of all, every date is a real date. A "real date" as in: movie and dinner, talking to her the whole time, having to check out her face without looking through the bottom of a beer glass. This new world can be mystifying, to say the least. But there are a couple of things you can do as a young adult to ensure that the next date won't be your last, unless, of course, you end up banging the girl—in which case you won't call her again anyway.

TIP #18: LEARN THE 1-2-3 PUNCH.

Now that you're in the real world, you'll need to familiarize yourself with the 1-2-3 Punch, better known as "Coffee, Drinks, Dinner." First date: coffee; second date: drinks; third date: dinner. This schema is widely accepted by virtually all women as the de rigueur method of dating, but, more important than the mechanics of it, you need to understand why women want it done that way. Thank God for this book.

a. *Coffee*—Somehow, a company named Starbucks became the largest date mecca of the last ten years. It's become so commonplace to go for coffee on your first date that if you don't ask a girl to do it, she'll think there's something wrong with you.

1. *Why do women want the coffeehouse?*

    i. *Safety*—Women are wary of men they don't know very well. Even if she knows you at work, she might not know you in a social situation. Meeting at the coffeehouse ensures that she's not dependent on you to pick her up or take her home.
    ii. *Timing*—A night at the coffee place can be as short or as long as she wants. If you're lame, she can down a latte and fake an emergency cell phone call before you've even finished sucking up the whipped cream on your capuccino.

iii. *Trendy*—Coffeehouses are considered sophisticated and trendy. Since women constantly feel stupid and have a tremendous need to fit in, the coffeehouse is perfect, because it gives them a false sense of security in both areas. It provides just enough interaction for her to decide if she wants to pursue you any further but not so much that she'll actually have to think, and thus expose herself as an idiot.

2. *Coffee goals*

i. *Touch her at least twice*—Not sexually, you pervert. But even a touch on the arm or the small of the back starts to knock those silly little thoughts of you two being friends right out of her vacant noggin.

ii. *Make her laugh at least once*—If you are even mildly amusing, you've significantly upped your chances of moving on to date number two.

iii. *Get her contact information*—How else will you ever get in touch with her?

b. *Drinks*—Having drinks works with women because it fosters the same comforting environment as the coffeehouse with a little bit more fun thrown in. She can drive there and leave by herself, so she's not feeling quite like a deer in headlights yet. However, since you've passed the coffee test, she's willing to get a little tipsy and see how attractive she finds you.

The number-one thing to remember about the second date is that *you absolutely must kiss her*. If you're not prepared to get your lips involved, you might as well just pack up your balls and head out of town. From the moment you see her at the bar you should be looking for your window of opportunity. If you're dancing, either watch for any welcoming signals or create your own, depending on your level of aggressiveness. Ideally, the first kiss will take place at a perfect "moment," e.g., at midnight on New Year's Eve, or the second that the Lakers win their fourth consecutive championship. But if it doesn't, screw it, you're a man—create a moment.[3] If the opportunity doesn't present itself during the date, you have no choice but to make the last-ditch effort at the car. At the end of the date, you have to walk her to her car. It's a responsibility that comes with having a penis. Once there, reach down to open the door, and then move in like an Army Ranger descending on a Taliban forward position. You will feel the terror of this moment right down to your heart. It will be thumping wildly as you walk towards the car and wonder whether you are about to encounter victory or abject defeat. That's why it's recommended to try the kiss earlier in the evening, because you won't have the same crushing pressure. If necessary, though, you *have* to go for it. Look at it this way, if you don't try now, it's worse than getting rejected, because you will forever fall into the "friend's zone," an area so treacherous and pain-inducing that we can't describe it without completely breaking down.

c. *Dinner*—Assuming that things go well over drinks, you should now be ready for the third date. This is the first true "date." She now feels comfortable being alone with you and kissing you. She not only will allow you to pick her up and drop her off, but she'll also get drunk with you. For that reason, this date is terrifying, since there is just one way to go: down. The only part of the date that you can't really screw up is dinner. Pick a nice place and

---

[3] Creating a Moment—If you're having trouble finding a good moment to slip the kiss in, try this smooth maneuver I picked up in college. I call it the "Competitive Kisser": I was at a club dancing with my date. It was the second time we had gone out, so I knew I had to make a move. Despite repeated subtle advances, I could never seem to get close enough to move in for the kill. Then I looked over and saw another couple going at it in the corner. I pointed over to them and laughed. She looked over and laughed, too. That's when I leaned over and whispered in her ear, "We can do better than that." Not wanting to get showed up by another couple, she smiled at me, and seemed to take it as a challenge. Before I could even smile back, she stuck her tongue so far down my throat that I was simultaneously receiving a rim job.

order lots of wine. After dinner is where you can really show your charm. You've been listening to this chick squawk for at least two weeks, so you should know whether she likes sunsets, horses, beaches, or something else similarly lame and chick-like.

Take her someplace unexpected that you know she will enjoy. Try and include as much alcohol as you possibly can. During this event, if you haven't kissed her for the second time; do it now. Then follow up with several more that unquestionably include tongue, even if the first or second kiss didn't. Ideally, you will be kissing all night, owing mainly to the booze you poured down her throat during dinner.

At the end of the evening, you must find a way to sleep with her. Merely dropping her off is not an option. Tell her you're too drunk, tell her the car won't start, ask if you can just get some water, anything to avoid driving home alone. Whatever you have to do, just get your ass in the same apartment with her. After that, try your best to close the deal. Even if she doesn't put out, you should at least get some heavy petting, and hopefully a blowjob. After this happens, sex is a foregone conclusion on the next date, which means that her time is slowly coming to an end.

d. *1-2-3 Timeline*—The dating timeline should go as follows: coffee should be done on a Tuesday or Wednesday; this will give you a couple of days to flirt via e-mail before Friday. On Friday, you should ask her for drinks at the beginning of the next week, say Monday or Tuesday. After drinks, you should ask her out on the dinner date for Friday or Saturday. All of this should be done before Wednesday, because another stupid chick rule is not to accept dates for the weekend if they are asked after Wednesday. This is an edict that came out of the heinously disgusting book *The Rules,* quite possibly the most pathetic, hideous, and ridiculous work in the history of American literature. Unfortunately, 90 percent of chicks have read that dumb-ass book and religiously follow its teachings, so deal with it.

e. *Random Dates*—Sometimes you can't plan the 1-2-3 Punch for a number of reasons: she works so much that you can't rely on her giving you three days out of her two weeks—or maybe she doesn't like coffee, Commie bitch! If that's the case, you'll have to come up with some other dating options that don't require the precise scheduling and forward thinking of the 1-2-3 Punch. Here are some of the things you can use in its place:

1. *Dinner and a movie*—Going out to dinner and a movie is kind of like the blue Brooks Brothers suit of dating—it's traditional, it's tough to screw up, and, no matter how hokey it seems, she'll appreciate you for your relative sense of style and grace. The slowest of eaters is going to be out of the restaurant in ninety minutes, and after that you've got two hours of blissful silence when you can relax, put your arm around her, and try to grab a little boob by the time the lights come up. You might want to avoid grossly masculine films, like pro wrestling, documentaries or anything starring Steven Seagal, if he's still alive. Your date will consider your choice of movies as indicative of your true nature, and if you're whooping for joy every time a minor character is shot through the eye, she may start having second thoughts about another date. A good restaurant before the flick is also imperative, because if you take her to Taco Bell for a ninety-nine-cent chimichanga she'll spend the entire movie figuring out how to ditch you before the credits roll. Here are a few ways to avoid this embarrassment:

   i. *Seafood place*—Seafood's good. All chicks like seafood, because they can maintain the illusion they're eating something healthy, even though that tuna was batter-fried for at least forty minutes before it saw her plate. You can also get out of a seafood place for less than thirty bucks per plate, provided you don't order the "Catch of the Day"—

which is basically what they call the spoiled shit they couldn't sell yesterday, now at triple the price.

ii. *Steakhouses*—No steakhouses. Those places are for old men and cigars. Men dig meat because it harkens back to the days when a man would wake up in his cave, put on a loin cloth, spend the rest of the day hunting and gathering, then club a woman over the head and drag her back to the dirt hole before sundown. Women, on the other hand, don't like steaks, because their rampant sensitivity won't allow them to enjoy something when they know it comes at the expense of tortured cows all over the country. (Another situation when women's emotions prevent them from putting a good piece of meat in their mouths.)

iii. *Bar and grill*—This is actually a tough call. Generally speaking, a bar is kind of low-class, and you could get poor marks. However, if it's one of those shi-shi, high-end places where you can drop twenty bucks on a glass of eighteen-year-old scotch, she might appreciate your ability to find a place with "character." Even if she doesn't like the place, drop four or five Cosmopolitans down her throat and it really shouldn't be much of a problem to get her naked.

iv. *Sushi*—Holy Christ, stay away from the sushi bars! First of all, sushi costs an arm and a leg. Nowhere but in America could somebody take two cents' worth of rice wrapped around a tenth of an ounce of salmon and charge nine dollars and seventy-five cents for it. Plus, no matter how much money you spend you're going to be so insanely hungry after you leave that you'll have no choice but to stop at a McDonald's drive-thru on the way home, spoiling your chances with the little filly. The second problem is that, because you're an asshole, you have no idea what the hell is in the sushi. Tamago, uni, futo-maki—what in God's name is this stuff? Women hate it when you don't know something, and you can

be sure that there will be some nineteen-year-old punk sitting
next to you who's practically speaking Japanese to the sushi
chef and making you look bad. If she suggests sushi, take her
back to her house and call Domino's on your way home.

v. *Anything ethnic*—Yes, yes, yes. Chicks love to think that
you're an eclectic, worldly guy with a lot of interests. Because
they're so dumb, they want to believe that their man can
expose them to a little bit of world culture. If you can find any
type of funky ethnic food—Vietnamese, Ethiopian,
Argentinian—anything off the beaten path, your chick is going
to think that you're a real stud. When you get to the place,
pretend that you know exactly what you're doing and order
with a certain sense of authority. Don't worry if they end up
bringing you a plate of frog testicles or mouse feces, just pour a
gallon of ketchup on it and tell her it's a local delicacy. If you
need to excuse yourself to throw up, that's entirely acceptable.

2. *Pro sporting event*—The NBA, NFL, MLB, (or the MLS, if
you're a Euro-fag), all of these make great dates. Is it because
chicks like sports? No, chicks hate sports, because sports has
nothing to do with makeup, waxing, or marriage. But they love
to know that you're a he-man who's way into sports. We think
that it's some evolutionary thing that makes testosterone-heavy
men more attractive to women. Somewhere along the
Darwinian trail, women must have realized that, if you're into
sports, you've probably got a decent-sized sack in your shorts,
and, therefore, they dig you. When you attend a pro sports
event, there is also the extra-added bonus that you have tickets.
This means that you either have a couple of bucks (because
tickets are ridiculously expensive these days) or you have
connections into the team, which is even better.

3. *Happy hour(s)*—Happy hour is one of those quintessential
American pastimes that requires you to drink yourself into a near

coma at 5 P.M. every Friday. You get free fried shit, one-dollar beers, and the opportunity to slur your words and spit on every business-suit-wearing chick in the place. After six or seven vodka-tonics, the chicks get better looking and you think you're funny. The best part about it is that your date will be doing the exact same thing. The fact that you will begin getting drunk literally the moment you step into the bar also shields you from having to come up with too much sober conversation. As the two of you laugh your way into early evening, the only potential obstacle for you to avoid is the possibility that you'll get a 9 P.M. hangover— owing to your early start—and the dry-heaves shortly thereafter at 11. Maintain some semblance of pace until you get her back to your place, where you are more than welcome to vomit a couple of times, if that's what it takes to get your dick hard.

4. *Clubs*—You're still a relatively young guy, and you shouldn't entirely dismiss clubs just because people there are going to start getting younger and younger every year. You still look cool and will continue to until you're about twenty-seven, so live a little. When you take your chick to a date at a club you've got a couple of built-in advantages. Hopefully, you know somebody at the door, so, when you bypass the entire line, your woman's going to think you're hot stuff. After getting inside, the music will blow up your eardrums, meaning that neither one of you can hear a word the other's saying. This will ease any conversational pressures you might have. Since you can't talk, you'll be forced to get on a dance floor packed beyond capacity, forcing the two of you to grind against each other.

5. *Theatre*—Chicks love the theatre. Why? They like to get dressed up, they like to believe that they're better looking than the other dressed-up women in the audience, and they love the fact that you've got to drop one hundred and fifty dollars for the same two hours of entertainment that seventeen bucks would've gotten you at the local movie house. This is a tough one to get around, and

the only advice we have for you is that, even though you will have to suck it up and go to a few plays to keep the peace, under no circumstances do you allow her to push you into seeing an opera. Operas are to an asshole what kryptonite is to Superman. About the only thing worse than sitting in an audience with a bunch of ancient, tight-assed, stuffed shirts while some fat chick screams at you in Italian for three-and-a-half hours is being dragged naked through a field of broken glass. If you don't want to take a swan dive over the balcony before the end of the first act, for the love of God, stay away from the opera.

Although the above examples seem relatively simple, we know that the date thing is a somewhat terrifying experience for the new adult, so, in addition to what we've already shown you, we've put together a little chart of some other niche dating experiences to help you with those particularly unique girls who you just don't quite know what to do with:

TYPE OF DATE	WHO RESPONDS	WHAT TO DO THERE
Horseback riding	Outdoorsy types and any chick from Texas.	Spit, take off after a rabbit, and avoid the horseshit in front of you.
Ice-skating	Northeasterners, twelve-year-olds.	Try not to kill yourself and don't wear a little pink skirt.
Picnic	Romantics.	Keep the ants out of the bologna sandwich and get her drunk.
Amusement park	Adventurous girls.	Don't puke on the roller coasters; pretend that you're not scared to death when you go through the third loop.

TYPE OF DATE	WHO RESPONDS	WHAT TO DO THERE
Fortune-teller	Freaky chicks.	Pretend that everything the fortune teller's saying is true, unless she says you'll never make money.
Bungee jumping	Out-of-control women.	Don't do number two in your pants (or number one for that matter).
Naked twister	If she agrees to do it, she'll respond no matter who she is.	Who cares, as long as she's playing?
Cook her dinner	There's not a chick alive who will not sell her soul for a man who cooks her dinner.	Have it catered.

TIP #19: FIVE BUCKS CAN GET YOU LAID.

f. *The Five-Dollar Date*—Face it, when you just get out of school, you don't have any money and it's tough to impress the chicks. How do you solve this problem? Actually, it's relatively easy, once you learn how to take five bucks and use it to stimulate all of your date's emotional pressure points. Don't forget that they're still young and inexperienced, too, so, although they've started to figure out that they should be searching for a man with means, they have not yet become the hardened, money-grubbing, gold-digging, high-class hookers that they will be once they turn twenty-seven or so.

It is important to note that these dates should generally be used on girlfriends. If you take a chick out on a five-dollar first date, you'll be lucky if she doesn't pretend to go the bathroom and sneak out a window. There is about a 5 percent chance, though, that a non-girlfriend will accept such a date so keep these in mind:

1. *Blockbuster Night*—The movie rental is God's way of supporting assholes. For just five dollars, you get two whole hours without the chick babbling in your ear. Yet, somehow she views this as quality time because you're lying on the couch and playing with her tits. In order to make the most of these joyous occasions, rent an older movie that doesn't cost as much as a new release. Your chick will probably *want* a new release, but you can impress her with your historical awareness by telling her that the '70s piece of dreck you're holding in your hand represents a true renaissance in filmmaking, and she will be pleasantly surprised at your apparent knowledge. In reality, you will never have heard of the movie you're renting.

2. *Ice cream*—Women *love* ice cream. They eat it constantly, especially when they are depressed. Buying a woman ice cream is like saying, "I understand you, and I want to make you happy," when, in reality, you're saying "I don't spend money when I jerk off into my sock, so I shouldn't spend more than five dollars on you either." Not to mention, there is a sweet bit of irony in the end of the relationship. Once you dump her, she will immediately look for consolation in the nearest bucket of Häagen-Dazs. She will then associate you with the ice cream, thus making her suffering twice as painful.

3. *A walk*—Walks are another fascinating chick phenomenon. Every single woman is a sucker for a long walk. It doesn't matter where it is—you could probably stroll around on an expressway and the chick will still be giddy. The reason is relatively simple: guys never listen to women, despite the fact that chicks want to do nothing else but talk to you about their day. When you go on a walk, she knows you've got no choice but to listen to her

prattle on about her problems, her life, and her morbid
fascination with her daddy—and she loves it. Just pop in your
earplugs and put on some sneakers. Walks are free, and at least
they will help keep that fatty ice cream off her ass.

4. *Jogging or working out*—This is a brilliant ploy and should be
used as much as possible. First, when women jog they tend to run
out of breath, which means they won't talk quite so much.
Second, men tend to jog faster, so, if your bitch keeps talking, you
can just pick up the pace until she gets winded. Third, it keeps
her in good shape while increasing her sex drive. Fourth, it keeps
you in good shape so you can still go out and bang other chicks.

5. *The zoo*—Chicks love kids. Chicks love animals. The zoo has
tons of both. Plus, the zoo is generally a family-related activity,
so your subconscious signal to her is that you are a stable,
committed guy who's looking to settle down. Try not to laugh
when this thought passes through your mind. She's also going
to think that you're romantic, creative, and a "real softie." Just
don't blow your cover by laughing your ass off when you see
one monkey raping another.

6. *The beach (or lakes, if you're noncoastal)*—We're going to assume
that, since you're an asshole, you're working out pretty regularly
and have a decent body. If that's the case, the beach is one of the
all-time great cheap dates. You can entertain her with stupid
games, you can bring along all the food and drinks without
seeming too cheap, and you can count on a full day in the hot sun
to weaken her ability to fight you off later that night. If, however,
your hairy back scares children, or if your gut falls down to mid-
thigh whenever you take off your shirt, you should probably avoid
any nudity that isn't masked by the dead of night.

g. *Weekend Dates*—Once you've had sex the first time, it is
important to establish that this will be the paramount activity in
your relationship. That's why you should take your woman to the

nearest weekend getaway immediately after sex enters the picture. Weekends are perfect because they eliminate all of the distractions of home, while allowing you to focus wholeheartedly on banging your woman into a bloody pulp. She will get drunk and kinky because, due to the relative newness of the relationship, she's still trying to impress you in bed. You don't have to worry about waking the neighbors during your howling sexual romps and, even better, you can run around naked, because nobody's going to walk in. After the weekend is over, tell her how much she turned you on and keep upping the ante until sex is considered an absolute necessity as soon as you wake up, right before you go to sleep, and two or three other times during the rest of the day.

h. *Impressive Dates*—Every guy is looking for that one perfect date, the one that's going to get a girl so hot and bothered she can't help but give it up at the end of the night. And almost every guy you talk to has his favorite place and his favorite sequence of events that he swears will work every time. Well, we're here to tell you that all of those stories are complete bullshit. Forget spending a lot of money, fancy dinners, or so-called romantic locations. They work a lot of the time, but they are usually better-suited to girlfriends, not just random chicks you're dating. If you want to get her wet, then you're going to need to put in some legwork and come up with something that is *relevant*, *original*, and/or *exclusive*.

1. *Relevant*—If you take a vegetarian to the nicest steakhouse in town, you're not going to score that night. What your buddies deem as the perfect date for their chicks holds no relevancy for yours. You need to remember the types of things that she's into and structure a date around those interests. If she loves the outdoors, a fifteen-dollar picnic will go further than a hundred-and-fifty-dollar dinner. If she likes horses, take her horseback riding, not hang gliding.

2. *Original*—Make sure that your "relevant" date isn't the same as the twenty dates she's had before. If she likes horses, and the

last six guys she's dated took her horseback riding, she's not going to get excited. Pump her for a little information and find out what she's done and what she'd really like to do. If you hit on one of her interests and do it in an original way, you're going to get some ass about nine out of ten times.

3. *Exclusive*—If you're like most guys and can't remember a word that your chick says, let alone what they're interested in, or you have the creativity of a peanut, then you'll need to find something exclusive. Exclusivity basically means that *you* have access to it, but nobody else does. It could be anything from tickets to a sold-out concert to reservations at a private club to an eleven-inch schlong. Exclusivity works because of the "friend factor." Her friends will *ooh* and *ahh* that she gets to do something that none of their boyfriends have ever managed to pull off. This should lead to "thank you sex" for making her look like the coolest chick in her clique.

GIRLFRIENDS—BECAUSE YOUR SOCK DOESN'T WASH ITSELF

Now, we all agree that no real asshole can be tied down to just one girl. Keep in mind that having a girlfriend does not limit you; in fact, it opens the door to getting more women than you can possibly imagine.

TIP #20: ASSHOLES ALWAYS NEED GIRLFRIENDS.

This is always an interesting contradiction in the life of an asshole. Your whole existence is based on banging new and different chicks, yet, during virtually every stage of your development, having a girlfriend is practically a necessity. Why is that? It's so you can always get laid—why the hell else would you let some witch make you spend money, chew you out constantly, and scream at you for drinking the last sip of milk?

Having a girlfriend also makes it easier for you to get other chicks. You might be somewhat confused. How does banging one girl lead to banging another? If this is your question, thank God you bought this book. The real trick to getting laid is (drum roll, please) *confidence*. Chicks can smell confidence the same way a rabid dog can smell fear. Conversely, girls can sense when you're desperate. It doesn't matter how, they just somehow know. Therefore, waking up every morning, twisting your chick like a pretzel, and poking her silly, is the best way to avoid giving off any "desperation vibes." If you walk in the bar fresh after getting some ass, the girls will know that you don't need anybody else, and it will make them want you even more—not to mention, if you know there's more ass waiting for you at home you can pick and choose at your leisure.

Okay, so you need a girlfriend. In school, as hard as you tried, a girlfriend, because of her proximity to your life, made it pretty damn difficult to bag other chicks. You had the same friends, lived in the same place, and went to the same bars. You practically needed to be a trained CIA operative to escape her little orbit. But now the circumstances have changed and the strictures have loosened up—this is one of the benefits of leaving the lock-down of educational life. You have more freedom of movement, and it's important that you take advantage of it, so as not to fall back into the nightmare of having to screw the same girl every... single... night. Even if she's a total disaster, you still need to have a girlfriend. Here are some more reasons why:

   a. *Guaranteed Sex*—At the end of a long day, you don't really care who you sleep with, as long as you get laid. Having a girlfriend eliminates the need to constantly hit the bar circuit hoping for that two-bit whore that will take you home.

b. *Girlfriends Are Relatively Cheap*—Even though you'll have to occasionally buy her presents, they will never add up to the cost of first dates. First dates are absolutely brutal on your wallet, and there's no guarantee at the end of the night. You might as well save that hundred and fifty bucks for a hooker, at least you don't have to *listen* to her.

c. *You Can Bang Even More Chicks*—Guys with girlfriends are immediately more attractive to other women. Women's little brains usually think, "If nobody else wants him, then why should I?" However, being seen with a girlfriend lets every woman know that you are desirable and highly sought after. We've already covered this on several occasions in this book, so you should be thoroughly familiar with the idea by now. If you're not, go back to page 1 and *start paying attention!*

d. *Experimentation*—If you stay with a girlfriend long enough, you can talk her into almost anything. Girlfriends are so silly that they may actually fall in love their boyfriends and feel the need to make them happy. This is difficult to imagine, but it's true. As she loves you more and more, she'll let you put it in her ass, tie her up, watch pornos, act out pornos, let you take pictures and video tape, and maybe, just maybe, bring another woman into bed and mow her box for your enjoyment. For this alone it is worth keeping her around.

e. *Girlfriends Are Good, New Girlfriends Are Always Better*—The day that your girlfriend feels comfortable enough to leave the bathroom door open while she's taking a dump or, God forbid, fart within one hundred fifty yards of you, it's time to pull out volume four of your little black book and start test-driving the newest models (pun intended). Ya see, getting a new girlfriend really is like buying a new car. At first, it's in pristine condition, gives off that great smell, and handles like a dream. Soon, though, after you're done abusing the exterior and grinding beer and cigarettes into the upholstery, you'll notice the once-smooth ride is now bumpy, treacherous, and downright scary. Once this happens, you need to get rid of the thing before you completely lose control and end up careening off a cliff. Chicks are the same. The first day you notice a scratch on her fender, you should be back in the showroom before she has time to wonder why her name has suddenly disappeared from your speed dial.

f. *Sexual Pinch Hitter*—Ultimately, your girlfriend's true purpose is to be your sexual pinch hitter, to stand in when you've taken your cuts at the scammers' plate but struck out swinging. Your girlfriend must be available when you come back home to the bench. What does that mean? It means that you are going to be a raging, pissed-off son of a bitch when you do see her, and you need her to be ready for the hate-fucking that you're going to want. We don't advocate any type of physical violence, so put away the brass knuckles and tire iron. However, a couple of strong smacks to the ass are acceptable. A little bit of hair-tugging is also tolerable if none of them come out by the root. It is entirely likely that you will never once see her face during the entire encounter. And, most importantly, you'll be engaging in all types of dirty, filthy sex talk which will likely include words such as "fucking bitch," "goddamn whore," "no-good slut," and the like. Your girlfriend must understand that her role in your life is to deal with these displays of affection with the utmost charm, humor, and acceptance.

g. *Different Circles of Friends*—Although you may have to spend a good deal of time with your girlfriend, it is critically important that you do not share too many friends, if any at all. If you both have the same friends, virtually nothing good can come out of it:

1. Her friends will be able to keep tabs on you.
2. Your friends will be less likely to get you other chicks if they know you're already banging somebody they associate with.

3. If and when you break up, it's going to be very awkward
   drinking beers with a group of people while your ex-bitch
   glares at you.

Having different circles is sometimes difficult, because your
friends will introduce you to many of your girlfriends in the first
place. If that occurs, simply disassociate yourself with that group
of people while you're banging this particular chick. Also, you
should try not to become too involved with your woman's friends or
let her become close to yours. Don't take her out on group dates
where she'll have a chance to bond with your buddy's girlfriend.
Only put them together in loud bars or clubs where the women
can't talk too much. It will make your life much easier when you
eventually dump her.

h. *Geography*—This one runs parallel to the "different circle of
   friends" advice. If your chick lives too close to you, like next
   door, you are entirely screwed. She can look out her window
   and spot the Volkswagen Passat of the tramp you picked up at
   the bar last night. She can stop by anytime she wants, and most
   likely she will do so when she can hear Dave Matthews music
   wafting out of your apartment. And she will continue to live there
   after you've dumped her ass. For this reason, you must *never*
   establish a semi-permanent relationship with a next-door neighbor
   or somebody who lives in your building (you are, of course,
   allowed to randomly sleep with them). There's nothing worse than
   riding in an elevator with your new squeeze while your hateful,
   furious, insane ex-girlfriend stands right behind you, staring
   daggers.

i. *When Is She Your Girlfriend?*—Oftentimes guys wonder when they
   should switch from just dating a chick to having a girlfriend. The
   answer is, you shouldn't care. Does it matter what you call her?
   Not really, since either way she's still the same hole, and you're not
   going to treat her any differently.

Whenever she wants to be called your girlfriend, go for it. It may be the only thing that you ever do to make her happy.

j. *The Overlap Theory*—This is an age-old piece of wisdom: "Don't give up pussy until you have new pussy." Roughly translated, it means that, even if your girlfriend is a hideous bitch, you should continue to nail her until you find somebody else. Under no circumstances do you ever want to be in a position where you come home alone and don't have someone available for a booty call.

BREAKING IT OFF—TRADING UP FOR A NEWER MODEL

Once you get into your twenties people stop going through the elaborate drama of dumping each other and enter into the simple world of just breaking up. "Dumping her" requires numerous conversations with friends to chart strategy, loud screaming matches in front of the neighbors, and months, if not years, of bad feelings. Breaking up, on the other hand, means you just stop talking to the bitch. That may be all well and good, but for you, the asshole, the most important piece of advice we can give you is, *don't let anybody break up with you*. It will damage your ego, sap your confidence, and leave you—for at least a little while—feeling like maybe you should become a "nice guy." Okay, that thought will probably only last for five to seven minutes, but, who knows, during that short pause you might encounter a hot piece of ass, so you have to be ready at all times.

TIP #21: BREAKING UP IS
NOT HARD TO DO, IF
YOU DO IT FIRST.

In order to make sure she never breaks up with you, you need to take the necessary precautions. Even if you think your chick is the greatest thing since K-Y Jelly, it's important that you jot down every one of her flaws while you're dating. During the relationship, refer to the list periodically in order to avoid falling completely in love with her, getting married, and ending up with only half of your stuff. At the end of the relationship, use this list as the reasons for dumping her. Why do you need a list? Because you've got to be prepared, in case, God forbid, she tries to dump you first. Here is the possible scenario:

It always starts with her saying something like: "This just isn't working out for me," or "I don't think we should see each other any-more," or "I'm screwing a six-foot-seven Samoan football player," etc., etc. Nothing on the planet can prepare you for the sick feeling you get in your gut after some chick, despite her numerous flaws, dumps your ass. Upon hearing these words, most men will turn into sniveling little bitches begging for another chance to know what they did wrong. Not you. Before she even finishes her sentence, you're going to jump in and say that it's not working for you either, and here are the reasons why . . . "You're too clingy." "You give oral sex like you're eating an Oreo cookie." "Your ass reminds me of flubber." You start reciting that two-page list from rote memory and, if you've done it right, you'll be going on and on for ten or fifteen minutes. It will be particularly devas-tating for her, because she knows that all of the things you're saying are true. Plus, the real beauty of this plot is that since she doesn't know you've been memorizing a list, she thinks you're saying them off the top of your head. If she believes her problems and failures are so blatant that you can just rattle them off without even thinking about it, she will be nearly suicidal. This is a great trick, because, although she's dump-ing you, she suddenly feels like the dumped. Not to mention, about halfway through the list, you start to wonder what you ever saw in her anyway, and it's that much easier to walk out of the room with your head held high.

When you get home, immediately call everyone you know and tell them that you broke it off and that she was crying like a baby. Don't mention that it was due to the ridiculously harsh and brutal things you said to her. She'll never repeat them, out of fear that people will find out what she's truly like, so your friends will naturally assume that she was crying because she couldn't live without you.

FEMALE FRIENDSHIP AND OTHER OXYMORONS

> **TIP #22: CHICKS CANNOT BE YOUR FRIENDS (REFER BACK TO TIP #2).**

If there ever was an oxymoron, it's female friendship. Females are not your friends. They never have been and they never will be. As a matter of fact, if you recall our second tip, chicks are the enemy. You should consider them as little more than tools in a box that you use to advance your own personal goals.

a. *Exceptions to the Rule*—At certain times you may act as if a woman is your friend, but it is only acceptable in the following circumstances.

1. *She has hot friends*—Any chick that can lead to additional chicks is worth a little face time. The key here is to make sure that you're getting the goods. Remember that if you're friends with the girl you don't want to have sex with her. If you don't want to have sex with her, she's probably a pig. If she's a pig, there's a strong possibility that she has a thing for you and won't introduce you to any of her model cousins. Don't fall into this trap. If she's not generating some promising leads, bail

immediately, or prepare yourself for all those times when she grabs your hand in public, tries to get you drunk, or slaps your ass in front of a girl that you're hitting on.

2. *It will help your career*—Odds are there won't be a woman in a superior position to you in any organization. However, if you happen to work in the fashion industry, and you aren't gay, then sucking up to your boss is a perfectly acceptable way to get promoted.

3. *You use her as bait*—If she'll go out with you in public, you can use her to reel in other chicks.

4. *You're trying to fuck her*—Taking the friend route is a great way to find out her intimate thoughts and insecurities. These can immediately be used to gain trust, and then to gain carnal knowledge.

b. *The Friend Zone*—The "friend zone" is where guys end up when they meet a chick but are unable to turn it into a physical relationship. Maybe she doesn't like to date guys at work, maybe she thinks you're nice but she's not attracted to you, or maybe you blew it and forgot to kiss her on the second date (you retard). Once you're stuck there, it becomes an interesting game of cat and mouse, as you continuously try to get her drunk and naked, while she tries to fight you off. Why would she do such a thing? We're glad you asked.

For women, having a guy friend has numerous advantages:

1. They get a sense of security by knowing a guy will protect them in times of need;

2. They get insights into a man's mind. This type of information is critical for a woman, because, generally speaking, she is too stupid to figure it out herself;

3. Men are brainwashed into buying dinner and drinks for a woman even if they're not dating; and

4. If a woman is with a guy, she won't be hit on by the other Neanderthals that are running around the bar.

As a male, none of these things have any relevance whatsoever. In fact, having a woman friend has almost nothing but disadvantages for a man:

1. If you're with a woman, you want to sleep with her. If you can't, you will soon lose your sense of confidence, adequacy, and self-esteem;
2. Women don't like to do any of the stuff you like, so you'll find yourself going to operas, flea markets, and other ridiculous events just to make her happy;
3. It's tough to talk to a woman about blowjobs and anal sex, so you can't brag to her about the date you had the night before; and
4. She's going to be very comfortable talking to you about her boyfriends, which just reinforces the concept that *she doesn't want you!*

Clearly, it is critical that you stay out of the friend zone. Here are the things you need to know.

c. *How to Avoid the Friend Zone*—Try to kiss her on the second date. If you don't, you're immediately a friend. If she kisses back, then you've just avoided a tremendous pothole on the path to pussy. If she rejects it, then you have two options: 1) drop her and don't look back, or 2) pretend to play friends while seducing her at every opportunity. If you're trying to accomplish the latter, here is how to get the girl:

1. *Always flirt*—Even though you are supposed to be friends, don't ever act like one. If she calls you on it, simply reply with

"What? I'm just kidding. Besides, the thought of seeing you naked makes me sick." Joke off everything.

2. *Lie about other women*—Even if you're not seeing any, tell her you are. Make sure to talk about all the wonderful things that you do for this mystery piece of ass. It's especially helpful if the phantom things that you do for your "girlfriend" are the things that your "friend" especially enjoys. For example, if your "friend" chick likes riding in fast cars, tell her you rented a Ferrari and took your "girlfriend" for a ride through the country. Then sit back and watch her face sink when she realizes that the only ride she's getting from her boyfriend is making her itch.

3. *Make her jealous*—Introduce your "friend" to any and every woman you know. If you're dating someone else, you should make sure the two women meet, especially if the meeting is unannounced. Next time you're supposed to see your friend for drinks, bring your new "girlfriend" along. The "friend" will immediately feel like the third wheel. This tricks her little brain into thinking that she wants to be with you, when, in reality, it's just that she would rather be with anyone than be alone.

4. *Encourage her to partake in slutty activity*—Get your "friend" to take home random guys from the bar. If she has a boyfriend and insists on talking about him, you should guide the conversation towards sex as much as possible. Once you and she are spending the majority of your time discussing sexual activity, she will begin to think of you when she's actually having sex with somebody else. Not to mention, it will drive her nuts that you don't care who she sleeps with. In the end, even if you don't get in her pants, you'll at least gain new understanding into a chick's warped views on sexual relations.

5. *Make her depend on you*—If you become her doctor, psychiatrist, counselor, friend, and confidant, she will not be able to live without you. Once this happens, just disappear for

a while and tell her you met an amazing woman that might be "the one." She will be miserable without you and do anything and everything to get you back into her life. Use your imagination from there.

E-MAIL—YOU'VE GOT PUSS!

> ### TIP #23: E-MAIL IS THE GREATEST DATING TOOL EVER DEVISED.

Let's repeat that—e-mail is the greatest dating tool ever devised. If you think it's just a useful business application, or a way to keep in touch, you're missing the boat. In the new millennium, he who controls the e-mail controls the chicks. E-mail provides a myriad of benefits above and beyond what the phone could ever deliver:

a. *Second Chances*—It is almost impossible to screw things up over e-mail because there is no tone of voice involved. If you accidentally write something offensive, you can say it was a joke. If you write something serious and she laughs, congratulations, now you're funny.

b. *Unlimited Wingmen*—Who cares if you're not witty? Who cares if you can't even form a sentence? We guarantee you've got a buddy with a great sense of humor who can write up a storm. Remember the movie *Roxanne* with Steve Martin, Rick Rossovich, and Daryl Hannah? Rick is an idiot with words, but Steve is a poet, albeit a hideously deformed beast. Steve writes poetry and sends it to Daryl with Rick's signature on it. And guess who ends up putting the wood to Daryl? Rick, of course, because even though he is a complete idiot, Daryl Hannah plays the role of the typical stupid slut that gets duped by devious men. If you have witty friends, suddenly you're sending witty e-mail. How great is that?

c. *You Can Save Everything*—How many times have you sat there staring at some chick's boobs while ignoring everything that's coming out of her mouth? Eventually, she'll expect you to remember something, and then you're really screwed. With e-mail, you can always read them later and pick up helpful bits of knowledge, e.g., the chick's last name.

d. *You Actually Get a Chance to Talk About You*—How many times have you sat there trying to get a word in edgewise as your chick dominates the conversation with her nonstop babbling? With e-mail, you can finally say what you have to say without worrying about her freaking out over her nails halfway through a sentence. The female also appreciates this aspect. Because she is slow and dumb, it is difficult for her to process things as fast as you say them. By writing them out, she can read one word at a time and move along at her own pace.

e. *You Become More Attractive*—It seems like every day that you hear about some loser who bagged a hot chick after meeting her in a chat room and finding out that they have all the same things in common. Face to face, it's nearly impossible for a shallow chick to see past your greasy zits and uni-brow. E-mail allows your inner thoughts and beauty to shine even brighter than the glare from your bald spot.

f. *She Can't Hang Up on You*—Let's face it, you're an asshole, which means you're going to screw up—a lot. In days past, your repeated phone calls would require you to suffer through the indignity of having her hang up on you. With e-mail, that's no longer a problem. As long as she doesn't take the drastic step of changing her address (which, don't kid yourself, could happen), she's got no choice but to read your pleas for attention, sex, or whatever else you're craving that day. She may not respond, but that's cool—you can just convince yourself that her DSL connection is down and might not be back up for six to eight months.

g. *You Can Send Her a Virus*—If you didn't manage to give her one in the bedroom, now's your chance to make up for it. After she dumps you, pay off some geek to write a computer virus. Hopefully, he'll figure out a way to e-mail naked pictures of her to everybody in her address book. It may not do anything productive, but it always feels better to screw her over one last time.

h. *Research*—E-mail also gives you time to research—you can gain critical information about her before you go on the all-important second date. If she likes sixteenth-century art, learn something about it. If she's from Minnesota, make fun of her for it. Joke and flirt as much as possible. This way, when you finally do sit down to have drinks, you'll be able to talk about something more meaningful than the smell of your farts.

CYBERSEX—I WONDER IF LUV2SWALLOW@AOL.COM LIVES NEARBY?

It is important to separate e-mail from Internet dating, because they are completely different. Using e-mail is an expected form of communication among people who know each other, dating or not. Scouring the Internet in search of a companion is a totally different story. To have access to hundreds of thousands of women and never have to worry about an opening line or breaking the ice in a conversation could be the greatest advance in the history of human relationships. The Internet has opened up a whole new world for the ugly, the lame, the inarticulate, and people who type really, really fast. In a chat room, a fat person can be Ally McBeal, a short guy can be Shaquille O'Neal, and an award-winning physicist could be a chick.

a. *Online Dating*—In the twenty-first century, even assholes use dating services. How could you not? They cost about fifty bucks, and you have access to 10,000 women. Who cares if 9,996 of them are heinous she-devils with hair on their butts and chronic halitosis? That's four whole chicks who you can bang at a mere twelve-fifty each. Shoot, a hooker's going to set you back a hundred bucks a throw. Dating services are easy; they all have pictures of the chicks, and, surprisingly, a ton of them are hot, and—despite the fact that every good-looking girl you see there has probably received over 15,000 e-mails in the last twenty-four hours—there's a shot at pulling some tail out of there. Although a lot of you might be shaking your head at such an admittedly pussy way of going about bitch-getting, what have you got to lose? Nobody knows you, and if you start banging Miss America, who cares how you met her?

b. *Chat Rooms*—Chat rooms are an interesting place to meet chicks, because you do have the opportunity to "pick them up." Furthermore, with hundreds of other dorks in the same room, you can get enormous satisfaction out of beating them to the punch by getting the telephone number of a girl whose screen name is "nogagreflex." In order to find a hot chick in this more complicated environment, you need to:

1. *Practice your typing*—The first and most important rule of chat rooms is that you have to be a damn fast typist. No matter how brilliant your comeback is to a sarcastic remark, if it takes you four minutes to type it out, the room has moved through three different topics by the time you're done. This is especially troublesome if your chick is publicly flirting with you, because there will be ten other dorks who are IM-ing her to death while you're trying to find the question mark key.

2. *Verify before you leap*—You know that chick in the chat room who describes herself as a twenty-two-year-old, blonde, 36-D,

bathing suit model from Fort Lauderdale? She's a man—or a 230-pound housewife in Des Moines. Chat rooms allow you to assume any identity you want, and, when it comes to entirely anonymous chatting, women will lie their asses off just as much as you. So, when you do succeed in getting some chick to agree to meet you at a bar after chatting with her online, demand a picture. If she sends you a baby picture, you're staying home. If she's supposed to be thirty-five and she gives you a shot of her as a cheerleader in high school, stay the hell away. There's nothing worse than walking into a bar, looking for your date and seeing a Kathy Bates look-alike making a beeline for you. If you're still trying to determine whether the Internet is a good place to pick up chicks, here are a couple of pros and cons, so your stubborn ass can figure it out for yourself:

PROS	CONS
You immediately open yourself up to millions of new chicks that you never would've met otherwise.	Every one of these chicks could be completely psychotic.
You can get to know a woman's personality before judging her by her looks.	Are you kidding me? You're an asshole! Looks are the only thing that matter. Half the time she talks you can't even hear any words coming out.
You could meet the woman of your dreams.	She could live in Detroit.
The perfect girl could work in the building next to you, and you would never meet her any other way.	You might fall in love with your sister under a fake e-mail name.
Cybersex.	Have you ever tried typing and jerking off at the same time? It's like trying to wipe your ass with your left hand.

In all likelihood, Internet dating will be the wave of the future. However, if you do it now, your buddies will never let you hear the end of it. If you are drawn to cyber-dating, try to only date local chicks. When something comes of it, you can always tell your buddies that you met her at the mall. The only exception is if you find yourself a supermodel. Then you can tell all your buddies to go to hell. You're fucking a supermodel, and it doesn't matter how you met her!

AGES 21–27 FINAL EXAMINATION

1. *A sharp-toothed beaver:*
   a. Can build a dam in under forty-five minutes
   b. Administers a sweet kind of pain when giving oral sex
   c. Will ruin your entire career
   d. Can make a man's dick look like a puppy's chew toy

2. *Weddings are good places to get laid because:*
   a. Women feel more secure about being single
   b. Every woman is looking for Mr. Right
   c. White makes chicks horny
   d. Every girl is drunk, sweaty, and utterly alone

3. *The only acceptable place to go on a first date is:*
   a. A candlelight dinner with scenic views
   b. A coffee shop
   c. A Japanese restaurant that will force her to sit on her knees
   d. A whorehouse

4. *Which is not an example of "periscope up"?*
   a. Sitting in the corner and blowing off any chick that looks at you
   b. Approaching a girl with a raging hard-on
   c. Grabbing three buddies and cornering a bunch of chicks
   d. Introducing yourself to a chick and buying her a drink

5. *When meeting a chick at a bar, you should buy her a drink:*
   a. Immediately after you introduce yourself
   b. Only after she has bought you a drink
   c. From across the room before you meet her
   d. Don't ever buy a girl a drink, because it is immoral, and girls that drink are icky

6. *Which is not the sign of a good wingman?*
   a. He gets you laid
   b. He likes fat girls
   c. He's irresponsible
   d. He has excellent beer goggles

7. *Repeat one-night stands are great for:*
   a. Finding yourself a girlfriend
   b. Getting a girl in every port
   c. Keeping yourself disease-free
   d. A woman's self-esteem

8. *The 1-2-3 Punch is:*
   a. The easiest way to knock out a screaming woman
   b. A lethal drink that combines 151, Rumpleminze, and tequila
   c. Dating, marriage, divorce
   d. Coffee, drinks, dinner

9. *Why should you let a chick decide to be your "girlfriend," as opposed to just someone you're dating?*
    a. Because you couldn't care less what she calls herself
    b. Because it won't stop you from banging other chicks
    c. Because it may be the only thing you ever do to make her happy
    d. All of the above

10. *When we say that "women are like tools in a box" we mean:*
    a. Tools are most useful when being shoved inside other women
    b. You only use women to further your own selfish goals
    c. If you let your buddy borrow tools, chances are they're gone forever
    d. Tools and women are essentially worthless without a man to use them

ANSWERS
1-c, 2-b, 3-b, 4-a, 5-b, 6-c, 7-b, 8-d, 9-d, 10-b.

Chapter Five

AGES 28–35

WELCOME MAT

Your late twenties to early thirties is a precarious time in your life. The most significant change will be the physical deterioration of your body. You begin to have aches and pains in places you didn't even know existed. Hair starts to disappear from your head and show up on your back. You don't have the strength, the stamina, or the endurance that you used to. All in all, you're a wreck. The thing you must constantly watch for, however, is that you don't let the degradation of your physical body affect your asshole mentality. Many older guys start to lose confidence, thinking they're less of a man than they were during their prime. They get soft, they start to believe that they should be nicer to people, to kiss somebody's ass so maybe they can move up another rung on the ladder. Bullshit!

If you're going to maintain that losing attitude, put the book down, start a knitting club or auction off your testicles on eBay. That kind of thinking is for losers, and we can't believe that a loser could have made it to page 136 of this book. You're now closing out your twenties and you've got to be prepared to work your ass off to be even half the asshole you used to be. And, goddamn it, if we have anything to do with it, you'll be up for the challenge. Even though responsibilities are starting to overwhelm you, many college girls think you're too old to date, and a family may soon screw up your dating patterns, we're going to make sure you are still the same prick you've always been. On your mark, get set, you're thirty.

TURN OUT THE LIGHTS, THE PARTY'S OVER

TIP #24: AGE THIRTY-FOUR IS NOT AGE TWENTY-FOUR.

How do you know when the good old days are really the good old days? Here are the ten most significant signs:

TOP TEN WAYS TO KNOW THAT YOU'LL NEVER BE TWENTY-FOUR AGAIN

10. You need to pull out long, curly nose hairs at least three times a day.
9. VH-1 seems way cooler than MTV.
8. You leave work early so you can catch *World News Tonight*.
7. Chicks ask you to help them with their homework, rather than just immediately jumping your bones.
6. Instead of trimming your sideburns, your girlfriend asks to shave your back.
5. Not basketball, golf.
4. When you're in the sun, your scalp gets burned.
3. You had no idea that Abercrombie & Fitch wasn't "in" anymore.
2. You still don't pay off your credit card's monthly balance, but now you know exactly how much it is.

And The Number One Way to Know That You'll Never Be Twenty-four Again—

1. After sticking it to her once, you're ready to go to sleep.

Guess what? You're thirty-three. It's over. No, not your life—dating the way it used to be. It might have happened at thirty-one, maybe it'll wait until thirty-four, maybe even twenty-nine if you're a friggin' loser, but it happened—your life changed and you're not a young, strapping buck anymore. Your slow, physical descent has accelerated recently, and the wild roller coaster of love you used to ride has come to a screeching halt. Yeah, sure, the mellowing of your social life will be tough to get over—kind of like losing an old friend, one that you occasionally had sex with—but a couple of attitude adjustments and a few modifications in your lifestyle and you'll be as good as . . . well, you're not going to be as good as new, but you'll be as good as you're going to get—and that's about all you can hope for at this age, ya old fart.

TIP #25: DON'T GIVE IN TO TIME.

All right, so you're ancient. What do you do now? You can't just curl up in a ball, gather five hundred issues of *Maxim*, *Stuff*, and *FHM* around you, and wait to die. What's next? Are you really consigned to a life of mind-numbing boredom with a wife you hate, kids who hate you, and a mortgage you'll never be able to afford? Well, actually, yes, you are, so it's perfectly acceptable if you need to be miserable for a little while. In fact, we highly recommend a good six-month mourning period, so that you can finally accept the fact that the fun part of your life is basically over and you've got nothing but drudgery ahead of you. You think we're lying? We wish you were right. Check out all of these things you're never going to do again:

- Midnight decisions to drive down to Mexico so you can get a tattoo.

- Daytona Beach, South Padre Island, Lake Havasu, or whatever spot you'd go to hang out with 25,000 drunk sorority girls. If you're over thirty and showing up at Spring Break, you might as well turn yourself in for statutory rape before you cross the state line.
- Hanging out in a fraternity TV room with four bros, six little sisters, a pony keg, and a pallet of condoms.
- Going to Vegas or Atlantic City, dropping only fifty bucks, and still thinking you had a great time.
- Having sex with someone under seventeen.

We could literally go on and on with these types of things, but we don't want to depress you any more than you already are. You're just going to have to deal with the fact that, as your twenties come to a close, an enormous metamorphosis is going to take place, and virtually none of the changes are going to be welcome. Sure, there's probably a few small tribes of people in sub-Saharan Africa who believe nose hair is attractive, but you're probably not going to run into them while you're hanging out at the local tavern. Read on for tips on how to identify and deal with the myriad issues that you'll now start to face. Try not to get too discouraged, though. Although you may be a shadow of your former self, chances are that every chick your age is sporting twice the shadow she was ten years ago, so it can't be that difficult to get a little action.

WHAT'S YOUR SIGN? CLOSED

We spend a lot of time writing about the different types of chicks you're dealing with now that you're old, the ways that you handle them, and how your body and mind must change if you want to continue to date women that inspire high fives from strangers in a parking lot. All of this is great information, but before we get to that you're going to have to

meet her first. Where do you find women now that you're in your thirties? She's not sitting next to you in class anymore. She's not lying
around the Winnebago, as you road-trip to some random college football game. She's not even at work anymore because they fired her for a
younger version that gives better head. So where is she?

Amazingly enough, all of the women that disappeared right after college will come back with a vengeance now. Women are everywhere, no
matter how hard it is to believe. If you think about it, to a certain extent,
there are more women available now than when you were in college. Back
then, everybody knew each other, you went to the same places every
night (because those were the ones who'd accept your fake i.d.). Damn,
you were practically in a rut! Now that you're out in the cold, cruel world,
you'll find that your neighborhood is probably bursting at the seams with
women who are too horny not to want to sleep with you, but too friggin'
scared to come right out and say it. Ay, there's the rub. Although there
are probably thousands of women within your little orbit every day,
they're just not going to grab your ass the way they used to.

When you hit your thirties, you've got to *work* to get women. It's a
battle. Every day, you put on your hard hat, grab an M-4 carbine and a
lunch pail, and you bust your ass trying to find the chicks that you're
going to be dumping in the next week or so. When you leave your
house, you're on the frontlines of an emotional battlefield, and you've
got to be badder than an Israeli soldier, more ferocious than the muja-
hedeen. In short, *you've got to be an animal!*

> ## TIP #26: AFTER AGE THIRTY, YOU'VE GOT TO BE AN ANIMAL TO GET CHICKS.

But you've got to be an animal in the right places, and you must
become more selective in picking your battlefield. Bars are out. If you

thought they were tough in your twenties, wait until you're using the same lines on the same chicks over the same drinks for the fifteenth consecutive year. The most well-adjusted of men have been known to kill themselves for much less, so you've got to evolve a little. Even the king of the assholes strikes out at bars the majority of the time, and at this age who needs the hassle? Never fear, though, because there are tons of places that you can be the same swinging dick you've been all these years. You're just going to have to sweat a little more than you're used to. But, who cares? You're an asshole. You'll make it happen. Here's where to go:

a. *The Supermarket*—The supermarket?! Have we finally lost it? Absolutely not. In fact, it would blow you away to see how much puss runs around supermarkets every single day. The fact that you've probably never seen the inside of one makes it a strange and mysterious place to you. But don't worry, they have a bunch of stuff you like to eat—frozen pizza, Kit Kat bars, and very bored, horny housewives. It may be disconcerting at first. All these strange foods and crazy packages. Where's the drive-thru window? How do I get some fries? But, if women see you in the supermarket, they automatically think that you're independent, healthy, and really, really trying hard to take on some domestic responsibility. Essentially, they think you're a pussy, when you're actually just after some. Isn't that great? You can throw her virtually any line that pops into your head, because she's not alert to your bullshit—she's just trying to show you how firm your tomatoes are supposed to be. Next chance you get, run out to the local food mart, grab a bunch of vegetables, and stand around, looking confused. The divorcees will be beating a path to your cart.

b. *Little League Baseball*—If you're an American, you played baseball as a little kid. If you're one of those Euro-fags who only played soccer, please return this book, we don't want your money. Now if you played baseball (which you did!), you know that you don't have to be some rocket scientist to coach it. It's not like football, where you've got eleven guys running all over and you've got to get them organized. In baseball, nine guys stand in the same place, and if a ball gets hit to them, they throw it to first. Why are we telling you this? Because you're going to go out and coach a Little League team. Little Leaguers are generally between the ages of six and fifteen, which means their moms are anywhere from their late twenties to their early forties—prime sex years, and perfect candidates for the prized classification of MILF—short for "Mothers I'd like to Fuck." If you're the coach, you've got an air of respect, an authoritative glow. Women die for this kind of stuff. And, because you're not coaching your son, the women will think that you like kids—a must for any mom who's looking for a man she can start banging. Plus, due to the fact that moms of Little Leaguers are going to be a little bit older, at least 40 percent of them will be divorced, which is good for you. It doesn't matter if you're not really into the game; put on a pair of faded Levis, an old baseball cap, and get your ass out to the park.

c. *Any Type of Class*—When we say class, we mean a nonschool type of class—like a class in photography at the camera shop. Maybe a class in sky-diving. Or even better, a class on human sexuality at the local community college. Chicks love to learn. We don't know why—maybe it has something to do with the fact that they're all so dumb. The coolest thing about being in a class with a woman is that she'll think you have common interests. This is a big one with older women.[4] Even though you took this class for the sole reason that you wanted to bang chicks, let her believe that

---

[4] Common Interests—Women always think you need to have common interests. It is a patently ridiculous argument, when you think about it. What man and woman really have common interests? How many women out there enjoy drinking twenty-four beers, eating an entire plate of buffalo wings, crying over the outcome of football games, blowing five hundred dollars in a strip club, and ripping farts so nasty that somebody in the room gets cancer? None—yet, almost every woman ends up with a man. If two people in a relationship really needed common interests, the entire population would be gay, because only people of the same sex really enjoy the same stuff.

she's found a guy who's somewhat similar to her. When you think about it, in a sense, you are. You want to bang chicks. She's a chick. What more do you need?

d. *Volunteer Work*—This is another great one, because people will think you're doing some noble, life-sustaining work, when, in reality, you're just trying to score some trim. Nevertheless, by volunteering for anything, absolutely anything, you will instantly be attractive to the women who have volunteered for the same work. You can be grotesquely obese, with one eyebrow on your head and ten on your fingers, but if you and that cute redhead both signed up to write postcards for the blind, she might just want some of your action. Make sure that you sign up for stuff that's going to attract hot chicks, though. Breast cancer prevention groups are always great, because hot women are usually concerned about their racks. Big name diseases—like Muscular Dystrophy and Lou Gehrig's Disease—are also good ones because, once the illness becomes attached to a celebrity, every women in town is jumping on the bandwagon to help out. There are some, of course, that you want to avoid: Save the Whales, for instance. Or Greenpeace. These types of groups attract the hair-under-the-arms, showerless, Grateful Dead, veggie burrito, LSD chicks who should all go back to Berkeley where they belong.

e. *Church or Temple*—Churches, temples, and mosques are truly the best places to pick up chicks when you're getting on in years. What's particularly nice is that the women you meet there will be of the same religion as you, so your parents aren't going to have a cow when their little Catholic angel brings home a pagan, devil-worshiping Episcopalian.

If you meet a girl at church, there's also a pretty good chance she's not some flighty ditz whose sole ambition in life is to be a face-cream model. Presumably, she's got enough substance that you can work with her. Sure, she's still a chick—which means she's going to be a pain in the ass—but at least on Sunday mornings you can take her someplace where she'll just shut up for a couple of hours. If you're a Jew, you've got it even better—you can take her to the temple on Friday nights and Saturday mornings, ensuring four to five hours of blissful silence. Girls with some spiritual experience also tend to be somewhat nicer, cleaner, and absolute monsters in bed. The women who spend the most time in places of worship will let the spirit out in a big way when they're behind closed doors. Trust us, "oh God" is something you will be hearing on a fairly regular basis when you bag one of these holy rollers.

COCKTAIL CHATTER ALWAYS
STARTS WITH A COCK

You're thirty now. Old topic starters like, "I'm thinking about graduate school, how about you?" and "How many interviews have you gotten so far?" don't hold quite as much weight as they used to. So what are you going to talk about? That's actually a much trickier question than it appears to be. Because, now that you've acquired a little age and experience, women are going to expect you to know about a bunch of stuff. The top ten RBI-producers in a season isn't going to cut it. These days, you are required to have a certain basic level of knowledge regarding a few key topics. If you have your bases covered when it comes to these critical areas, you can walk into walls the rest of the time, and women will still think you're intelligent enough that they may let you into their pants.

TIP #27: KNOW WHAT THE HELL
YOU'RE TALKING ABOUT.

It's important to be able to work some of your topics into the conversation in a cool, subtle manner. If you're standing around at some martini mixer, and everybody's talking about a political election, your contribution that "I never cared much for Picasso's cubist period" is going to leave the air a little flat. This is why you must develop a broad base of knowledge that cuts across class and socioeconomic lines. You never can tell when you're going to be hanging out with a bunch of rich aristocrats talking about tax relief, or when you'll be stuck with the starving artist klatch, discussing beat poets from the '60s. You must be prepared for all of these various and sundry groups, and even if you're not real hip to their conversation you'll need to know enough to bullshit your way around. Because, as we probably don't have to remind you, no matter what the size of the group, there's sure to be one or two young chicks who you can take home if you play your cards right. Here are the basic concepts you need to know:

    a. *Wine*—Trust us, all wines taste the same. The "experts" who claim to know the difference between two vintages based on smell or taste are lying through their teeth. If you gave them tangerine Gatorade, they probably couldn't distinguish it from a '98 Beaujolais, so don't sweat if you never really understood what constituted a good wine and what allegedly tasted like beetle dung.[5] However, as long as your date digs wine, you should know how to fake it. Here's how:

---

[5] This story is true evidence of the complete hypocrisy that pervades virtually every wine "expert." I swear to God, it's true. I was in the room and saw it with my own eyes. This is not an urban legend, like the gerbil in Richard Gere's ass, or the quart of cum in Rod Stewart's stomach. Sorry about that visual. Anyway, my girlfriend from a few years ago (who am I kidding? she was some chick I was sticking for a couple of weeks) bitched at me to go to a wine class. Thinking I might learn something that would help me get laid when I eventually decided to dump her, I agreed. We met this friend of hers who swore he practically invented grapes. He went on and on about wines this and champagne that and all the trips he'd taken to the wine country and ladeda-dada. I tuned him out about ninety seconds in, but that's not the point. Here is the point: We tried about three different glasses of red, the teacher told us about them, and we supposedly learned a new nugget that will impress people at cocktail parties. After that, the friend excused himself to go to the bathroom. The next glass we were given, while he was out of the room, was a spoiled wine, which the teacher explained will give us an idea what types of things you should *not* be looking for in a good wine. I swear, after the teacher told us about the problems with this wine, the loser walked back in, sat down, drank the spoiled stuff, and started falling all over himself about how great it was. "The bouquet! The tannins! This is roses in a bottle," he screamed. When he found out that he was drinking the equivalent of grape vomit, he left the class at the break and we never saw his fat ass again.

1. *Lines*—Use a line like "this '97 Cabernet is delicious because the conditions for growing the grapes that year were ideal." She's guaranteed to think you're a cultured, sophisticated genius, even though you have no idea what you're saying.

2. *Swirl the glass when you get it*—This is a favorite of wine connoisseurs—they're served a glass of wine and, almost reflexively, they swirl the contents around in their glass, even though none of them could tell you why they do it in the first place. However, virtually all chicks have seen this happen and believe that a guy "in the know" will always swirl. So, our recommendation is to swirl every glass that's ever set in front of you. If she asks why you're doing it, you just smile as if you have some hidden reservoir of knowledge, secure in the fact that she's as clueless as you are.

3. *American wines rule*—Drinking California wine is the only acceptable choice for any asshole, which brings us to another important point: *Fuck the French!* In all the world, there is not a more loathsome and arrogant group of people than the French. If you're French and reading this book, we hope you get a paper cut. The French will dispute the fact that California wines are the world's best, but the Frogs have gotten their asses kicked in every war that's ever been fought, so why in God's name would you believe *them*? Anyway, what you want to take out of this is that when you're perusing the wine list before you eat you should mention the fact that you prefer California wines, because they produce a fuller, richer, more refined taste than the French wines. Your date will have no clue what you're talking about or what a "more refined taste" means, but she'll be too embarrassed to ask.

b. *Art*—If you think the pseudo-intellectuals are bad when it comes to wine, they can't hold a candle to the supposed art "experts" who run around out there. Nobody—we repeat, *nobody*—has the slightest clue what they're talking about when it comes to art. Forgeries have hung in the world's finest museums for years before people realized they were piece-of-shit copies worth about two cents. In the '70s, the New York Metropolitan Museum of Art, one of the premier art institutions in the world, had a painting of a Campbell's Soup can gracing its walls. Are you kidding me? The point of this is that art appreciation is truly the highest form of nonsense in the world, and there is no way that we could give you any real advice regarding what to say when you and your little tramp are checking out some pictures. Therefore, when you're in the presence of both art and a woman, just put your chin in your hand and silently stare at the piece. If she asks what you think, you say, "I'm just so overwhelmed by it. I'm trying to come to an appreciation of what the artist was telling us." And then sigh heavily as you drift into deep comprehension. You don't know what you're talking about, but neither does your date, so you're safe in the fact that your woman's going to think you're a deep thinker, and that's an extra arrow in your quiver as you try to get her into the sack.

c. *Politics and Government*—These conversations are huge. They can kill your shot at getting laid, or they can land you in bed before you have a chance to go out to dinner. It's extremely difficult to come up with a couple of shorthand notes that will allow you to seem knowledgeable about politics and government, because it really depends on the political leanings of your chick.

For instance, if you tell a woman that you believe in helping children by funding more programs for their early development, she should be impressed by your sensitivity, warmth, and caring for kids, right? Not if she's a rabid right-wing Republican. If she's on the far right, she's for small government, and absolutely hates taxes, so, in her mind, she's not thinking about your opinion on helping children, she just thinks you want to suck her for a few more tax dollars to create another government-sponsored bureaucratic organization that's going to screw the kids up anyway.

Then what do you do to impress her? It's easy. Ask questions.

Don't ever express an opinion until you're sure you know what she thinks. After she tells you her point of view, you slightly modify the words she used and give the same point of view right back to her. Even if you're just a parrot, her knowledge that you two have the same beliefs will be infinitely more important than your ability to offer creative insights into the political process. Here are a couple of examples:

1. YOU: Gee Susie, did you hear that the state of Texas just executed that gang rapist the other night?

   SUSIE: Yes, I did. Isn't it disgusting that the government can sponsor murder?

   YOU: I couldn't agree with you more. A government that commits murder to punish murderers is unbelievably hypocritical.

   SUSIE: Can I give you a blowjob?

2. YOU: Hey Christy, were you watching the President's speech where he talked about raising taxes to expand the government's welfare plan?

   CHRISTY: I did, and I'm appalled that he wants to sock us with another tax increase when businesses are having so much trouble making ends meet right now.

   YOU: I know, isn't it horrible when he tries to sacrifice the needs of the companies that make our economy grow so he can waste money on the lazy, shiftless poor?

   CHRISTY: Will you ravage me like a wild pig?

See, it's easy to develop political ideas once the woman has given you the answers to the test. Just make sure you know what she thinks, feed the same drivel right back to her, and you're set for at least the next four hours.

d. *Sports*—Even when women are not into sports, they believe their man should be. A post-pubescent fascination with sports is

considered to be highly indicative of male virility and the lack
thereof will inevitably make you appear, um, effeminate. We
imagine that you're a sports fanatic if you're an asshole, but there's
a possibility that you avoided it for some reason—like, if you suck
at sports. It's cool when a woman doesn't know that the Rams are
a football team; if a man doesn't, you really have to wonder if his
father ever made him put on a dress. But this doesn't mean you
should be studying the box scores every day to figure out the
latest National League stolen-base leaders. That's worthless trivia
that might be great if you're trying out for an ESPN game show
but are almost entirely useless when trying to scare up some new
trim. However, regardless of your level of interest in sports, you
can get by with just a modicum of knowledge.

1. Know which teams are good in the big three: football, baseball,
   and basketball. Hockey's starting to be a little more popular,
   but since Gretzky retired, who the hell really cares? You also
   need to know a couple of the top players and enough rules that,
   when the referee or umpire signals something, you can explain
   to your woman what's going on.
2. You must also understand point spreads and virtually all gambling
   permutations. For some reason, chicks like gamblers. It's probably
   because women think of gamblers as bad boys with a lot of
   money. A woman finding those two qualities will be as happy as a
   man who just found a mute stripper that moonlights as a
   professional chef. Therefore, it's a good idea to let the woman
   believe that you engage in recreational betting, even if you're really
   taking out a second mortgage to try and break even.
3. You must watch *Monday Night Football* every week. Even if
   Dennis Miller comes back and sucks so bad you want to
   scream every time he starts blowing sunshine up the ass of
   whatever coach gave him a team jacket that afternoon. *Monday
   Night Football* is one of those American institutions that is so

widely accepted, even most women will watch it. If your chick actually wants to check out sports on TV, and you don't, the relationship might as well be over, because she'll never believe you're a heterosexual again.

HER PLACE

We know what you're thinking: if she takes you to her place, you've scored a huge victory, right? Yes, and no. You're a little older now, so you're going to have to be a little smarter, too. Sure it's great to be brought inside her little realm, but you've got to be aware of what's going on now. Remember that, as much as you hate to admit it, the woman you date at this age could end up being Mrs. Asshole, and even though you'd rather endure an afternoon of getting caned by a Singaporean executioner before bringing up the term "marriage," you have to be evaluating her as much as she's evaluating you. Therefore, when you go to her place, you might not want to just jump in the sack as soon as you've walked in the door. You've got to be on the lookout for a couple of things to make sure this doesn't turn into another disaster:

TIP #28: BE AWARE OF YOUR SURROUNDINGS.

a. *Is Her Place a Mess?*—If yes, get the hell out of there. If she didn't even have the foresight to clean her house after knowing that you were coming over she's either: a) too stupid for you to be involved with; b) a disgusting pig who'd never be worth shit as a wife, or; c) a man. Any of the three should have you running for the hills before she gets back from the bathroom.

b. *Does She Have Food in the Refrigerator?*—Another litmus test. If she doesn't have food, that means she doesn't like to cook. Or worse, she's going out every night, which will be a real pain in the ass once *you* are picking up the bill. If she's not making anything but toast and reservations right now, do you think that's going to change when your old, fat, hairy ass is hungry? Hell no. Get out right now.

c. *Is It "Too" Clean and Perfect?*—Clean is good. Maniacally perfect is the sure sign of a sick mind. For instance, if she has all of her cat figurines pointing the same direction, she could be a bunny broiler. If her table remains permanently made with Wedgewood china and antique silverware, you're looking at a very high cost of admission to get into the game. If she has her bed made with "hospital corners," she's not going to swallow. All of these things are important to notice right now. The day after you're married is a lifetime too late.

d. *Pictures of Her Ex-Boyfriend*—You think it's tough to beat out the guys who are still calling her? Think about how brutal it will be to defeat a memory. Every day that he's gone, he gets better looking in her mind. If *he* dumped *her*, oh Lord, every time you don't bring her to orgasm will be another chance for you to compare poorly to his long-gone supersperm.

   If the pictures are of a deceased boyfriend, run, don't walk. Remember John F. Kennedy? What did he do during his two-and-a-half-years as president? He got his ass kicked at the Bay of Pigs, the Commies built the Berlin Wall under his watch, and he couldn't get a civil rights bill passed to save his life. But after he died? He became quite possibly the greatest hero in the history of the American presidency. That's the same way your potential chick remembers her ex. If she's still thinking about a dead boyfriend, her vagina may as well be boarded up.

e. *None of the Above*—If you can't find anything that jumps out at you as a sign of a seriously diseased mind, you should mount that little girl as if she's the second coming of Secretariat.

AVOID THE "M" WORD AT ALL COSTS

The single greatest danger that you must face as the years start to pile on is the dreaded "m" word—marriage. Everybody you know is thinking about it. Your parents are wondering when you are going to get yourself together and settle down with a nice girl. Every unmarried woman in your life will be sizing you up like a three-hundred-pound offensive lineman at the NFL combine. Your buddies, who are certain to be dropping like flies at this time in your life, and their shrew-like wives will constantly be trying to set you up with "the one." You shouldn't completely blame your friend, though, because he at least has the right idea in mind—he doesn't care whether you find the right girl, he just wants you to become a couple so he can have you over to watch football games and drink beer while "the wives" go into the other room and talk about what assholes they married.

> ## TIP #29: AVOID LIKE THE PLAGUE ALL CONVERSATIONS REGARDING MARRIAGE.

There's not a woman alive who can hit the age of twenty-five without going into some kind of toxic shock syndrome when she thinks about scoring a husband. Once they've hit the quarter-century mark, women will employ all manner of trickery to get themselves hitched. Biting the tips off of condoms, getting their boyfriends a job in the family business, buying new boobs—these are all things that women do to trap a man. Most non-assholes out there will fall for these petty antics. Not you, though, you're not biting.

As you swim through the shark-infested waters of potential matrimony, the warning signs are everywhere and your internal chick radar should be going off like a siren at a Mississippi speed trap. You must know the difference between when women are trying to get you hooked into marriage and when they've got their heads on straight, i.e., when they know that your relationship will be nothing more than cheap, tawdry sex. Here are a couple of tips on how to know when the vile woman sitting across the table from you is on the express lane to her impending nuptials, or at least thinks she is.

a. *She Uses the Word "Marriage" or "Wedding" During the First Three Dates*—Okay, maybe you think this is an easy one, but it's not as simple as it sounds. She doesn't necessarily have to be talking to you about marriage. The mere mention of the word indicates a Freudian obsession and should be your first clue to get the hell out of there as soon as you can. For example, if she says:

1. *"When I was a bridesmaid at my cousin's marriage . . ."* Notice she used the word "marriage" instead of "wedding," which is a chick-style Jedi mind trick that is supposed to spur your thoughts of a lifetime of marriage, rather than the one-day wedding. The only thing it should spur is your need to get another drink, and make it a double.

2. *"Marriage is such a crazy thing."* She might try to throw you off by insinuating that she's not ready for marriage either, or by discussing the philosophical disadvantages of marriage. *Warning! Warning, Will Robinson!* This is a cover-up. Don't fall for it. She may be pretending that she doesn't want to get married, but we guarantee that if you propose to her that night she'd be on her cell phone reserving two tickets to Vegas before you got to dessert. By pretending she's uninterested in marriage, she is merely probing you to find out where you stand on the idea. If you're smart, you'll play along, because

even though you're certainly not going to marry her, it could get you laid.

3. *"I was watching TV the other night and saw the most lovely wedding."* Again, she's using the guise of conversation to bring up the dreaded topic. This is a rather clumsy and blatant attempt, though, and it is entirely acceptable to tell her that the date is over and you're taking her home. When chicks are subtle or cool about bringing up the topic of marriage, you should probably roll with it, since they clearly know they're treading on thin ice. When it's this ridiculous and overt, she's too stupid to hang out with anyway, so you might as well send her packing right now. Unless, of course, you haven't had sex with her yet, in which case you should play along until you've gotten her at least once.

b. *She Asks About Your Personal Finances*—Asking about money is a certain death question. Even if she's not looking to get married, she's a money-hungry, gold-digging bitch who should be kicked to the curb immediately. The best way to deal with this type of woman is to tell her that your portfolio is worth about eight figures conservatively, watch as she gets all excited, then excuse yourself to go to the bathroom and never come back to the table.

c. *She Wants to Take You to Her Friend's Wedding*—Always be wary of situations like this. If you had to go to a wedding, asking one of your stable of women to accompany you would not be a hidden request for commitment. You just need a date. Women are incapable of maintaining this type of emotional distance. If they want you to take them to a wedding, any wedding, it is almost assuredly a hint that you should be thinking about a possible betrothal to her.

You will know for sure if during the wedding she continuously chatters about how beautiful it is, how wonderful the couple is, and how amazing the rest of their life is going to be. She will likely spend most of the time holding your hand, looking into your eyes, and trying to be as wife-like as possible. She is already trying to maneuver you down the aisle, and you must stay on your guard. The good part about this is that you are absolutely, 100 percent guaranteed to get laid when the wedding's over. The raw emotion and romance of a newly minted commitment is an aphrodisiac like no other. Prepare yourself, however, for the emotional hangover that comes the day after. Your date's friend will be married, but your date is not. Plus, she just gave you five to seven hours' worth of sex and she thinks you owe her something. They *never* give you something for nothing.

d. *She Refers to You as Her "Boyfriend" After Less than a Month of Dating*—Many women do this, and it is not always a sure sign that they're looking to get married immediately. Some of them try it for pure guilt purposes, i.e., to make you stop sleeping with other chicks. This is pretty much expected, and provided that you continue banging as many women as you can, it's relatively harmless. However, it could show a deep-seated desperation for a commitment, and may foreshadow an oncoming conversation regarding where the relationship is going. If she asks "where are we going?" less than six weeks after you meet her, you must immediately leave her house, tear up her telephone number, and forget what she looks like.

e. *Diverting the Conversation Away from Marriage after Six Months of Dating*—Diverting a conversation away from the topic of marriage is relatively easy when a chick is stupid enough to bring it up in the first couple of dates. It starts to get tougher when you've been going out with her for a while. When you start hitting the six-month barrier you'll likely be dodging a barrage of marriage innuendoes and hints on a daily basis. As the relationship drags on, it gets progressively more difficult to avoid the topic, so you may have to be very creative. If, God forbid, she's older than thirty, there may be nothing you can do to avoid the "come to

Jesus"[6] conversation, other than moving out of the house under the cover of night, changing your telephone number, or simply buying her a big-ass car. But there are certainly a lot of things you can try before you have to give in. Here are a couple of ideas that are worth a shot:

1. *Buy her something*—The marriage question is less about the actual institution of marriage than it is about the commitment, or lack thereof, in your relationship. What a woman is really talking about when she brings up the "m" word is whether or not you're ready to agree that she can have something for her very own, i.e., you. Truth be told, she *can't* have you, because you're a friggin' asshole, and it's highly unlikely you're going to do something as stupid as that—unless her father is the CEO of a Fortune 500 corporation. However, if you give her something else, e.g., a necklace, she can make the connection in her own head that she actually has gotten something. The mere fact that she now has some bauble that she can use to evidence your "love" to her friends will give her a reason to be happy for a short while. While it won't give you permanent peace, it'll probably buy her off long enough for you to find a new girlfriend.

2. *Take her on a vacation*—Again, remember that the conversation regarding marriage is not necessarily about marriage, it's about commitment, i.e., you doing something for her just because she wants it, not because it's good for you, too. An entirely acceptable short-term substitute for the marriage talk is a quick

---

[6] The "come to Jesus" talk has nothing to do with religion. It merely refers to the point in time when she demands that you guys have a conversation regarding the direction of your relationship. "Coming to Jesus" refers to your bellying up to the bar of commitment, much like born-again Christians give themselves over to their Lord. Interestingly enough, the phrase was allegedly coined during the time of Jesus Christ, when that whore Mary Magdalene tried to lock Jesus up for a long-term commitment. His refusal to be tied down was one of the first recorded, and most revered, acts in the history of assholes.

trip to some tropical paradise. You're doing something for her, just for her, and, more importantly, she can tell her friends afterward about all the romantic evenings you had together, even if all you really did was drink Mai Tais and bang each other silly. It should be comforting to you that, at the same time that you are providing what she considers to be a complete gift for her, you are forestalling any continued talk about marriage and getting three to seven days worth of nonstop sex. Ah, the joys of asshole-dom.

3. *Clean something*—It's pretty much a sure thing that you haven't done so much as clean a plate in the last five years. Once again, marriage conversation is not necessarily about marriage, it's always something else. One of the things she's probably pissed off about is that you are taking her for granted, because she does everything around the house while you sit on a La-Z-Boy recliner watching football, eating pizza, and farting. As noted above, she can't let herself believe that she's giving you something for nothing. They *never* give you something for nothing, and she's worried that, with her cleaning, cooking, and straightening up, you think she's little more than a free maid. Even though you probably do, if you immediately jump up and start doing some dishes, (a) she'll realize you're sharing in the household duties and that maybe you're actually going to take on some responsibility, and (b) she'll be less inclined to bitch about doing the housework if you occasionally do it, too. And the best part about it is, after you wipe off a bowl, you can sit back down and watch the rest of the game in peace.

4. *Feign interest*—An extremely dangerous move, and only one to be attempted by the brave. Pretending that you're interested in getting married when you're not could be a good move if you believe it will placate her and she'll drop the subject for a little while. However, this is a highly unlikely scenario. Once a woman knows that you're thinking about marriage, she will

grab on like a pit bull. Expect a flood of Tiffany's catalogues, Wedgewood china patterns, and sample invitations coming into your life. Plus, when you dump her in a month or two she's going to be crushed beyond all recognition. If your tolerance level is extremely high, and you operate with virtually no conscience, feigning interest in the "m" word will at least let you avoid a bunch of high-decibel arguments. Otherwise, it's a prescription for disaster.

GIVING IT THE OLD COLLEGE TRY

Ultimately, the real issue you have to face when you approach your thirties is the same question you had to face in your twenties: how do I bang college girls? This becomes a much more vexing issue as you get older. When you're twenty-three, everybody you hang out with is in their early twenties. Eventually, no matter how bad your persistent acne, there are too many women around for you not to stumble onto some dumb sophomore who thinks you are God in really baggy pants. Life is a numbers game and, one or two years out of college, they're stacked in your favor. Once you're getting up there in years, though, you can't just run off to a kegger or drop by a football game to score chicks. The day you hit thirty a translucent mark appears on your forehead that is visible only to dogs and sorority girls. They know you're checking them out, (the girls, not the dogs) they know you'd give your right testicle to have them for one night, and they know that if they play their cards right you'll buy them stuff even if they don't put out. At this point, your odds of getting them into the sack are as good as winning money at a Vegas slot machine. Zero.

It's very easy to give up on young girls at this age. You're in your late twenties, early thirties, and you start thinking that you need a girl who is mature, a little more settled, maybe one with a good job. *No!* You need college chicks, nineteen-year-old models, law school students. Do not let the pounding drum of societal acceptance skew your goals. Do you remember when you were in college, and half the hot sorority chicks were bragging about their date with a thirty-year-old real estate broker? Do you remember how pissed off you were? Can you believe there was a time you envied a thirty-year-old real estate broker? Well, now he's you, and you've got to be up for the challenge.

If you are willing to settle for any random thirty-five-year-old, it's time for you to get rid of this book and pick up a *Better Homes & Gardens*. However, if you're ready to go for the gold, we're right behind you. Please understand that you will have to alter your style. Some guys might think that if they have to start doing things differently they're no longer a true asshole. But, remember, being an asshole isn't great because you're an asshole, it's great because you can get dumb chicks to blow you while you're watching ESPN and eating red vines. Whatever it takes to get women is perfectly acceptable. Always keep that in mind and make the right adjustments when necessary. Here's how to do it:

> ## TIP #30: JUST BECAUSE YOU'RE THIRTY-TWO DOESN'T MEAN YOU CAN'T GET SOMEONE WHO'S TWENTY-TWO.

a. *Pretend You Don't Want to Get in Her Pants*—All right, this is generally good advice for banging chicks at any age, but, when you're past your thirties, it becomes especially important. Chicks in their twenties know that they are at the top of their game. Their boobs are firm, their asses are tight, and they've got ten years before everything drops to their knees. They are absolutely positive that, not only does their shit not stink, but that you'd eat a mile of it to get to their ass. And what do we do when some chick thinks she's God's gift? We treat her like we don't care if she's got diamonds in her muff.

When she thinks you don't want her, she'll be determined to make you realize that you should. She must show you that, yes, she's worth something; that yes, her ass is tight; that yes, her boobs are firm. If you don't agree, she starts to think that maybe, maybe . . . maybe they're not! Once she needs your approval to get her self-worth back, tell the fat lady to start warbling. To get to this point, you should really, really work the "I-don't-want-you" angle. Toy with her for a few weeks. Tell her you're not ready. You don't want to go too fast. The best line to use is "this could be something really special and I don't want to mess it up." That'll nearly kill her. Then, when you've got her literally panicked, terrified that no man will ever want her again, you take her out, throw a couple beers down her throat, and work that little monkey like the organ grinder's bitch that she really is. And then, never call the stuck-up trash again. Score one for the old guy.

b. *Be Husband Material*—The biggest reason that young girls like older guys is because of their alleged stability. If a girl tells you she's not interested in getting married, she's either lying, gay, or grotesquely overweight and can't find herself a man. Every woman on earth is pre-programmed from birth to constantly search for the guy she can glom onto and make miserable for the rest of his life. Even in college, a woman will be attracted to a man who might take care of her so she can engage in more thoughtful pursuits like having her legs waxed, eating brie, and banging the pool guy. Simply put, she'll want you because you are better marrying material. It's more likely that you'll sweep her off her feet and walk her down the aisle than the twenty-one-year-old guy who wants nothing more than to bed her down in a room with four of his buddies watching from the closet.

You must cultivate the idea that the more she thinks you're her future husband, the less likely she is to deny you what you really want: sex. Play up all the angles. Tell her how much you love kids. Speak longingly about the joys of growing old together. Wax poetic about the "one" that you are looking for. That's right, lie your ass off. Lie, lie, lie, lie. Because the second she believes that *you* might be the one, her panties are flying across the room faster than an F-14 Tomcat. And remember, since she's twenty-one and you're thirty-four, you don't want to get rid of her too quickly. Make sure all your buddies see her, tell them how much sex you're getting, and then dump her like yesterday's news.

c. *Financial Stability*—It always comes back to cash, doesn't it? Well, when you're talking about women, yes, it does. Deal with it. Again, remember the three things that young girls are looking for in older guys: stability, stability, and stability. Stability does not mean asking her for an extra buck so you can super-size your fries. If she wants some dork who can't afford a pitcher of beer, she can knock on the front door of the neighborhood fraternity. You've got to show her that you can bring home the bacon, fry it up in a pan, and then buy her a Porsche. Okay, maybe not a Porsche, but certainly a pansy Miata.

If you've got cash, that's great. If you don't, just lie through your friggin' teeth. If you've subscribed to a magazine in the last ten years, it's likely that you can't go two days without getting at least ten promotions for Visa gold cards in your mail. To a twenty-year-old girl, a gold card is the world's most powerful aphrodisiac. She doesn't have to know that your cards are so maxed out that they weigh almost two pounds each. She sees a gold card and she becomes convinced that Spring Break is going to be in Mazatlan this year.

d. *Go to the Gym*—Obvious? Probably. Young chicks stay away from fat guys, no matter what their age. Unless, of course, the guy has money, in which case he could be Jabba the Hutt and still pull tail. Since you already know you have to stay in shape, we'll just give you one extra hint. Since you're in your thirties, there will be times when you're not in tip-top condition. Work, life, money, and a bunch of other problems always seem to conspire against your continued fitness. So, when you do find yourself packing on an extra ten or fifteen pounds, start going to a gym about ten miles away. Let all the out-of-town chicks see you when you're fat. Once you've worked yourself back to respectability, come back to your neighborhood gym where the aerobic chicks won't remember you sweating your fat ass off after three minutes on the treadmill.

e. *Hide Your Baggage*—Your baggage? Hide your set of Samsonite carry-ons? No. Hide your love handles? No—well, actually, yes, but that's not what we're talking about either. Your emotional baggage, Sonny, hide your emotional baggage. College girls don't understand that after you've dealt with a couple of hundred women your bitterness quotient will be reaching maximum density. Find a thirty- or thirty-five-year-old chick, and *they* get it. They know that if you've had a couple of bad relationships you're a little wary of getting into another one, and you may just have the emotional Star Wars defense system up. In fact, the more experienced ones realize that this is a good thing, i.e., you're not some Pollyanna geek who walks through life about to get pummeled by the next breakup.

But the youngsters don't get it at all. The sorority girls are all alike—they think that every man who pops into their lives will be Prince Charming, Prince William, and the fag formerly known as Prince all rolled into one. Don't let her know that you've been screwed over by every Tomasa, Dixie, and Harriet for twenty miles. Try not to let on that you're so bitter that you reek of lemons. Just hold her hand, look deep in her eyes, whisper sweet nothings, and screw her over ten times worse than you ever got. If you're already on your way to Hell, then you might as well go for the penthouse.

f. *Get Over It. Don't Be So Picky*—Feel free to bang as many pigs as you can get your hands on. When you're standing around the water cooler telling your coworkers about the twenty-two-year-old you had this weekend, do you think they're gonna ask if she was a size four? Hell, no. They're probably at home with their miserable wives, pondering their miserable existence, and wondering if they're going to be able to afford to send their miserable kids to college. You, on the other hand, are screwing college girls! The mere concept alone will send shivers through their spines as they worship and exalt you. Truth be told, even if they saw you with an ugly beast, as long as she had some Greek sorority letters on her sweatshirt, they'd still be jealous. See, we told you there were some good things about getting old.

RESPECTING YOUR ELDERS

Generally speaking, the advice we give all guys in their thirties, especially their late thirties, is obvious: bang as many young chicks as you possibly can. Even if you can't get them as easily as you used to, the chase alone is going to keep you younger than any "spinning" class at your gym. Plus, occasionally you'll take home some blonde cheerleader who can barely spell her name, and that should be enough to get you through the next month or two. However, although this is surely sound advice, there are a number of older men who not only don't want to deal with naïve little girls, but actually would rather hook up with somebody even older than they are! This seems shocking. Many of our readers would be appalled to know that this could possibly be acceptable asshole behavior.

Amazingly so, it is okay. Screwing chicks who are a decade or two older than your already old ass is not necessarily a horrible thing. Remember, as we've said all along, you can hold firm to the core asshole beliefs forever, but, if you want to be a true renaissance asshole, you've gotta know when to bend the rules a little. Banging your head against a wall so you can bang young girls can have its sweet, sweet rewards, but, once you hit thirty, moving up an age class in your women can turn out to be a solid move. (Please note that hitting on older women before you're thirty is pathetic. Any twenty-nine-year-old out there who can't bag himself a sorority girl on a fairly regular basis is a geek, a pussy, or both.) Actually, there are a ton of reasons why it's fun to go after some more, ahem, "experience," and we're nothing if not enlightened when talking about scaring up some new trim.

TIP #31: OLD CHICKS SCREW. A LOT.

a. *You Can't Teach an Old Dog New Tricks, But It's Sure Fun to Let It Sniff Your Ass When You First Meet*—Old chicks screw. A lot. Young girls are a whole different deal. Even when you know the tricks, college girls are going to make it a battle. You've got to break down their resistance, kiss their ass, all sorts of stuff that you know is going to be hard work. Forty-year-olds, on the other hand, have long since given up the fight. They've been beaten, bruised, and dragged through the relationship mud so many times, they don't care what you look like or what kind of car you drive, as long as you're ready to munch a little rug. Plus, the forty-year-olds know they don't have much time left. If they let you get away, it's not much longer before they're buying support hose and dental adhesive, and at that point, sex is something they're only getting via the produce aisle of the local supermarket. And remember, she's always a light switch away from being twenty years younger.

b. *Independence*—How many times have you woken up at a sorority house and had to sneak out the fire escape to avoid the chick clinging on you for the rest of the day? It's a nightmare, ain't it? Now if you've got yourself a forty-year-old woman? Trust us, she doesn't want to see you within a hundred miles of her house, once you've pushed her ankles past her ears a couple of times. She's busy and doesn't need you to clog up her hectic day. She's got a ton of work, because her asshole boss will only give her credit if she does twice as much as her male counterparts; she needs to make sure her daughter's going to her dentist appointment; and she's got makeup, hair, and nails appointments that she's got to squeeze into her schedule before she goes to her next kick-boxing class. The only way that she's going to want to spend time with you is if you promise to color her hair, shave her moles, or administer her weekly Botox treatment. Most likely, she'll be out the door before you're finished wiping your dick off.

c. *Cash*—Another well-known fact about older women is that they generally have a bunch of cash. If they're single and in their forties, they're most likely milking their first husbands dry while pursuing pseudo-successful careers in real estate or cosmetic sales. An older woman's own income, plus the blood money from the ex-husband who traded up for a newer model, plus the fact that she's not spending a dime of child support on Junior, adds up to a whole bunch of coin after a while. And don't forget, she's bitter as hell that her fat husband dumped her for a little girl, so nothing would please her more than to take his money and shower it on you. This could mean anything from new Air Kobe Bryants to a weekend in the Bahamas. But work it right—if she thinks you're taking advantage of her, she'll spread her largesse on the next youngster smart enough to know where his bread is buttered. Buy her some flowers occasionally and smack her in the ass when she wants. She may be old, but she's still a chick, and therefore she can't help but being stupid enough to fall for the same old tricks.

d. *Food*—Old chicks cook like a mofo. Most of the time they can't get dates and they're too embarrassed to go out by themselves. Accordingly, they are constantly cooking. That stuff you see on *Sex and the City*, where all the chicks go out to eat with each other five times a day and don't have a piece of bread in the house? That may be true today. But five years from now, Carrie, Miranda, et al. will be gourmet chefs, as gravity takes effect on their bodies and they don't have a single friend left.

Because old chicks like to cook, they always, always have food in the refrigerator. This is especially rewarding because, as you can see from section (b) above, she's out the door once she's done with you. If you're smart, you can hang back when she goes to work and raid her fridge the second she's gone. Bring an overnight bag and shove it full with roasted chicken, apples, and a couple quarts of orange juice. Since you couldn't cook a burger without the George Foreman Grill, this may be the best you're gonna get until you can find a McDonald's.

HOW TO KEEP MAMA HAPPY

Please understand that we're not trying to sell you on old chicks. It is our undying duty to foster the idea that all guys, no matter their age, should be schtupping barely post-teen women as much as humanly possible. But, in the interests of fairness we think it is incumbent upon us to give you all of the options, especially when it means you might rack up a few more notches on the splinter that is your bedpost. If we are going to advocate this type of search, we also have to give you the specifics on scaring up a fortyish woman. How do you do it? Where do you go? The answers, as usual, are right here:

a. *Go to Museums*—Why stare at pictures of birds, trees, and statues when you can walk out to the park where girls are lying around practically in their underwear? Because old women dig culture. It doesn't matter if you don't know the difference between a Gauguin and a Go-Fish. Offer to take some old chick to a

museum and she'll be so impressed, she might just drop you a
hundred dollar bill on the car ride over.

b. *Drink Wine*—This is one of those Euro-fag things that has
caught on big in the U.S. over the past few decades. Everybody's
gotta be a wine connoisseur, everybody's gotta know the
difference between a '97 Cab and a '98 Beaujolais. Whatever.
Give me a Coors Light and a big-ass pretzel and I'm way happier
than any of those cheeseball, stuffed shirt, classless losers could
ever be. But facts are facts, and if wine gives you a better chance
to hook up, we're sure not going to tell you to order a pink
lemonade. Now, many of you might be intimidated about
choosing a wine because you, like us, are smart enough to prefer
beer. However, you shouldn't worry, because, in reality, nobody
knows what the hell they're talking about when it comes to wine,
especially the French. All wines taste pretty much the same when
you're sober, and, two glasses into it, you couldn't tell a
Sauvignon Blanc from a pail of warm mule piss. Just make sure
that the next time you're over at an old chick's house, you show
up with a bottle that costs more than twelve bucks. You'll be sure
to get double that back in sex.

c. *Once You've Given Them the Wine, It's Time to Dine*—
Thank God for dinners. Can you imagine what we would do if we
had to hang out with other people when we're not eating? When
it comes to forty-year-old chicks, it is crucial that you take them
to great restaurants. Remember that they're cooking their asses
off when they're home, so they know good food. A quick trip to
Coco's for strawberry pancakes just ain't gonna cut it for a woman
who bakes chocolate soufflés in her spare time. Read some
magazines and find out where the cool places in town are. Get
ready to drop a hundred and fifty bucks, including the wine. It'll
be worth it just to find out what she'll make you for breakfast the
next morning.

d. *Let Them Bitch*—Chicks spend virtually their entire lives listening to people bitch. Their boyfriends, their husbands, their kids, their parents—every person in a woman's life will eventually look to her for guidance, support, blahblahblah, blahblahblahblah. Women in their forties are tired of listening, they don't want to hear about anybody else's shit anymore. They don't care about your lost goals, your painful childhood memories, your sack of worthless emotional baggage. They want to talk about their own stuff. Go ahead and let them. If you listen to a forty-year-old woman talk about her own problems for ten minutes or more, there's a good possibility that she's not only whipping up a quick filet mignon after she blows you for the next three hours, but she's running down to the local mall to get you a whole boatload of clothes before you leave tomorrow morning. Oh, you don't have to actually listen for those ten minutes, just think about something pleasant, like sleeping with a girl fifteen years younger than she.

BANGING A WIFE WHO'S NOT YOURS

Now that you're approaching thirty, or might be in your thirties, there's a good chance that you're going to be around married women all the time. What does this mean? Well, it means that you should do everything in your power to start banging married women as often as possible. But this is one of those life-altering issues that requires you to fundamentally change your attitude and actions in order to succeed. Married women comprise a whole different subset of chicks, one that doesn't necessarily conform to the normal set of rules and regulations. Like any defined set of women, there are a ton of positive and negative traits that you have to deal with. Here is the short list:

POSITIVES	NEGATIVES
They have kids, so you know they'll fuck.	They have kids.
They're used to dealing with boys who, like you, whine when they don't get their way.	They punish boys who whine when they don't get their way.
Their husband probably got them a gold card.	Their husband will see the statement with five charges at the Tropical Nights Hourly Motel.
You can bang them in the minivan.	Your friends might see you driving in a minivan.
They don't want to be your girlfriend.	You can't just call her at home whenever you want a blowjob.
She can't be seen with you, so she probably won't want to go out that much.	Since you can't take her to a movie, you might have to talk to her for an entire evening.
She's not in it for a commitment.	She's in it for some other reason that she probably won't tell you until it's too late.
Her husband doesn't sleep with her anymore, so you get to have freaky sex.	Her husband doesn't talk to her anymore, so you have to listen to all of her bullshit problems.
She doesn't want to have kids with you.	You have to look at pictures of her kids every time she comes over.
You are her fantasy.	You're gonna go broke buying all of the sex toys that she wants.
You don't have to call her every day.	She gets to call you every day.

Another interesting phenomenon about married women is that they actually speak a different language than single women. A single woman is generally quite bitter, and regardless of what you say she will hear it in the most negative light possible. A married woman who is talking to you is obviously on her way to divorce and desperate to get out. Accordingly, when you speak, your every word will be interpreted as an emotional safety net to her. She will believe that your sole purpose in life is to save her from her current predicament, and that nothing would make you happier than to marry her and give her a house that is at least 1,500 square feet bigger than the one she currently half-owns. Based on these varying interpretations, you'll often find that you can say the exact same thing to a single woman and a married woman, but they will hear two entirely different conversations. Here are some examples:

WHAT A MAN SAYS	WHAT A SINGLE WOMAN HEARS	WHAT A MARRIED WOMAN HEARS
Let's go back to your place.	Let me come over, sleep with you, and never call you again.	Let's go relieve the babysitter and bring Lincoln Logs, so your children aren't bored.
My salary is $100,000.	You can have $50,000 of my $100,000 salary.	My salary is great, but it would be a lot better if we combine it with your alimony check.
Isn't this wine fantastic?	Drink another bottle so I can get you naked.	Please drink as much as you want, I'll take care of the kids when you pass out.
Will you take off your clothes?	I will never call you again.	I can't wait to see the beauty of a woman who has conceived two miracles.

WHAT A MAN SAYS	WHAT A SINGLE WOMAN HEARS	WHAT A MARRIED WOMAN HEARS
That was the best sex I ever had.	That was the best sex I ever had.	That was the best sex I ever had.
Will you marry me?	You will never have to work again.	Can we suck your husband dry by continuing to date until the child support payments stop, and *then* get married?

The reason we're giving you a bunch of charts, but virtually no advice, is that we can't decide whether it's a good idea to sleep with married women or not, so we're taking the cheeseball way out and not telling you anything. Just go ahead and figure it out on your own. Good luck.

WHO WILL BE MRS. ASSHOLE?

Granted, being an asshole requires an almost unholy commitment to doing things that you want to do, versus doing things that she wants you to do. This is something that should start early in your development and will pretty much continue throughout the rest of your life. However, as we often say in this guide, being an asshole does not mean that you always have to be an asshole. For example, being an asshole to your boss, while it may be your biggest dream, is probably not going to lead to the success you'll need to be able to bang as many chicks as possible.

This is also true of marriage. While we are well aware that it is much more preferable to sleep with a different chick every night for the rest of your life, very few of us are Gene Simmons from Kiss and are afforded that luxury. At some point, you're going to have to settle down. Don't fret, though—marrying a woman doesn't mean you stop being an asshole, it just means that some of the rules and regulations must be altered to continue down the path of true asshole enlightenment. Why, many of you ask, would you ever settle down, when there are always going to be women who will sleep with you, no matter how old, fat, bald, wrinkled, cynical, or bitter you become? There are a lot of reasons:

a. *All Your Friends Are Married*—This is truly the reason why everybody you know, and you, too, are going to get married by the time you're forty. There is virtually nothing better than being single . . . as long as you have people around to enjoy it with. Once your buddies are gone, taking care of their kids, building new rooms onto their house, shopping for baby furniture, what are you going to do, hang out with them at Baby Gap? How much weight do you think your opinion holds, when the question is whether to get the pink shammy or the blue quilt for the new baby's room? Sure, for a year or so you can look for new friends, but the ones you make after you're old are never the same as the buddies who have been around for five, ten, fifteen years. Face it, you're not the same. You're bald, you get tired early, you can't drink like you used to; you're pretty much a loser. Who would want to hang out with an old bag like you? Once you've experienced the solitude of going to the movies alone, you'll pick up the next mail-order bride catalogue to see what kind of bargains are available in Botswana.

b. *Somebody's Going to Have to Take Care of You When You're Old*—This one's big, too. You're only in your thirties now. You still pee when you want, and you're not even close to wearing dark socks with sneakers. But wait till you're sixty, buddy boy. By then, you're going to be a complete mess. At that point, if you've still got your bowels under control, you should convert your game room into a shrine for the almighty that spared you the pain of watching shit dribble down your leg. And if it's not bad enough that you're gonna be taking dumps into a bag, how do you think it'll look if you're still trying to scam college chicks?! Hell, past retirement age, you can be arrested for that. So right now, while you still have a bicep left to flex, you should be thinking about who's going to take care of you.

c. *Being Forty and Never Having Been Married Is An Immediate Red Flag for Most Women*—Read any candy-ass, perfumed, chick shrink book, and somewhere within the dreck about female orgasms, withholding oral sex, and the quest to remove thigh fat will be a statement that says, roughly, "If you find a good looking, successful, intelligent man who's forty and never been married, *watch out!*" Whether or not this is true doesn't matter. If chicks think you're screwed up, you are. Perception is reality. Based on this universal assumption, you must get married before you're forty. Really, you should get married by around thirty-eight, so you can already be divorced by forty and get back to some serious banging . . . unless you meet the following criteria:

1. You've got ten million in the bank, in which case you're so busy getting blown by half the female population of Sweden, you don't have time to find a wife.
2. After forty, you can still pull nineteen-year-old tail on a regular basis. You, Hugh Hefner, and the Rolling Stones are about the only ones in that club but, hey, anything's possible.

TIP #32: GET MARRIED BEFORE YOU'RE FORTY.

d. *You Must Go Forth and Procreate*—If the world is such a great place with one asshole, think how much better it will be with a couple of little assholes running around and wreaking havoc. As exciting as it is to stomp all over the world for sixty or seventy years, you should never forget that six or seven decades is nothing in the great big scheme of things. Assholes think big. If you want to really make your mark, you have to put your seed out there and generate one hundred to two hundred years' worth of pricks. Think about that for a second. You alone can be responsible for the sexual conquests of virtually tens of thousands of women, just by fertilizing one solitary chick. You may not be Wilt Chamberlain, but he's dead, so you should be proud.

e. *You Can Still Bang Other Chicks When You're Married*— Well, we've been pussyfooting around this fact for a couple of pages or so. The coolest thing about getting married, and the reason why it's not such a bad thing to contemplate, is that you don't have to stop screwing other chicks. Who ever said you did? It's a well-known fact that a wedding ring attracts more women than a "Going Out of Business" sale at Bloomingdale's. You walk into a bar with a gold band and every chick in the place is instantly drawn to you like little hooker moths to a flame. They think you're safe, they think you're stable, and they're sure you haven't had a good blowjob in years. Flash a platinum card every once in a while and you'll have them standing in line to wipe the scotch off of your chin. Don't get carried away, though, and think it's actually you. It's always pathetic when a guy gets a little bit of attention in a bar and, all of a sudden, he thinks he can dump the faithful little wife. Not a chance. The second you take off the ring, those chicks will be crossing the street to avoid you. As long as that wedding band's on your finger, your sex life is just an eighty-dollar hotel room away. Lose it, and you're just another dick trying to get lucky. Enjoy.

Okay, so now you understand that there must be a Mrs. Asshole in your future. It's a devastating realization, so don't feel bad if you think you might break down for a few minutes. It'll hurt for a little while, but when the pain subsides you can still go out, nail a couple of college sophomores, club a baby seal or two, rip the transmission out of a '74

Camaro, and everything will be just about back to normal. Eventually, though, you've got to find her and, trust us, it ain't easy. It's tough enough finding a woman who you don't want to beat over the head with a stick every time she opens her mouth, much less finding one who you can listen to for the rest of your life. Accordingly, there's a bunch of stuff that you have to look for in a wife. You don't need every one on the list, and you're certainly free to add some more if appropriate, but the following represents just about everything you could ever want out of a woman, presuming that she instinctually understands that, even though you're married, you will be cheating on a regular basis:

   a. She thinks it's funny when you fart

   b. She enjoys having sex with women almost as much as men

   c. She watches *SportsCenter* regularly

   d. You come home and she's drinking beers by herself

   e. She swallows

   f. She learned how to cook at the Sorbonne in France

   g. She has a rare throat disorder that only allows her to speak when spoken to

   h. Her father is the CEO of a Fortune 500 company

   i. Her father, the CEO, is about to die, and she has no siblings

   j. She was a supermodel but gave it up because she just wanted to be a mom

   k. She loves it when you go to strip bars because you come home all sexed up

   l. She's a recovering nymphomaniac, but she constantly relapses

   m. She doesn't believe a man should ever change diapers

   n. Keeping the house clean makes her feel like more of a woman

   o. She's always wanted to be a porn star, but never got the opportunity

   p. She has no gag reflex

   q. No matter how hard she tries, she just can't help bringing other women to bed with you

r. She demands to take a ten-month vacation while she's pregnant, because she can't stand the thought of looking fat in front of you

s. She underwent full-body electrolysis because seeing hair on her skin makes her nauseous

t. Her Olympic Gold Medal in gymnastics didn't stop her from growing to five-foot-eight

u. She enjoys playing waitress whenever your buddies come over

v. She can't watch a movie with a death count of less than one hundred

w. She never let that whole "Miss America" thing go to her head

x. Every man you've ever met has offered his house in exchange for a pair of her dirty panties

y. The mere thought of cheating on you causes her throat to swell shut

z. NASA is studying her tits and ass to gain an increased understanding of anti-gravity

We were just kind of kidding with the above list (no, we're not), and we realize that it's tough to make those categories apply to most women. But we're not going to leave you hanging. We've come up with the definitive thirty-question quiz to determine whether or not the woman you're sleeping with is marriage material. Please do not be put off by the fact that these tests are usually seen in the froufrou pages of a thousand chick magazines, like *Cosmo* and *Women's Digest*. If taking a stupid little exam saves you from the pain and misery associated with marrying a complete bitch, don't ask any questions.

> ## TIP #33: WHATEVER YOU DO, DON'T MARRY THE WRONG GIRL.

WHAT-GIRL-TO-MARRY TEST

(The number after each answer is a point total. At the end of the test, add up all the points and see where your girl ranks)

1. *How often does she like to have sex?*
    i. More than once a day—10
    ii. Once a day—8
    iii. Once a week—5
    iv. Once a month—1
    v. Once a year—(−10)

2. *Is she into anal?*
    i. Yes—7
    ii. No—4 (Can't blame her if she's smart enough to know that sex isn't supposed to hurt.)
    iii. Begs for it—10

3. *What is her blowjob style?*
    i. Swallows—10
    ii. Spits on stomach—5
    iii. Won't do it—0
    iv. With teeth—(−10)

4. *What is her opinion on sex toys?*
    i. Doesn't like 'em—2
    ii. Likes 'em when she's drunk—4
    iii. Has a Honda generator under the bed—10
    iv. Has outfitted your basement with a dungeon—4 (Could be cool, but it's going to be tough to explain the black eyes and whip marks to your coworkers.)

5. *What type of sexual positions does she enjoy?*
   i. Missionary only—1
   ii. Only the golden triangle: missionary, doggy, her on top—7
   iii. Hangs from chandeliers—8
   iv. Refuses to have sex unless you're bound and gagged—0
   (Assholes do not let women tie them up, under any
   condition.)

6. *How much money does she make?*
   i. She doesn't work—5 (This is not necessarily bad if she's
   going to cook for you, clean for you, and generally be
   your slave.)
   ii. $25K or less—0 (She's got a job, but she's obviously
   failing at it or has virtually no skills. Why doesn't she just
   stay home, take aerobics classes, and bang you silly every
   night?)
   iii. $25K to $100K—7
   iv. $100K or over—2 (Although it's not enough so that you
   can stop working, she might make more money than you,
   and then she'll be more difficult to control.)

7. *Is her family rich?*
   i. They don't have jack—0
   ii. They own their own home—4 (Not much money there,
   but you'll have a place to stay if you get fired for jerking
   off to the Internet.)
   iii. They are rumored to have big money but you can't tell—
   10 (If they're rumored to have it, they probably do. If
   they don't tell anybody they have money, then they
   almost assuredly have it. If they were running around
   talking about their cash, you can bet that they're actually
   leveraged up to their eyeballs and are just trying to
   impress people.)

iv. They own an island off of Aruba—4 (Sure, it's great that they have money, but you'll never be as rich as Daddy, and you are therefore doomed to a life of hearing her tell you what a loser you are every single day.)

8. *What is her earning potential?*
    i. She's a housewife—5
    ii. She's a doctor/lawyer type—8
    iii. She's a hooker—0
    iv. She still hasn't paid off her student loans or the $50K on her visa card—(−10)
    v. She's the CEO of a Fortune 500 company—0 (She is too powerful and will eventually start treating you like a woman.)

9. *How much money does she spend?*
    i. She uses coupons and, even then, thinks groceries are too expensive—5 (This could be bothersome if she doesn't want you to buy cool stuff. Then again, she won't spend your money.)
    ii. She pays off her credit card balances every month—8
    iii. She's got a personal shopper at Tiffany's—6 (She's a materialistic pig, but the fact that she can afford it is worth a couple of extra points.)
    iv. She shops like Imelda Marcos—(−5)
    v. She has enough money to shop like Imelda Marcos—10

10. *Does she play sports?*
    i. She played high school sports—10 (She's active, athletic and knows that Shaq isn't a little house in a bad part of town.)
    ii. She played college sports—5 (She may be a little too masculine and there's a good chance she's going to eventually leave you for another woman.)

    iii. She trips over her own feet—3 (She will definitely not be able to golf or play tennis with you on vacations. But it is kind of cute watching her stumble around.)

    iv. She's a member of the WWE—(−5) (She's on steroids, she's probably got a bigger dick than you do, and she hangs out with guys who are twice your size.)

11. Does she watch sports?

    i. She likes *Monday Night Football*—6

    ii. She doesn't mind making nachos when your buddies come over to watch the game—7

    iii. During Game Seven of the World Series, she wants to watch *Shabby Chic* on The Home & Garden Network—(−10)

    iv. When you wake up, she's already got *SportsCenter* on—10

12. Does she care about sports?

    i. She thinks Tiger Woods is cute—5 (It's good that she knows who he is, but a little disconcerting that she could like a Cablinasian.*)

    ii. She hides your remote control on Sunday morning—0 (This is a crime punishable by death in several countries.)

    iii. She asks how many baskets the Yankees scored in the last game—2 (At least she's trying.)

    iv. She knows the name and stats for every running back who played for the Dallas Cowboys since 1961—8

13. How often does she drink?

    i. Never—5 (What is she, a nun?)

    ii. Socially—8

*Caucasian-black-Indian (or Native American)-Asian.

iii. Every night—if you're under thirty—9; over thirty—2

iv. If nobody's around, she'll drink nail polish remover—(−10)

14. *When she's done drinking, she:*

    i. Hands her keys to somebody sober enough to get her home—8

    ii. Belches violently and demands one more shot for the road—4

    iii. Passes out on the barroom floor and, after she comes to, spends the rest of the evening trying to find her skirt—0

    iv. Wakes up in the back seat of a Chevy low-rider, wondering why her private parts smell like guacamole—(−7)

15. *What does she drink?*

    i. Water—6

    ii. Cosmopolitans—7

    iii. Beer—10

    iv. Grain alcohol—(−5) (She's too hardcore, and you're going to have to pay for her liver transplant.)

16. *How often does she cook?*

    i. You don't have to go into the kitchen to know that dinner's gonna be good—7

    ii. She burns soup—2

    iii. She thinks Julia Child is an amateur—10

    iv. The only thing in the refrigerator is the number for Domino's—0 (You could do that yourself. What do you need a wife for?)

17. *How's her face?*

    i. Girl next door—7

    ii. Most of your friends want to do her—8

    iii. Pig—(−5)

    iv. Supermodel—5 (Supermodels have a very high
          admission fee. If you don't kiss her ass she can find some
          rich European prince who will. Bang supermodels, don't
          marry them.)

18. *How's her body?*
    i. Aerobics instructor—6 (See Supermodel face above.
       Also, if she spends that much time working out, she's an
       airhead, and, in ten years, she's going to be fat anyway.
       At that point, you've got a friggin' moron who's also fat.
       And forty years until you die.)
    ii. Calls Richard Simmons and asks for help—(−10)
    iii. Can't tell if she looks more like Ally McBeal or Olive
       Oyl—0
    iv. Walking down the street, she gets at least two double
       takes per block—8

19. *What cup size are her boobs?*
    i. A—2
    ii. B—5
    iii. C—10
    iv. D—8 (Great when you're dating, but in ten years she'll
       be tripping over the sloppy bastards.)
    v. More than D—(−5) (She'll be starring in porn movies
       within two years.)

20. *How often does she read?*
    i. Occasionally she'll buy a Danielle Steele
       paperback—7
    ii. The last book she read was *See Jane Run*—0
    iii. She quotes Dostoyevsky—3
    iv. She's illiterate—(−10)

21. *What does she know about the world?*
    i. She reads a national magazine, like *Time*, once a week—7
    ii. She reads *The New York Times* every day, even if you live in Des Moines—3 (Way too smart for you.)
    iii. She's not sure who George Bush is—(−5)
    iv. She quotes the *National Enquirer*—2

22. *What is her level of education? (Points depend on* your *level of education.)*
    i. If she finished graduate school
       • If you can't spell—0 (Too smart for you.)
       • If you got a GED—2 (Still too smart for you.)
       • If you finished high school—3 (Probably too smart for you.)
       • If you finished college—10 (Marrying up, good work.)
       • If you finished grad school—2 (You're both too smart. You'll wind up arguing about some arcane topic every night for the rest of your life.)
    ii. If she graduated college
       • If you can't spell—0 (You'll never have anything to talk about—you can't have sex twenty-four hours a day forever.)
       • If you have a GED—6 (Marrying up—but probably too far up. Not bad, but make sure she's a community college girl.)
       • If you finished high school—9
       • If you finished college—10 (perfect)
       • If you finished grad school—5 (You'll most likely believe you're smarter than she, and eventually she's going to resent it.)
    iii. If she just got out of high school
       • If you can't spell—6 (Well, you're both pretty much on the same level, but you guys have no hope of ever making money, and sooner or later she's gonna be pissed about it.)

- If you got a GED—8 (You're both losers, but you deserve each other).
- If you finished high school—4 (If you don't mind the fact that both of you are working at Safeway for the rest of your lives, you're cool.)
- If you finished college—2 (You know she's an idiot. You're only marrying her for her tits—which will be at her ankles in ten years.)
- If you finished grad school—1 (Please. Go write a doctoral thesis or something.)

iv. If she earned a GED

- If you can't spell—9 (You guys will make millions robbing banks.)
- If you got a GED—2 (You'll be fine, until you pop out a couple of kids whose genes consign them to a life of petty larceny.)
- If you finished high school—1
- If you finished college—0 (If you're a college grad and you couldn't score anything better than a chick with a GED, you've got no hope.)
- If you finished grad school—(−5) (Your parents, who are still paying off your student loans, will kill you.)

v. If she can't spell her name

- If you can't spell—5 (You'll probably both be happy in the trailer park.)
- If you got a GED—2 (The inbreeding alone will spell certain failure.)
- If you finished high school—0 (You struggled through algebra to have to deal with somebody like this?)
- If you finished college—(−5) (If she's an English supermodel, we'll give you a year with her. Otherwise, you've lost your mind.)

• If you finished grad school—(−10) (We hope you married her for some anthropological study you're doing.)

23. *What does she think is funny?*
    i. Comedy shows—7
    ii. Farting (yours, not hers)—10
    iii. George Stephanopolous' witty remarks on *Meet the Press*—3 (Too smart for you.)
    iv. In her eyes, nothing in this horrible world could be funny, ever—(−5)

24. *What type of house does she want?*
    i. Three-bedroom with a white picket fence—7
    ii. She can't imagine not living in an apartment—2
    iii. Her bags are packed and ready to move to Beverly Hills—(−5) (Any money you make is gone before it hits your bank account.)
    iv. She just wants to get off the street—0

25. *What type of personality does she have?*
    i. Agressive—5
    ii. Bubbly—4
    iii. Quiet—9 (They're monsters in bed.)
    iv. Intellectual—2 (How could you think of anything to say to her?)
    v. Just a nice girl—7

26. *What kind of conversations does she have with you?*
    i. She agrees with everything you say—4 (You will be bored, eventually.)
    ii. Everything you say is stupid—0

   iii. She'll show you why she's always right—(−5)

   iv. She doesn't care, as long as you bang her once a day—9

27. *How does she act with other people?*
     i. Friendly—7
    ii. Loud and obnoxious—3
   iii. Wallflower—3
   iv. She hides when people come over—0

28. *How does she treat the waiter? (Why do we care? Because that's exactly how she's going to treat you in six months.)*
     i. Rude—0
    ii. Nice—8
   iii. Demanding—2
   iv. What waiter?—(−5) (If she is such a friggin' princess that she can't be bothered with addressing the waiter directly, prepare yourself for a lifetime of drawing her baths and feeding her peeled grapes.)

29. *Does she want kids? (This is a litmus test. All normal chicks want kids. If a chick doesn't want kids, there's something screwed up with her chemistry. Plus, it's a sure thing that you'll eventually have them anyway, at least by mistake, and then you're going to be stuck taking care of the little monsters.)*
     i. Yes—10
    ii. No—(−10)

30. *How many kids does she want?*
     i. One—2
    ii. Two—8
   iii. Three—5
   iv. More than three—0

Where Does She Rank?

225+—Impregnate her immediately. She's way too good for you and could definitely marry somebody with better looks and more money than you will ever have. Planting your seed may be the only way to get her down the aisle.

185+—Great catch. Unless you've got a slew of supermodels queuing up to lick your balls, then you should probably lock this one down.

125+—Marginal, but she'll do in a pinch. If you're over thirty-eight and have no massive inheritance coming your way, she's probably the best you're going to get. If you're younger than that, you can probably do better.

75+—Keep looking. Don't even buy her a drink.

50+—Bitch. Shove it in her ass once and never call her again.

Below 50—Shoot her. Shoot her dead. Juries will view it as a mercy killing.

PROPOSING LIKE AN ASSHOLE

Unfortunately, you're no longer allowed to club a woman over the head and drag her back to your cave. These days you actually have to ask a chick to marry you. But, before you do, keep this in mind: no matter where you propose to your girlfriend, she will instinctively love that spot for the rest of her natural born life, so you'd better choose carefully. Here are a few favorite places to consider:

a. *Baseball Games*—Many ignorant people believe that the electronic score boards in center field were designed to help fans keep track of the game. This is completely incorrect. In actuality, the electronic score board was designed by an asshole so that his fellow assholes could propose to their girlfriends. When a woman looks up during the seventh inning stretch and sees "Will you marry me?" she will be forced to uncontrollably love baseball for the rest of her life. This, in turn, will eventually matriculate into love for other sports, thus providing her husband with a lifetime of happy weekends—not to mention, if the bitch has the audacity to turn you down she'll get booed by 35,000 people.

b. *Denny's*—If you propose to her at Chateau de Spend All of Your Money, it will immediately become "your special place." It may seem like a good idea at the time, but every year thereafter you're going to have to blow another two hundred dollars to keep her happy. That's why you should propose over a Grand Slam Breakfast at Denny's. When you come back for your yearly visit you're saving a bundle, and she's thinking the scrambled eggs taste like caviar.

c. *Las Vegas*—What better place to propose than Sin City? You're going to be there at least a dozen more times in your life, and chances are your wife won't be accompanying you. Instead, you'll be with your buddies dropping twenty dollars a lap dance, or nailing some dishrag whore you plucked out of the Golden Nugget. The point is, every time you take off for another bachelor party or weekend of debauchery, your wife will think it's romantic that you spend so much time in "your special place."

d. *Skydiving, or Other Dangerous Activities*—Nine times out of ten, getting married is a huge mistake. No matter how many people's opinions you get, only The Man Upstairs knows if you're making the right decision. That's why you should propose while plummeting thousands of feet down to the earth. If it wasn't meant to be, God still has a chance to blow a hole through her parachute.

AGES 28–35 FINAL EXAMINATION

1. *When you hit thirty:*
   a. You are at your sexual peak
   b. Your hair migrates from your head to your back and butt
   c. Your vertical leap increases by nine inches
   d. You no longer have to worry about making money

2. *In your early thirties, supermarkets are:*
   a. The only place where you can find nutrients that will clean your colon
   b. An eyesore on the way to McDonald's
   c. A place so full of tits, it should be referred to as a mammogram
   d. A great place to use coupons, in order to save money for retirement

3. *Picking up on chicks who are ten years older than you is:*
   a. Only a good idea when you're eleven years old
   b. Perfectly acceptable under the right circumstances
   c. Punishable by death
   d. Fine, as long as you're claiming to be twenty years younger than you actually are

4. *When you're thirty-two, twenty-two-year-old chicks are:*
   a. A dish best served cold
   b. Unattainable
   c. Just as normal and pleasant as they always were
   d. Still willing to bang you if you play your cards right

5. *The perfect woman:*
    a. Demands that you buy her tampons
    b. Doesn't swallow
    c. Laughs when you fart
    d. Expects jewelry on her birthday

6. *A woman whose apartment is so immaculately clean that you can eat off the toilet:*
    a. Has serious issues that you should avoid
    b. Probably wouldn't mind if you spilled popcorn in bed
    c. Will think it's funny if you put a beer on the table without a coaster
    d. Should be pursued to the ends of the earth

7. *If you're a cool, good-looking guy over forty who's never been married:*
    a. Women think you've aged as well as a fine wine
    b. Nobody wonders why you haven't gotten married
    c. Your father has no doubts that you're heterosexual
    d. Chicks think that you're a freak

8. *Old chicks screw:*
    a. A lot
    b. A little
    c. Off the tops of pickle jars without your help
    d. To make sure their hips still work

9. *Opera is:*
    a. A great place to spend a night
    b. The closest you'll ever get to Hell on Earth
    c. A notorious hangout for hot, young chicks
    d. Spelled "k-i-l-l-m-e-p-l-e-a-s-e"

10. *All women are looking for single men in their forties because:*
    a. White chest hair is an unbelievable aphrodisiac
    b. Saggy balls are fun to play with
    c. It's nice to date someone who can name the original cast from *M*A*S*H*
    d. Women will avoid single men over forty like a yeast infection

ANSWERS
1-b, 2-c, 3-b, 4-d, 5-c, 6-a, 7-d, 8-a, 9-b, 10-d.

Chapter Six

MARRIAGE

WELCOME MAT

Marriage. The word alone conjures up images of such intense pain that it's difficult for us to write about. Everything, and we mean everything, changes when you're married. Responsibility used to be a word you only saw at the end of beer commercials—now your entire life is nothing but responsibility. What a disaster! While single life was a series of meteoric ups and downs, married life generally remains on a relatively even keel, provided that your wife continues to put out and you manage to stave off bankruptcy.

You've got to be ready to change with the times. Although there are many ways that you can keep your asshole tendencies intact, there are very few that are going to remain in a pristine, unchanged state. For example, you're still going to try to bang other chicks, but it will be done under much different circumstances than before. Your former compulsion to be in tip-top physical condition will slowly melt away. It's not all bad, though. Sure there are a couple of good things about being married, we just can't think of any off the top of our heads. Sorry.

TAMING THE SHREW

You finally did it, huh? You had to give up a life of banging chicks, scoring new tail, and hooking up in Burger King bathrooms for *what*? So you could wake up next to the same face for the rest of your life *and* give away half your stuff? Have you gone absolutely out of your freakin' head?!

All right, all right—if you read the last section you know that we aren't totally against marriage. There are a lot of good reasons to get married, and, although temporary insanity is one of them, it's more important that we guide you through your soon-to-be-ex-marriage than it is to rip you for not having the sack to stay single. Besides, even though you're married, you can still be a total asshole and maintain some semblance of dignity while laughing at friends who are being pecked to death by their hens. The most important thing to remember about getting through this turbulent time is that marriage is a lot like anal sex: most of the time it's a lot of fun, but you occasionally have to deal with some shit. Here's what you have to expect:

WHAT YOU'RE USED TO	WHAT TO EXPECT NOW
Banging a variety of chicks.	The same face, every second of every minute of every hour of every day of every week of every month of every year for . . . the . . . rest . . . of . . . your . . . freaking . . . life. How's *that* sound?
Poker nights with your buddies.	Dinner parties with two couples who bitch the whole time about how much they miss their kids.
Oral sex.	Headaches. Lots of headaches.
Dropping everything and running off to Vegas for the weekend.	"Honey, we've got the gas bill, the phone bill, a mortgage, and the electric bill.

WHAT YOU'RE USED TO	WHAT TO EXPECT NOW
Dropping everything . . . *(cont.)*	How can you possibly think about throwing our money away over a stupid little football game?"
Playing golf.	Watering the lawn.
Drinking yourself into a coma.	A glass and a half of Chardonnay before your wife freaks out because the baby sitter hasn't answered the phone in two rings.
Beer posters on the wall.	Matching bathroom towels.
A refrigerator full of Samuel Adams and a half-green jar of mayonnaise.	Fruits, vegetables, and batteries organized alphabetically in the door shelves.
Internet porn on an AOL account.	Internet porn on a DSL. See, not everything's bad about marriage.
Friday afternoon Happy Hour.	Having tea with your wife because she saw a TV special on the British and she no longer thinks you have enough culture.
Sex in the afternoon.	The afternoon.
College football on Saturday, NFL on Sunday, DirecTV "all-access" season pass the rest of the week.	*Shabby Chic* on Saturday, *Home Beautiful* on Sunday, and *Oprah* every fucking day after that.
Blowing your money on booze and clothes that you don't wear.	Your wife blowing your money on booze and clothes that *she* doesn't wear.
Strippers and hookers.	Strippers and hookers. (C'mon, who're you kidding? This is what keeps marriages going.)
A BMW.	A . . . dare we say it . . . minivan! No, no, say it ain't so. Annulment! Annulment!

Sounds pretty exciting, huh? No, it sounds like a miserable, boring nightmare. The lows are never that low, the highs are never that high, you just chart a course down the middle and pray that your kids don't turn out to be rapists. Boy, did you make the right choice.

YOU'RE MARRIED—STOP SUCKING IN YOUR GUT

There was a time in your life when working out meant something to you. But you weren't doing it because you had some weird fascination with sweat, strain, and morning stiffness (muscle stiffness, not the other kind). No, you worked out because you needed to stay in shape to bag chicks. Chicks dig biceps, and you would suffer for hours underneath a curl bar, as long as you knew that you'd score some action later that evening. But now you're locked into sex and, whether or not you've got a sixteen-inch bicep or a sixteen-inch love handle, you can get laid anytime you want.

The point of this is that you don't have to be in shape anymore, and, Jesus, what a relief that is. You'll be at McDonald's so often that you might add six cents per share to their earnings this quarter. From now on, everything will be cooked in two to four inches of pure vegetable oil. Hell, you'd deep-fry water if you could figure out how to avoid the splatter. Light beer?! You piss on light beer now. You shouldn't be drinking any beer that you can't get down without a knife and fork. Make sure that your wife revels in the folds you're creating. Even if not, who cares? After all the pain and suffering she's caused you, she deserves to drown under the newest fold of skin hanging beneath your tricep.

However, it must be known that your wife is absolutely forbidden to gain more than 10 pounds after the wedding—unless, of course, she's pregnant, in which case fifteen pounds will be tolerable as long as ten come back out with the baby. We actually have a buddy who put a weight clause into his prenuptial agreement. (God bless you, Steve.) After all, you pay the bills and buy the cars and deal with ridiculous issues like PMS and hot flashes. You're entitled to sit on your fat ass sucking down jalapeño poppers and using your gut as a safety net for fallen Doritos chips. What the hell has your worthless wife ever done to garner such privileges?

DATING YOUR WIFE

The words "dating" and "wife" probably don't belong together in the same sentence, but there they are. You guessed it, we're going to tell you why. Although the divorce rate is currently hovering around 60 percent, *theoretically,* marriage is a life-long adventure. If you go into a marriage not thinking it will last forever, you might as well flush half your money down the toilet and shoot yourself in the head right now, because it will save you a lot of hassles down the line.

So, assuming that you honestly believe you'll spend a lifetime with this woman, *you are going to have to work at it . . . hard.*

> ## TIP #34: YOU'LL HAVE TO BUST YOUR ASS TO MAKE YOUR MARRIAGE WORK.

Marriage is not easy. The cute things that she does when you're dating become downright intolerable after a couple of years. Here are some examples:

WHAT WAS CUTE WHEN YOU WERE DATING	WHAT IS DISGUSTING NOW THAT YOU'RE MARRIED
The cute way she would nibble her food.	She sounds like a cow chewing her cud.
The endearing way that she would get out of bed, but leave the bathroom door open and talk to you while she was in there.	You have to listen to her pee every night.
She was always trying to save you money.	She never buys you a goddamn thing.
She'd sneak up behind you and start rubbing your package.	"Jesus Christ, honey, will you leave that alone, it's the last two minutes of the fourth quarter!"
She always spoke her mind and challenged you intellectually.	She never shuts her trap.
She was extremely close and loving with her family.	Is her mother coming over *again?*
She loved to try new hair styles to change her image.	"Who are you today, Little-Fucking-Orphan Annie?"
She loved to just run out of the house and do something crazy.	Now she leaves you with the kids every night.
She had a kick-ass job.	She makes more money than you.
She thought it was funny when you farted.	She thinks it's funny when she farts.
She was always ready to throw a party.	She's drunk before you get home from work.
She was so beautiful when she slept.	She snores louder than a Portland lumber mill.
She loved to give blowjobs.	She constantly reminds you how many blowjobs she *used* to give you.

As should be painfully clear from the above examples, marriage will be taxing on even the most patient man. If you don't try really hard, you're sure to become bored with your marriage and resentful of the witch who sleeps next to you every night. When you're single, this means it's time to find the next tramp. When you're married, this means you better figure out a way to get things resolved, or you're sleeping at a Motel 6 for a couple of months. Here are a couple of things you might want to try to ensure that the marriage you intended to survive a lifetime doesn't end up lasting about as long as Phil Mickelson's Sunday assault on the Masters leaderboard:

a. *Date Your Wife*—This seems like a contradiction, but it's been known to work wonders. Establish one night every week when you guys go out on a real-live date, the whole nine yards. Not only can this be fun, but for at least one night you can forget you're married and pretend you're scamming chicks again. Plus, the fact that it's a sure thing should inspire some cool memories. Anyway, each date should consist of nothing less than dinner, a movie, and a backseat blowjob in a deserted parking lot somewhere. Chicks dig that kind of stuff, and it should work for you because, as we stated, you eventually get a blowjob in the backseat of your car. If you really want to step it up, tell her to wait for you in a bar and then go pick her up. Make her fight you a little bit, maybe even slap you after you grab a boob. Even though it's hokey, you'll both probably get a kick out of it, and all the dudes around you will think you're a stud. Just like the good old days.

b. *Weird, Kinky Sex*—Whips, chains, videotapes, graphic pornos, exotic vegetables, Astro-Glide, a two-liter Coke bottle—anything goes. The same muff over and over again for years can make you downright asexual. But if you paint it up with caviar and mustard, or shove a stapler in there once in a while, it can be a big turn on for everybody. Your wife may object at first, as she'll feel like a street-walking, dishrag whore. But once you've left her on the bed, gasping for breath after her eighth orgasm, she'll eventually come around.

c. *Frequent Weekend Trips*—Not everybody's lucky enough to live in Southern California, where you can go to the beach on Friday, ski the mountains on Saturday, and play golf in the desert on Sunday. (Sorry about that shameless plug for our home state.) But, wherever you are, it's certain that you've got a few cool spots not more than a couple of hours' drive away. Go there a lot. Even if you're not completely thrilled by the scenery, a weekend trip is little more than an excuse for forty-eight straight hours of hot, vicious banging. If you're not strapping a U-Haul to the back of your car loaded down with sex toys, you're not doing the job. We want your wife walking bowlegged from Sunday night to Tuesday morning. She should be sweating sperm when she goes back to the gym on Monday.

d. *Board Games*—Don't laugh. Monopoly, Scrabble, Clue—they're just as fun to play now as they were when you were a little kid. And the best part is: women get horny when you're down on the ground playing children's games. It's another one of those strange cultural phenomena. We're not real sure why chicks think it's so sexy that a man will play a kid's game, but we think it has something to do with that mothering instinct thing again. There's nothing in the world that brings out the "woman" in a woman more than the thought of kids. The idea that you still have a lot of kid in you (even though you're a fat, bald, old asshole) gets those estrogen glands pumping like an Iranian oil derrick. You probably won't have gotten much past Baltic Avenue before she jumps across the floor and starts pulling your pants down. Run with it— don't worry about the fact that you would've kicked her ass had she finished the game.

MONEY AND SEX

If you do get a divorce, it's two-to-one odds that either money or sex will be the reason. If Rodney Dangerfield were here, he'd say that money and sex is always a problem in a marriage—she's going to charge you too much. Money and sex are such enormous issues that they should each have their own section. But, money and sex are kind of like chicks and misery—one is always running pretty close behind the other—so we're combining them into one.

> ## TIP #35: DON'T LET MONEY OR SEX TEAR APART YOUR MARRIAGE.

a. *Money*—Nothing—*absolutely nothing*—summarizes the very ethos of money, and women's true feelings toward it, better than a song that radio stations used to play in the early '80s. We can't remember the name of the chick singer (and we'll probably be sued when we don't attribute it properly) but the lyrics went something like this:

> *The best things in life are free,*
> *But what they are, I don't need—*
> *I want money*

Truer words haven't been spoken since 1987, when Gordon Gecko told us all that "greed is good." Virtually every chick in the universe is trained to recite the same ridiculous lies when confronted with a conversation about money. "Oh," she'll say, "I don't care if a man has money. I just want somebody with a good sense of humor who'll love me and care for me."

Excuse us, but *bull-fucking-shit!* That is the biggest crock ever, and it is astonishing that women continue to believe that anyone would buy such pure nonsense. All women want money. All men want money. *Everybody* wants money, and you know what? There's nothing wrong with that! From the day you were six years old and realized that with an extra couple of bucks you could get the big-ass, cool Mattel car, instead of the cheap piece of shit with the crooked wheel, you knew you wanted to have money. Since everybody wants cash, why do women think their claim that "I would take a vow of poverty for a husband who cares about me" is believable?

Here's why: women know that if they admit to wanting money they might be considered gold-digging leeches, not more than a level or two above a Tijuana street hooker. They would rather lose a limb than let that story get around, and, if necessary, they'll jump on a grenade to squelch the rumor. Unfortunately, once you're married women have less of an obligation to hide their inner feelings and they start to let them loose. They don't need to continue to hide all that pent-up garbage they've been concealing for the last couple of years. And we guarantee you that the first "reality" she's going to spring on you is her complete and total obsession with money. The day this happens is usually the same day that you begin asking your buddies whether they know anyone in the Mafia. Bet on it.

The all-time marriage killer is the conversation where she tells you that you don't make enough money, or that you're spending it on the wrong things. This is a devastating insult, because it strikes at the core of your masculinity—your ability to raise and maintain your family. If you can't even support yourself, your wife, and a kid or two, the argument goes, you must be completely hopeless. There's not much advice we can give you on making more money—you either have a good job or you don't, and assholes are no different from anybody else. However, there is a surefire way to know that she won't ever give you a hard time about what you have and what she gets: establish from Day One that, regardless of how much money you make, you are not going to be a regular at Tiffany's or Cartier.

To be an asshole, you've got to control your world. One of the most important aspects will be controlling the monetary flow between you, your wife, and the bank. This is so critical we're going to make it an official tip:

> ## TIP #36: EVERY SIX MONTHS, BUY HER A CHEAP GIFT.

What do we mean by this? It simply means that you should keep your wife's consumption down to a level that you can afford. If you were to get her a fur coat every three weeks, she will come to expect a fur coat, and when you *don't* get it for her she'll get so pissed off that she'll probably screw the neighbor as soon as you leave for work. Remember, you've got to mold your wife's spending habits so she doesn't question the amount of money you make or use on her. If she's not used to living like the Queen Mum, she won't bitch if your standard of living falls below that level.

The ultimate point is that whatever you buy for your wife, keep her expectations as low as possible, so that no matter what she gets she's happy. If, God forbid, the economy hits another rough patch because a thousand twenty-four-year-old arrogant, know-it-all, snot-nosed Internet kids come along and blow twenty trillion dollars again, your standard of living will not be severely impaired, and your wife won't whine because the next-door neighbors' computer is worth ten grand more than your house.

b. *Sex*—The battles fought over sex are bad enough when you're single; when you're married, it can turn into all-out war. The biggest problem is that men and women look at sex in fundamentally different ways. Women give sex to get love, men give love to get sex. If you're single, that's a pretty fair exchange. If you're married, though, it can turn into a emotional tug-of-war that just might land you in a hotel for a couple of nights while your wife eats chocolate-fudge ice cream and cries on the phone to her mother back home.

> ## TIP #37: WOMEN GIVE SEX TO GET LOVE. MEN GIVE LOVE TO GET SEX.

You've got thirty or forty years with this woman, and your views on sex have got to change if you want to survive without being Lorena Bobbitt-ed. Gone are the days when you could just run roughshod over the woman, secure in the fact that if she didn't like it you'd be on to the next girl so fast it would make her head spin. You've now got to be concerned with her pleasure, her needs, her bullshit. This could be a tough transition to make, so we're not going to tell you it's easy. It's an all-encompassing shift in your life, but one that could prove extremely beneficial, as you continue to regale your buddies with the sexual intensity of your life, while they wonder why they haven't gotten any in two months.

There are a lot of problems that come up with a married couple's sex life: you want it too much, you don't want it enough, you don't do the right things, you don't wait for her to finish, yadda yadda yadda. The list goes on and on, and if we were to get more graphic, we'd probably puke before you do, so we'll leave it at generalities. However, no matter how many different issues arise, they all spring from the same dilemma: you're not listening to her and responding to her needs. In the next chapter, we're going to give you a whole bunch of helpful hints on how not to listen to your woman during important stuff like football games and dinner. But when it comes to the bedroom, if you don't want to be forced to jerk off seven times a day to fulfill your sexual requirements, you'd better be ready to step up to the plate and let your wife have her say.

TIP #38: LISTEN TO YOUR WIFE IN THE SACK.

Because women give sex to get love, if you dominate the sexual process to the point where your wife feels excluded, her inability to give you sex will translate into the death sentence, i.e., her inability to receive love. As ridiculous as it may seem, chicks must have love to survive. Once your woman feels like she's not getting love anymore, guess what happens then?

You're right—the two of you are sitting in front of a judge trying to figure out how to split up the season tickets to the local NBA team. Being an asshole is great, until it destroys your entire life. When you're at that point, it's probably not a bad idea to throttle back a little. The point is, you can still dominate her and smack her on the ass, but just know that there are some moments when you might have to suck it up and say "I love you" or something equally stupid. It's okay, we won't give you any demerits for making her happy. Just don't make us watch.

HOW NOT TO LISTEN

Okay, okay, we know, we just had a little moment of sensitivity back there. Don't bitch, it only lasted for a few pages, and you're past it with minimal psychological injury, you whiner. But now that we've gotten in touch with our feminine side and advised you to listen to your wife when you guys are in bed, we're back to our old selves, and we're going to give you the corollary to that tip:

TIP #39: DON'T LISTEN TO HER ANYWHERE ELSE.

Ask any ten women what they dislike most about guys, and seven of them will say the same thing: men never listen. We've got news for you—there's nothing wrong with that. Between televised sports, going to the bathroom, taking a nap, and watching porn, guys don't have the time or the inclination to listen to what women have to say. However, since you're not talking, and most women are too dumb to come up with something interesting to talk about, you'll find yourself in a curious dilemma: you're stuck with this chick for the next thirty to forty years, you don't want to talk to her, she's got nothing to say that you're interested in but you've got to come up with some type of conversation during the next 360 months or you just might kill yourself. Prior to marriage, the solution is easy: dump her. After marriage, the growing numbers of divorce lawyers and "deadbeat dad" laws make this a little bit more difficult. So, what to do? Unfortunately, you're going to have to figure out a couple of tricks to make her think you're listening, when, in fact, you're just trying to find out whether the Rams beat the point spread last week. And here's how to do it:

a. *Have Her Sit with Her Back to the TV*—This one's relatively easy. As long as the TV is behind her, you can look just past her ear and continue to check out the score. You will be completely intent while she's talking. Even though your gaze is slightly off-center, she'll be so happy that you're listening, she won't even notice when you're watching John Madden diagram another play. There could be geometric issues, though, so you have to set up your living room, den, or TV room to ensure that there is a place for her to sit appropriately. The easiest way to accomplish this is to get a big-ass, overstuffed chair with a big-ass, overstuffed footrest. When you sit your woman down on the footrest, it will appear as if you're trying to get close by sitting her just a few feet away from you. Of course, you're doing it because the closer she is, the better sight lines you have to the TV—but let her believe whatever she wants to believe. As a chick, that's her right.

b. *Ask Her to Write Down the Issues Before You Have a Conversation*—If she writes down a few notes about whatever's clogging her pea-brain, you then have the chance to stare down at the notes while she's blathering on. It will look as if you're comparing her conversation to the notes she's written when, in reality, you're just checking your watch to see how much longer this is going to last. At your next job interview, you'll notice that hiring personnel use the same trick. They scrutinize your resume as you speak. You think they're trying to learn about your past, but really, they're just trying to stay awake. With your wife, you might want to throw in a noncommittal observation, like "I notice you're having issues regarding my hygiene." You don't actually comment on what she said, you just repeat what's written. Chances are pretty good that she'll spend the next fifteen minutes babbling mindlessly at the perceived slight while you take a mental vacation secure in the fact that she thinks you care what she's saying. Ha!

c. *Practice Your Throw-Away Lines*—Although she'll be mildly annoyed if you constantly don't listen to her, she'll flip her lid if, when you do allow her to drag you kicking and screaming into a serious conversation, she sees that you're not really trying at all. We are well aware that you'll spend a majority of your time daydreaming during these little tête-á-têtes, so it's important that when the inevitable "are you listening?" comes screaming at you you're prepared. Here are the best lines to parry her conversational thrusts:

TIP #40: PRACTICE YOUR
THROWAWAY LINES.

1. SHE: "Are you listening?"

   Your response—"Honey, I'm sitting here with you. I'm trying
   to understand. Some of these issues are difficult for me."
   (This is another cool Jedi mind trick, because you're playing
   upon her instinctual nurturing skills. By telling her how hard
   it is for you, she'll believe that you need her help. Then,
   she'll immediately transform herself into Mother Hen, forget
   about the fact that she was pissed at you, and try to help
   you get through *your* troubles. If you can form a tear when
   you say the "difficult" line, you're not only home free, but
   you may turn the brutal conversation into some solid
   sympathy sex.)

2. SHE: "What did I just say?"

   Your response—"Sweetheart, I need a little time to let it
   sink in. There are so many thoughts and emotions running
   around in my head, it's hard for me to comment without a
   little time to reflect." (The important part of this line is
   the word "emotions." You don't really have emotions,
   because you're an asshole and you don't give a rat's ass
   about anything. Your pretending that the conversation has
   had an impact on you is infinitely more important to her
   than your having anything thoughtful to say about it. She
   just wants to know that you care. Once you've established
   that you do, you can go back to watching the game and
   drinking beer.)

3. SHE: "What do you have to say for yourself?"

Your response—"I really don't have anything to say. What I did was wrong, and it's something I'm going to have to deal with. I just hope that our relationship is strong enough for us to get through this." (These lines are more notable for what you *don't* say than for what you do say. If you're an advanced asshole, you'll notice that *you never said "I'm sorry."* Refer back to page 19 for one of our most important tips: never, ever, ever say "I'm sorry." If you *do* apologize, she wins. And if she knows that she's won, she'll hammer you worse than MacArthur did the Phillipine Islands during WWII. Just allude to the strength of the relationship and commit yourself to making it work. Her biggest fear is that the relationship will fail. If that happens due to chick insecurity, she'll believe it was because *she* failed, not you. Playing on a woman's lack of self-worth is the quickest way to absolve yourself of blame for whatever dumb-ass thing you've just done.)

4. SHE: "Does that mean anything to you?"

Your response—"Of course it means something to me. You're the most important person in my life, and what you say means everything to me." (It almost brings tears to our eyes, knowing that you can spout completely meaningless drivel and chicks will eat it up like a lapdog. You have no idea what she just said. How could you? You weren't listening. But when she hears you talking about how important she is to you, there is virtually no way that she's going to be able to hold back blubbering, uncontrollable tears. And once she's crying, the immediate threat is over. She'll probably even apologize for getting mad. Most likely, she'll throw her arms around you, tell you how wonderful you are, and run into the kitchen so she can start making a monster dinner. This gives you a few minutes of freedom to call your girlfriend and cancel your date for the night.)

BECOMING YOUR WIFE'S PSYCHOLOGIST

In a perfect world, getting married would magically erase all of your chick's insecurities with the same efficiency that a Martini erases her morals. But the reality of the situation is that even though she's married she's still a chick, which means it doesn't take more than one glance at a Victoria's Secret billboard to send her self-image plummeting faster than Wile E. Coyote chasing that damn Acme truck off the cliff.

When you were single this wouldn't have been an issue. You'd simply stock up on porn and hunker down at your house, while she consulted Dr. Ben and Jerry, working through things on her own. But now you're married and you can't escape her insanity. You certainly don't want to waste your time comforting her, especially when there's a football game on TV or a pizza being delivered, so you've got to anticipate what's going to happen and do something about it before it spins out of control. Things like yeast infections, dying family members, or pancreatic cancer don't hold a candle to a woman who has just realized that she is either (a) fat, (b) old, or (c) unattractive. These three problems will be the bane of your existence, and it's important that you handle them with the same foresight, tact, and patience that you would use trying to nail an eighteen-year-old virgin supermodel. The warning signs are usually pretty blatant. You just have to be ready to hop into action when the situation calls for it—kind of like an emotional backup quarterback. Just remember that working through your wife's crises is like working on your golf swing—you've got to try smoothing it out, no matter how badly you want to snap the little fucker in half.

TIP #41: BE PREPARED FOR YOUR WIFE'S INSANITY.

a. *She Thinks She's Fat*—Women's lives are based on their weight. Read three pages of *Bridget Jones's Diary* and you'll realize that if your wife had the choice between gaining three pounds or losing both her legs, you'd need to start shopping for a wheelchair. Anorexia is the teenage girl's Little League, and it doesn't change much as she gets older. If your wife averages less than four nervous breakdowns per year—all due to some realization that she's gained seven ounces in her sleep—consider yourself lucky. However, as usual, there's a bunch of stuff you can do when the appearance of a granule of cellulite sends her over the edge.

1. *What to do:*

   i. *Buy her clothes with vertical lines*—All chicks know that the only reason to buy vertical lines is to look skinny. But women are clothes whores, and when you bring home a two-hundred-fifty-dollar Lane-Bryant-DKNY-Guess-Chanel-Gap-whatever she won't care that the stripes resemble prison garb more than haute couteur. In fact, she'll be so excited with her new blouse that she'll subconsciously disregard the idea that the only reason you bought it for her was so that she doesn't look like a sow.

   ii. *Let her get on top during sex*—With her back arching, her stomach will be slightly stretched and won't look quite as big. Heaven forbid she's on the bottom and her gut bunches up. Or even worse, she's on all fours looking back at the fat rolls hanging past her gunt.[7] If that does happen, immediately remove all the sharp objects from the house.

iii. *Do a little banging in the shower*—The thing about weight gain is that she's not going to think she's pretty anymore. You put the wood to her . . . the right way . . . and she'll forget all about it. Shower sex is always great sex, and she'll forget her other problems for a few minutes. Also, because you're in the shower, the water makes you keep your eyes closed so you don't have to see what a fat pig your wife has become.

iv. *Buy a bunch of fruit*—Chicks are into fruit. Just look at their fascination with gay men. But when you bring back a couple of bananas, she won't consciously notice that you're trying to get her to eat healthy. She'll just be psyched that you're finally paying attention to your diet. Once she's knee-deep in apples and peanut butter, you can get the hell out of there and get yourself a Big Mac.

2. *What not to do:*

i. *Don't take her to a restaurant!*—Even assuming she appreciates the night out with her man, she'll spend forty-five minutes grilling the waiter on how many fat calories are in the light caesar salad dressing. Plus, when your steak shows up and she's got four garbanzo beans on her plate, prepare yourself for a cascade of tears roughly equivalent to the white-water rapids on the Colorado River.

ii. *Don't buy her a gym membership*—You think, "Hey, I work out at the gym. I'll just pretend like I want her to spend

---

[7] Gunt—the fat pouch that forms beneath the belly button at the intersection of the gut and the cunt.

more time with me." No, no, no, no! Gyms are good for guys, because they can just walk onto a basketball court and have nine new best friends. You get health-conscious chicks together and it's like seven cats fighting over the last ball of yarn. A woman can't be in a health club for more than five minutes without knowing the bust size, shoe style, and hairdo of every other chick within fifty yards of her. And you know, you just absolutely know, that the second your fat-ass wife walks in, the high school cheerleader tryouts will be starting in the aerobics room. Your wife will be so devastated by the sight of all those skinny people that she may never be heard from again.

iii. *Don't go to the movies*—Why do you go to the movies? To see the film? Of course not—Hollywood hasn't made a good movie since *Porky's*. You go to the movies so you can eat popcorn, JuJuBes, and stale nachos while drinking a seventy-six-ounce Coke. Even if she can manage not to spend the equivalent of the Brazilian GDP at the snack stand, she's going to have to listen to the sound of every other horse chomping away like it's their last meal. It's going to be too much for her to handle, and she just might run out the door and swan-dive into the cherry Icee vat. Stay the hell away from the movies.

b. *She Thinks She's Old*—This is one of those inevitable things. It doesn't matter how hot you think your wife is, in ten years, when her tanned skin starts turning into beef jerky and her ass drops a yard and a half after the second kid, you'll know the salad days are over. Unfortunately, so does she. But women don't care about the fact that they can't shoot a jumper anymore, or that they now pee eighteen times a day. No, what they're worried about is that if they're old, *nobody gives a shit about them anymore!* That is much more serious and will cause a woman more anxiety than you can possibly imagine. Ever notice that nobody wants to give Grandma a ride home? How must Grandma feel about that? And when your wife interviews for that managerial position, do you think hot flashes are going to be a positive or a negative trait? Is she going to be in a real great mood after she experiences one while eight guys are asking her if she can handle the next IPO? Your wife is moving into scary, uncharted territory, and her reactions can be drastic. This is a tricky time, and you've got to be prepared.

1. *What to do:*

   i. *Take a beach vacation*—Remember the old days, when you would go on vacation to ski, horseback ride, golf or play tennis? It's over. Deal with it. Probably the worst thing you can do is try to bring back the good old days by working up a little sweat. You think it's bad for you that you can't hit a drive 275 yards anymore? Well, she's a chick, so even in her best days, she still sucked. Now, if she gets the ball past the tee box, it's a miracle. Instead of your old sports vacations, go to the beach. Chicks like the beach. She thinks it's romantic, she doesn't have to do much, and she'll be convinced that you really do love her. Then, when the old bag falls asleep, go down to the hotel disco and flash a platinum card at a twenty-year-old.

   ii. *Take her anywhere that smacks of culture*—When a chick gets old, she knows her body's going to hell, so she tries to believe that her maturing, expanding mind is making up for it. We all know that's ridiculous, but you're married to the woman, so you've got to accept it. When she goes to museums, art galleries, and musical theater, she lets herself fall under the spell that she's an intellectual icon with a wealth of experience and sophistication to make up for her saggy-ass boobs.

    iii. *Buy her a computer*—The things she used to do—raise the kids, take care of the house, endlessly berate you—are not really available anymore. The kids are gone, you guys are too old to mess things up anymore, and she's finally realized that you couldn't care less what she says as long as she can make a decent pot roast and hand you the remote control. She needs something to take up her day. A computer will open her up to a whole world of information, and she can spend hours screwing around on the Web while you watch sports and pick your nose. If you're lucky, she'll start having cybersex with some cheeseball in Wisconsin and you can finally have a little peace.

2. *What not to do:*

    i. *Don't try to do the strenuous things you used to do*—When guys are out of shape, they work out and try to get better. When chicks are out of shape, they generally cry for an hour or two and then stomp off to Häagen-Dazs to drown their sorrows. It might seem normal that if your wife is feeling old, you should take her out to the tennis court or running track and get her back on the saddle, so to speak. Wrong. If she gets tired after one game of tennis and remembers that it used to take four, she's going to be a wreck for the rest of the afternoon. Plus, she'll probably run away crying, and you'll still have to pay for the hour of court time.

    ii. *Don't take her shopping*—Where do you shop? Probably at the mall. Who goes to the mall? Teenage girls. If you want to send an old chick over the edge, there's no faster way than to put her face to face with a bunch of tanned, firm, energetic, boy-crazy teenage girls. Whether she's thirty-three or sixty-three, she probably still looks at herself as a teenage girl, and being reminded that she can barely make her way up a flight of stairs is going to crush her, especially when she sees some high school sophomore taking three steps at a time to chase after the varsity quarterback six stories above. Keep your woman at home where she can look at old pictures of herself and remember what it was like before varicose veins took over her life.

iii. *Don't comment on your own rapidly aging body*—She's your wife, remember? If you're getting old, then she sure is getting old, too. You may think that explaining your deterioration will make her feel better, because she's not as bad off as you are. And you're probably right for about six minutes. However, that night, when you're asleep and she's pacing around pre-menopausal, she's going to stare at the parts of your body that you pointed out—sagging balls, concave chest and a cue-ball head—and realize that she's as old and pathetic as you are.

c. *She Thinks Other Women Are Better Looking than She*

1. *What to do:*

Get rid of any chick magazines lying around your house—Chick magazines, like *Cosmopolitan* or *Vanity Fair,* are brutal for anybody. Hundreds of pages of the most flawlessly beautiful creatures who have ever lived. Even though 87 percent of every picture is air-brushed, who cares when you're staring at an ass that looks as if it's practically carved out of marble. When your woman starts freaking about not being pretty enough, these magazines might as well jump up and strangle her. But that makes sense. Here's what doesn't make sense: If you just lost an important baseball game and saw a *Sports Illustrated* on the coffee table, you'd throw it away, because you wouldn't want to hear about *sports* for a few days. If a chick thinks she's ugly and sees Christy Turlington on the cover of *Vogue*, she'll literally stare at the picture for five days, comparing Christy's every curve, feature, and aspect to herself, no matter how painful it is. Chicks revel in their own pain and insecurity, and instead of just moving on they will wallow in misery for days or weeks on end. The only way to get them out of their funk is to get rid of the magazines yourself. We'll excuse you if you want to jerk off to a couple of covers before you actually throw them away.

2. *What not to do:*

God forbid, don't look at other women, at least for a few days— This should be pretty obvious, but you'll be surprised at how hard it is to do. Remember that you're an asshole and you spend virtually every waking hour checking out chicks. You can't buy a can of beer or run into McDonald's without sizing up the chick taking your order. It's instinctual. But, if your woman has suddenly decided she's not good-looking enough and you so much as catch a boob out of the corner of your eye, her chick radar will lock on like an AWACS cruiser. The hell you'll receive will make you wish you were in lockdown at Leavenworth. Please, for the love of God, focus for the next couple of days on not even thinking about checking out other chicks. Once she's come to her senses, you're free to ogle at your convenience, but, until then, we're worried about you.

JAILBREAK

Just because we told you to get married doesn't mean you actually have to spend time with your wife. To do that, you'd have to give up time with your girlfriend, your buddies, and hookers, which is entirely unacceptable. Nevertheless, it's tough to get out of the house by telling your wife, "Honey, I'm going out with Christy, the bisexual stripper with the huge fake rack." Here are some of the ways for you to get away from the shrew for a few solitary moments of silence or just to find yourself a strip bar.

TIP #42: LEARN HOW TO GET AWAY FROM YOUR WIFE.

a. *Blame Work*—This is always the number one reason to get out of the house. You've got a meeting; you're having dinner with a customer; your boss needs your help to get him on the Internet at 3 A.M., etc., etc. Work is a great excuse, because your wife thinks it will help you make more money, which, of course, is half hers. Let her entertain the illusion. The only thing to be careful about here is the kind of job you have. If you dig ditches for the city, it's pretty unlikely you're going to be called in at night for a "seminar." Or, if you drive a bus, nighttime "proficiency tests" are also pretty tough to get by the missus. Just make sure your work-related excuse is within the realm of possibility, and that you don't come home smelling like strippers, and you should be fine.

b. *You Forgot Anything*—Forgetting stuff is always a convenient way to run out for a little while. Your keys, your wallet, your wife's IUD, these are all good. Of course, if you "forgot" your keys, you probably shouldn't pull them out before you get to the car. Also, if it's your wallet that's allegedly sitting on your desk back at work, make sure it's not in the back pocket of your jeans for your wife to see as you head for the door.

c. *Classes*—An absolute classic. Sign up for a class in something. Photography. Screenwriting. Nude sculpting. Anything. The content doesn't really matter, but it would be best if you knew something about the subject, because you're never going to attend a lecture, and if your wife asks what you've learned, you could be screwed. Also, try to pick a hard-core masculine class so that your wife doesn't decide that "it would be fun" if you took it together. Iron working and welding comes to mind. If your wife bitches about the fact that you'll be out of the house one night a week, remind her that you're trying to expand your horizons and broaden yourself so you can enrich your relationship. That should shut her up for a while. Again, make sure you sweat the small stuff, though. If she wants to see your textbook, or God forbid, audit a lecture, you could be totally out of luck when you don't even know where the building is, so make sure you have contingency plans.

d. *The Emergency Phone Call*—Have one of your buddies fake a call about a horrible automobile accident. You'll have to go to the hospital immediately. This is not only very dangerous, but must also be used sparingly. The first problem is that your wife may want to come—chicks are into that whole "let me help you heal" thing—so the buddy should be somebody she only knows slightly. She has to recognize the name for credibility, but not be so close that she cares whether he or his mom dies that night. Secondly, make sure your wife doesn't know the person who's allegedly been hit. If it's your pal's sister who's purportedly unconscious, it's not going to help your situation when your wife runs into her at a spinning class the next day in the gym. Finally, remember that this one will cause chaos and drama at your house. If somebody's getting hit by a car twice a week, your wife will eventually figure it out. Therefore, this should not be used more than once or twice a year, max, and usually only when you have to attend a really big event, like a bachelor party with three lesbians and a tri-headed dildo.

e. *Honey, I'm Going Out with the Boys*—Hiding right out in the open is usually a solid tactical move. Although most women will mildly object to you carousing with a bunch of psychotic, drunken buddies, if you tell her you want to hang out with a few friends she probably won't say "no" out of fear that (a) you'll think she's a controlling bitch and you might seek out a warmer, gentler woman in retaliation, or (b) she's turning into her own mother and you might seek out a warmer, gentler woman in retaliation. If you play it right, not only will she say it's fine for you to go out, she might actually encourage you to hang out with your friends, even though your "friend" is really a twenty-two-year-old blonde toll booth operator you met going to work the other day. The only danger here is, of course, when you go drink beers with your buddies, you don't end up with lipstick stains on your underwear, so, as always, be careful.

CHEATERS NEVER PROSPER . . . UNLESS THEY'RE MARRIED

Throughout your life, you're going to run into a lot of oxymorons, i.e., things that are inherently contradictory. Fried ice cream, for example. Military intelligence is another that springs to mind. Happily married. Female orgasm. But the biggest, most insanely paradoxical concept in your life will be the fact that you are a complete asshole, and yet you will ultimately get married. It really doesn't make sense when you think about it. Your life is committed to making sure that everything you do goes entirely against the grain of what women say they want. Then, out of the blue, you do the one thing that every woman, from the day she pops out of the uterine canal, is desperate for: marriage. How will you reconcile these inconsistent concepts? That's easy—you'll cheat.

Don't kid yourself, there's simply no way you're going to spend the next thirty or forty years with the same woman and not desperately long for every piece of ass that comes within a hundred yards. You know it. Your wife knows it. Everybody knows it. They all expect that you're going to stray on occasion, and if you don't they'd probably think you're a fag. As far as your wife goes, she married an asshole—a guy who's essentially been treating her like garbage for the past couple of years. *What*—she thinks all of a sudden you're going to change because of that two-dollar piece of tin around your finger? She knows just as well as anybody that you're gonna cheat—shoot, she probably started banging you when you were cheating on a previous girlfriend, so don't get your underwear in a big wad when you finally realize (two or three days after your honeymoon) that it's time to start spreading that seed around.

Don't worry that you won't be able to find somebody to cheat with. Women who are willing to bang married guys simply aren't looking for the same things that they look for in a young, single guy. Even if you weren't much of a stud before you got married, your demonstrated willingness to commit makes you infinitely more attractive in the eyes of other women—even if they're not the ones you're committed to. It's one of those weird, single-minded chick fantasies. They sit around with their friends for hours, saying things like "he's such a wonderful father, a wonderful husband, so responsible, maybe he'll buy me a condo." The fact that he's the husband of another woman and the father of somebody else's kids never enters the equation.

TIP #43: YOU CAN CHEAT, BUT BE DISCREET.

The most important part about cheating, though, is that you've got to be discreet. Just because everybody knows you're going to cheat doesn't mean you have to throw it in their faces. Being unfaithful to a wife was the first instance of the "don't ask, don't tell" policy. As long as you're careful, and not too obvious that you're sticking it to a variety of twenty-year-olds, nobody will care. But let yourself get photographed by *The National Enquirer* once—just once!—with some floozy model gutterslut, and you'd better run for the hills, because all hell is about to break loose.

a. *How NOT to Get Caught:*

1. *Hookers*—Despite what you hear, prostitution is *not* the world's oldest profession. Being married is the world's oldest profession, and it beat prostitution by about forty-eight hours. We're not sure if it was Adam and Eve or some African Bush People who were the original married couple, but we do know that it was less than a week before the first husband got so tired of his chick nagging him to sweep the dirt out of their cave that he ran off to the nearest woman, offering her two pterodactyl feathers for a little poontang. Thus was born prostitution in all of its glory. Hookers, unlike college girls, know that their livelihood is based on their ability to keep their friggin' mouths shut, which makes them infinitely superior as cheating partners. This alone is worth the price of admission. If you've ever felt a pang of guilt for going to see a hooker, by the way, take comfort in Hugh Grant. Even though Hugh wasn't married, he spent ten or so years with Elizabeth Hurley, the absolute hottest piece of ass who has ever walked this earth. Despite being able to poke that goddess on a regular basis, he still ended up with a black, skanky streetwalker named Divine nestled between his legs in the driver's seat of a rented Buick. If the luckiest guy on the face of the earth needs a whore, no court in the land would convict if you do, too.

2. *Business trips*—Business trips are the biggest scam in the history of infidelity. Why do you really need to fly across the

country to meet some dork in a restaurant for fifteen minutes just to sell him whatever worthless garbage you're peddling at the moment? The truth is, you don't. The business trip was invented so you could bang chicks. In fact, the business trip was the precursor to the infamous "border rule," which recognizes that anytime you cross a state border your marriage vows are temporarily suspended. The concepts of cheating and business trips are so totally intertwined that you would not be considered out of line for trying to cash in your frequent flier miles at the local brothel. Simply put, travel is good; travel to underdeveloped, whore-sponsoring locales like Bali, Amsterdam, and Malaysia is much, much better.

3. *Bachelor parties*—This is truly the only part of the wedding that you should expect to enjoy with gusto, and the perfect opportunity for an escape from the sexless hell that is your marriage. The mere concept of a group of guys getting together for a night of strippers, hookers, lethal combinations of recreational drugs, and assorted long, cylindrical vegetables is almost too much for the asshole to handle without slipping into a state of unconscious ecstasy. In your thirties, nights out with the boys become much tougher to come by, and bachelor parties are the one place where virtually all of your friends (even the uptight, henpecked married ones) will party like they're back at a fraternity kegger. The unbridled mayhem of a well-executed bachelor party is music to the ears of a professional asshole, but, despite the fact that the actual night of the party should be a bacchanalian haze of booze, cigars, silicone breasts, and unpeeled bananas, just remember that there are a few rules:

i. No cameras. Repeat, *no cameras*—cameras are to the bachelor party what the Rodney King videotape was to the Los Angeles Police Department. If anybody brings a camera, especially a video camera, you are legally permitted to beat him to within an inch of his life. And then laugh at him when he can't finish his shot of tequila.

ii. There must be a VCR in the room playing porn all night long. True assholes will watch nothing but anal.

iii. If the strippers don't do a girlie show—complete with a two-headed dildo—you do not have to pay them.

iv. The bachelor should black out before 1 A.M., at which time you are obligated to write all over his face with a permanent marker.

4. *Cell phones*—The blackest day in the history of infidelity was the one that saw the introduction of the answering machine. It wasn't forty-eight hours later that the first dumb-ass twenty-three-year-old girl left a message on her married boyfriend's machine and caused the first recorded (no pun intended) answering-machine-related divorce. In the twenty-first century, however, it is considered de rigueur to give out your cell phone number. You can pretend as if you're giving her some secret access to the most personal aspects of your life, when in reality you're just hiding her from your fat, bearded wife.

5. *Stay away from college girls*—This might be a tough one to swallow. The whole point of being an asshole is that you can bang your way through Delta Gamma no matter how ugly you are. Unfortunately, this is one of those times when you're going to have to bow down to the practical realities of your situation. College girls are freaks. When you break up with them, they drive by your house to see if you're home. They look in your mail. They watch you take your kids to school. They are compulsive, obsessive, neurotic, and tortured. That's why they're so fun to screw—because they're out of their flippin' minds. You can be doing her doggy style one minute and she's barking at the moon the next. Now that's a party. Regrettably,

since you're married, you've got to dump her at some point, because you sure as hell are not going to give up half your stuff for some nineteen-year-old dunce who's probably taking on four guys every time she darkens the door of the local fraternity house. Besides, if you do end up with her, when you send her packing, she's going to be parked in a Volkswagen Jetta outside your house for the next two months, if you're lucky—ten months if you're not. There's nothing worse than sending some chick to the minors and coming home two days later with a bunny boiling on your range. So just suck it up and find yourself a twenty-five-year-old, you'll be much better off in the end.

6. *Love in the afternoon*—If you're planning on doing a little illegal lovin', do it in the afternoon, for God's sake. A little lunchtime soiree is quick, you've got a great excuse to leave her after forty-five minutes, and, best of all, by the end of the day the sex smell will be gone. Don't forget—*women can smell sex.* They're like St. Bernards that way. Hell, they should have a little keg of condoms hanging from their necks. If you go out with your "other" woman at night, after the obligatory two hours of pounding, you smell like a *Vanity Fair* scratch-and-sniff ad. How are you gonna get that past the wife? "Oh honey, I was at Nordstrom's buying you a chinchilla coat, and then the lady behind the counter spritzed me." Yeah, right. Your chick is calling the divorce lawyer before you've finished the sentence.

b. *How to Do the Things That Would Normally Get You Caught, Without Getting Caught*

1. *Going out locally*—Now that you're married, you've settled into a community, and it's likely that you know a lot of people in your general vicinity. You go shopping at the same places, dine

at the same bars and restaurants, and see a lot of the same faces as you go through your day. This is great when you need to borrow a cup of sugar or want somebody to go watch the high school football game with you. Unfortunately, it sucks when you've just bagged a smoking-hot twenty-two-year-old piece of ass, and everybody is asking you why your wife is home knitting while you're out sucking down a third martini with this little trollop. What to do? It's relatively easy. You've got a bunch of options:

   i. Always carry a textbook when you take her out. If anybody asks, she's a local college student and you're giving her a little tutoring help. Don't tell them the real subject is sex education.

  ii. Get her a fake i.d. with your last name. She's now your cousin visiting from Montana. It'll be especially exciting when you let your river run through her.

 iii. Have her carry a little notebook and write down virtually everything you say, except for the stuff that can get you arrested. If people start to whisper, you just hired yourself an assistant—ass being the operative part of the word.

 iv. Don't ever go out to eat. Go to bars, go to clubs, go anywhere, as long as food isn't involved. If you're not sitting at a booth eating with the girl, there is always the possibility that she just came up, started talking to you and you're being polite. You can pretend that you have no idea who she is or where she came from, and all you really have to do is make sure her head's in your lap when you drive away.

2. *Phone calls at home*—Although the cell phone largely takes care of this problem, chicks are generally not smart enough to remember to dial your mobile number every single time. If they

can remember it seven times out of ten, you may have just bagged Alberta Einstein. When she ultimately does call you at home, don't ever have her hang up the phone. Hang-ups immediately trip your wife's chick radar, and she's going to know something's up. Write out a telemarketer's speech in big block letters and paste it next to every phone in your girlfriend's house. Once she hears your wife pick up, your girlfriend should immediately start reading about how "yes, you, too can sign up for AT&T's long-distance service for just half the price," and your wife will immediately hang up the phone.

3. *The nose knows*—The most curious part about cheating is that you'll rarely get caught in the act. However, afterwards, when you go home reeking of Escape, or some other similarly disgusting perfume, the ever-present chick radar can immediately distinguish between the smell of a disinterested bar patron and the peculiar scent of a woman who just spent the last twenty minutes with you in the back seat of the Ford Explorer. How? Who the hell knows how? How can a dog run into a forty-acre stretch of shoulder-high reeds and come back with a duck in his mouth? How can a shark in the Indian Ocean smell the cut on your finger when you dive into the surf off Malibu? It's just one of those things that's developed in women over the past 40,000 years—kind of like her ability to walk into a jewelry store and immediately fall in love with the necklace that costs more than your car. Therefore, you need to make sure that you have extra cologne—the kind that you use every day—in your glove compartment.[8] No matter how clean you think you are after you've been with your girlfriend, you'll

[8] Mötley Crüe, the '80s heavy metal band, raised the act of getting a chick's smell off you to a true art form. When one of the band's members poked a groupie and a girlfriend was coming over, he would simply rub Taco Bell products on his genitalia to erase the scent. Apparently, chalupas worked best.

reek like sex, and you've got to get your own stink back. Put it on before you drive back home and leave the windows open so it's not quite as strong when you make it to your house. If you walk in smelling like you just stepped out of your morning shower, it's going to be a long night.

c. If You Do Get Caught, How to Get Out of It

TIP #44: DENY, DENY, DENY.

1. *Deny, deny, deny*—The Rastafarian singer Shaggy released the true "denial anthem" with his smash hit, *Wasn't Me*. In the song, he's banging his next-door neighbor, and even though his chick walks in on him he just says, "Hey, it wasn't me." Who cares that she's watching it happen, "it wasn't me"—and he ends up not getting in any trouble whatsoever. *Deny, deny, deny.* Chicks don't want to believe that you're cheating on them. You can have seven lesbians walk out of your bedroom carrying a pallet of K-Y, but if you tell your wife that they're plumbers, she'd rather believe you're telling the truth than contemplate the fact that you might have more fun with an army of sexed-up hookers than her. Don't *ever* underestimate the female ability to deny reality. This is how women can buy *Cosmo* every day, stare at the most gorgeous human beings that have ever existed, and somehow still believe that their husbands are hot for them. Don't fight it. Use their complete disdain for the truth to work in your favor. Deny, deny, deny.

   Although denial is the preferred method, there is the possibility that your chick, unlike the rest, has an IQ above room temperature and refuses to dismiss what is smacking her in the face. In that unfortunate event, you'll have to call in the reserves. However, only use any of the following under extreme circumstances.

2. *Feel worse about it than she does*—No, you don't actually feel worse than she does. Just pretend that you do. Sample lines:

   i. "Honey, how could I have done such a horrible thing? I don't deserve you. I don't deserve to live. I should just kill myself."

   ii. "My God, my God, my God! I can't believe how disgusting I am. I feel dirty. I've thrown away everything that's good in my life. I should just kill myself."

   iii. "It was terrible. She can't hold a candle to you. I lost my mind for a split second, and I am doomed to everlasting damnation. I should be tortured until the end of time for such a horrible, horrible act. I should just kill myself."

   Don't ever forget women's instinctual nurturing tendencies. They're used to never-ending pain, misery, and torture, because they have to deal with assholes like you on a daily basis. But when they see somebody else suffering, some reserve parachute of emotions just overwhelms anything else that might be going on in their own heads. If your wife thinks you need help, you could've just been caught with the Lindbergh baby and she'll still rush to your side. You might even want to practice forming a tear in your eye, so the words you say have more of an effect. Try pulling fifteen or sixteen nose hairs out at a time and that should do the trick. That's only three or four more than you normally pull out in a day anyway, so who really cares?

3. *Get her a day at the spa*—Actually, the amount of time you have to get for her will vary, depending on the severity of your transgression. If you got drunk at a Christmas party and pecked some hot secretary, one day will probably suffice. If

you were caught fully making out in a coatroom closet with the new intern, you might have to get your wife a week at the spa with honey-mustard oil treatments and deep-tissue toe massages. If your wife walks in on you as you're fitting the neighbor with her new ankle earrings, oh Jesus, you might have to move your wife into a condo at some resort in Puerto Vallarta.

4. *A preemptive walkout*—This move is not for the faint of heart. You've got to have nerves of a cat burglar and balls of radioactive titanium. To fully understand this trick, you've got to think back to when you were single. Remember when you were going out with that little girl and you didn't think it was going too well? You decided one night that you had to end it, and you made the call to her house to break it off. Out of nowhere, she dumped *your* pathetic ass. All of a sudden, you were in love with her, you had no idea anything was wrong, and you were willing to do virtually anything to get her back. After two months of unreturned phone calls, an extra fifteen pounds, and the temporary restraining order, you finally gave up.

Well, that exact same thing happens with chicks, and it doesn't stop just because you're married. If your wife catches you cheating, she's going to be so pissed, she'll be ready to dump your ass right there, right then. Unless you do it first. If you simply tell her that the affair was really indicative of the fact that you've lost that lovin' feeling, she's going to be sent into an emotional vortex, stunned at the sudden loss of her husband, her life, and surely, her self-esteem. She'll be so desperate to get you back, she'll entirely forget that twenty minutes ago you were getting blown by some skanky college girl in a Pearl Jam t-shirt. The danger, of course, is that she calls your bluff and goes outside to start cutting the SUV in half. This is known as a zero-sum game. Gutsy move if it works, two years of litigation hell if it doesn't.

5. *Tell her it was her fault*—There are very few women out there who are not filled with self-loathing and complete disdain for themselves. Mostly, that comes from a society that tells them if they're not built like Pamela Anderson or look like Christy Turlington, they are completely worthless. Because images of sex, beauty, and perfection are showered on them from the day they're born, chicks become programmed to believe that they're completely screwed up, and you can use this trait to turn virtually anything against your woman, even your own cheating. If your wife catches you with somebody else, you simply explain that if she were more attentive or more loving you wouldn't be forced to seek it elsewhere. This will set off an estrogen chain reaction that will quickly move your wife's mood from anger to self-doubt to fear to panic that not only are you right, but that once you leave, she's not good enough to get anybody else. She'll be so busy trying to figure out what she did wrong and searching for a chick magazine that will teach her how to be normal, she'll probably forget what sent her there in the first place.

ONE WIFE + ONE BABY = WAY MORE THAN TWO HEADACHES

Having a pregnant wife is the true asshole conundrum. Your wife is bearing your child, the one who will carry on your hopes and dreams, your name, the living embodiment of everything you hold dear. At this time in your life, you need to care for your woman, make sure her every need is satisfied, embrace her so that your progeny can develop into the singular being that you pray for every night. But she's a goddamn chick, and she's stupid, and she wants stuff from you, *all the friggin' time*. Pickles, ice cream, Big Macs with hot sauce—what the hell is going on here? You think you might shoot yourself if her fat ass rolls over and whines, once again, "Honey, I have to go to the bathroom. Can you get me a sardines-bacon-and-Jell-O sandwich?"

But, as we've stated over and over again, this is just one of those instances when the true asshole realizes that he's got to suck it up and make the best of a trying time. She's your wife, that's your kid, deal with it. Treat her like garbage now, and it's guaranteed that your son will be born with two heads, or, even worse, he'll be born a girl. Are you ready to go out and buy tampons when your daughter's thirteen, she has her first period, and Mom's on a business trip? Of course you're not. So, you've got to make it through the next nine months by reining in all of your instincts to smack the little woman silly when she asks you to make her cinnamon-salsa toast in the morning. It won't be easy but, hey, we weren't the dumb asses who decided to get married in the first place, so don't bitch at us. We will, however, come to your rescue and give you a couple of helpful hints to get through this painful and sleep-deprived time.

a. *Hire a Midwife*—Get yourself a full-time pre-nanny, someone who will sit there and listen to your wife squawk for forty hours a week so you can play golf, get drunk with your buddies, and forget the fact that you've got to pay $175,000 for the soon-to-be little punk's college education in eighteen years. If your wife has full-time help during her pregnancy, she's also less likely to object when you decide to keep the slave chick on permanently when your monsters are born. Your wife will undoubtedly resist hiring a maid who actually lives with you. "Ooh," she'll say, "what if I want to walk around naked? How can I with someone always . . . being there?" The fact that your wife hasn't walked around naked since she was a sophomore in college will not enter into the equation at all and you shouldn't bring it up. It'll just piss her off more.

For whatever reason, chicks all believe that having full-time help will somehow diminish your need to have them around. Chicks need to be needed. If somebody else is cooking, cleaning, and giving you secret blowjobs in the pantry, what do you really need a wife for? Her insecurity quotient, already pushing maximum density because she's gained fifty pounds in the last six months, might just blow the eyes out of her head. However, your wife is at her weakest point when she's pregnant, and if you get her used to having Magdalena dust the house every day she probably won't be able to imagine having to actually do work again once the kid's born.

b. *Get Close to Her Mom*—Okay, her mom has always hated you because you are a complete and total asshole. Can you blame her? It's difficult for Grandma to be real helpful when she's spent the last couple of years hoping that you would get hit by a cement truck. But now is the time to mend those fences and get her on your side. It's not that tough. You know how to do it—lie your ass off! Tell her how much you love her and how wonderful it's been having her in your life. Don't laugh when you say it, of course, or that could blow the whole deal. Send flowers. Fix her leaky roof. Teach her how to program the VCR. If you can get her on your side, there is literally no task too dirty or disgusting for a grandmother to take on when she feels like she's being helpful. Whatever it takes to get the full grandmother tornado sweeping through your house, do it. Once you've got Grandma to the point that she can actually be in the same room as you without wanting to vomit, she'll become a one-woman cleaning, comforting machine. Your wife just blew chunks on the rug? Have no fear, Grandma will buy a steam cleaner. Your wife wakes up at 4 A.M. yearning for caramel ice cream and an anchovy pizza, her mom's got Domino's and Baskin Robbins on speed dial. Get your mother-in-law on your team and you'll be sleeping like a baby for the next nine months.

c. *Tell Her She Looks Hot*—This may be a lot harder than it sounds. Your wife has gained forty pounds, she doesn't bathe half the time, and she's perpetually surrounded by Twinkie wrappers and pizza boxes. This is the worst she's looked since you guys met—she knows it, you know it, everybody knows it. You know what? It doesn't matter. When you wake up every morning, stare that monster right in the eye and tell her that she's the most gorgeous woman you've ever seen. You might think that she'll see through your veiled attempt to placate her, but, amazingly, she won't. When your wife is pregnant, she is at her most womanly. Her female hormones are increasing so rapidly that she's practically sweating them at this time, and any chick tendencies she had before multiply ten times over. If, prior to her pregnancy, your wife was happy when you told her she was pretty (even when she looked like death warmed over), you do it now and she'll practically nominate you for sainthood. She will be so overwhelmed by your thoughtfulness, it's possible she might even shut up long enough for you to finish watching the game with your buddies before she asks you to run down to the 7-Eleven to pick up sunflower seeds, pork rinds, and Spam.

ASSHOLE JUNIOR[9]

Being an asshole is a great thing; raising an asshole is an experience that you will cherish for a lifetime. Just imagine your son never being bothered by the pain, misery, and torture of chicks, never lacking self-confidence, and never absorbing even a single body blow from the insanity that is the female mind.

We know that you're going to want to start peppering him with information the second he's old enough to understand words: "dump her before she dumps you," "stop calling within thirty minutes after

---

[9] This section is only applicable to those of you with sons. Given that we view infant women as little more than the future pincushions of infant assholes, we don't feel qualified to counsel you on raising them. We can offer only this slight piece of advice: keep her the hell away from anybody who's read this book.

you've slept with her," "pretend like you don't care about her," and so on and so on. But remember that his little budding brain does not have the experience that you have, and he probably won't be able to act appropriately until he's grown up a little. You have to give him the "Asshole-Lite" treatment until he can handle the real thing. We hope like hell that you're not stupid enough to bring him along too fast and screw him up for life.

> ## TIP #45: DON'T INDOCTRINATE YOUR KID TOO EARLY.

Here are a couple of rules that you'll have to keep in mind during their childhood:

a. *Encourage Them to Play with Little Girls*—This will be painful. You're letting the infidels inside the gate. Cozying up to the enemy. These are the same women who will spend the rest of their lives trying to make your son's life a living nightmare . . . and you're inviting them into the house. What the hell? Unfortunately, boys have to learn how to socialize with girls before they can treat women like garbage and make them fall in love. If your boy does nothing but destroy toy soldiers with his buddies, he'll start regarding women as aloof and mysterious, and it will be difficult for him to close that distance when he's forced to ask them out. Plus, he's got to be well-rounded. Smashing his little friends in the head is great, but if that's all he knows he won't be able to dial it back when he's forced to lie his ass off to a woman about how much he loves museums. Keep him out there interacting with all of the children, not just the boys. Let him learn how to relate to people, show him the proper way to be sensitive to other kids' needs, and then, when he's old enough, explain to him why that's all bullshit.

b. *Teach Him to Play an Instrument*—It's probably true that you spent a fair amount of your childhood beating the crap out of the boy who carried the violin case. We don't encourage this type of behavior, but we're also realistic, and we know we're dealing with a bunch of friggin' assholes. However, which guys get more puss than any group in the history of mankind? Rock musicians, without a doubt. Take, for instance, Marilyn Manson. Are you kidding me? They use pictures of his face to scare little Japanese children into doing their homework. Yet, he continuously pokes the finest women in the world. The list of hideously deformed rock stars who get nothing but the finest ass is unbelievably long: Ric Ocasek is married to Paulina Porizkova, for God's sake; the lead singer from Warrant got that *Cherry Pie* chick; Nikki Sixx and Donna D'Errico. If you even want to be in the running for Father of the Year, you'd better give your kid the same opportunity. Sure, he'll hate you now for making him practice, but when he's twenty-three and brings home his first Playboy Playmate of the Month, he'll walk up to you, plant a huge kiss on your cheek, and tell you that you're the best goddamn father who's ever lived.

c. *Have Him Playing Sports Before He Can Say His Name*—It's a pretty good bet that your kid isn't going to be a professional athlete. Unlike musicians, athletes have to achieve a certain level of success in order to attract women. Face it, your kid's star will probably flame out around high school, if he even gets that far. Maybe Tiger Woods benefited from receiving his first set of golf clubs at the age of nine months, but since your kid doesn't have any Cablinasian in him, he's probably out of luck. However, none of that matters. Your boy must play sports to be cool. If he sits around reading and playing with Legos, he could turn out to be too femme to help you pick up chicks after you divorce his mother. Even worse, if he's not out there in the dirt, screaming at umpires, and throwing beanballs at his buddies, he won't develop the competitive fire he'll need to chase chicks. Athletics keeps him in shape, teaches him how to perform under pressure, and don't ever forget, chicks dig the long ball.

d. *Hold Off on the Asshole Game Until He's at Least Twelve*—Your boy's going to start having problems around the time that he discovers he has a penis. The inevitable chaos that will ensue might encourage you to start explaining some of the asshole facts of life when he's sent home crying from kindergarten. Don't do it. You think it'll help, but it won't. Kids will interpret things differently, and here's what'll happen:

1. YOU SAY: "Don't play with the little girls, they're not like us." HE HEARS: "Grow up to be gay."
2. YOU SAY: "You shouldn't treat the girls well, they don't respond to it." HE HEARS: "Beat the crap out of little girls, and when they cry do it some more."
3. YOU SAY: "Blow the little girls off and they'll come around." HE HEARS: "I'm not allowed to go to any more birthday parties."
4. YOU SAY: "To get what you want from a girl, lie your ass off." HE HEARS: "If my parents ever ask me a question, lie my ass off."

See, none of these things come out right in the twisted little world of a seven-year-old. Instead of teaching him to be an asshole, just make sure he understands the four G's that he'll need to develop into a teenage stud:

1. Grades
2. Girls
3. Guitar
4. G-Sports (No, not G-Spot. We actually wanted to say sports but couldn't come up with a good way to say it using a "G." Work with us.)

MARRIAGE FINAL EXAMINATION

1. *When you're married, you should expect to:*
   a. Drink as much as you always did
   b. Not care as much about making money
   c. Deal with a lot of stuff you never worried about when you were single
   d. Get no flak about watching football all weekend

2. *During marriage, money:*
   a. Grows on trees
   b. Is something that could be a real problem if you're not careful
   c. Will never come between you and your wife as long as she's a hooker
   d. Is just something to count when you're bored

3. *To get out of the house, you should:*
   a. Ask your wife if she knows where the condoms are
   b. Make sure you come home the following day smelling like Jessica McClintock perfume
   c. Have your girlfriend pick you up
   d. Hide right out in the open

4. *If your wife catches you doing something you're not supposed to do, you should:*
   a. Apologize profusely
   b. Give her cash to leave you alone
   c. Deny, deny, deny
   d. Get another wife

5. *Cheating on your wife is:*
   a. The wrong thing to do, because you might get caught
   b. Expected
   c. Not a problem, as long as you tell your wife
   d. Something that your neighbors will think is cool

6. *When your wife thinks she's getting fat, you should:*
   a. Have sex in the shower
   b. Come home with a few pints of Häagen-Dazs
   c. Ask her if she wants her stomach stapled
   d. Tell her that you always thought Mama Cass Elliott was a piece of ass

7. *To properly raise your son, you should:*
   a. Tell him to smack anybody who doesn't listen to him
   b. Pull him out of kindergarten if the teacher makes him play with girls
   c. Wait till he's twelve to explain the asshole facts of life
   d. Never let him touch a guitar

8. *If your wife is eight months pregnant, you should tell her:*
   a. To drop a couple of pounds
   b. That she's beautiful
   c. To leave you the fuck alone
   d. That her mother is no longer allowed in the house

9. *Sex during marriage should be:*
   a. As outrageous as you can make it
   b. Extremely conservative
   c. Nonexistent
   d. Something you do once a year at most

10. *You should force your kid to play music because:*
    a. Joining the high school band will build character
    b. Somebody's got to be the next John Tesh, and he might as well be it
    c. Only a rock star can get two supermodels to blow him while the Playmate of the Year rims his asshole
    d. The music blaring out of the basement will help you sleep at night

ANSWERS
1-c, 2-b, 3-d, 4-c, 5-b, 6-a, 7-c, 8-b, 9-a, 10-c.

Chapter Seven

DIVORCE AND DEATH

WELCOME MAT

There is no welcome mat for this section. What the hell is welcome about divorce or death?

WHAT ELSE DID YOU EXPECT?

It doesn't matter how wonderful, beautiful, smart, rich, or fantastic you told everybody your first wife was, she wasn't anything more than a first wife. You're an asshole, and you've got to bang chicks, drink beer, and generally not give a crap about anything. The only reason you got married was because all your friends did, you figured you needed to have a little child asshole, or just in case somebody has to clean your colostomy bag when you get old. But despite all that, ya wanna hear something crazy? You'll probably get married again!

At this point, you're probably getting a little bit confused. First, when you're in your twenties, we tell you never to get married. Then, when you hit your thirties, we tell you to get married. Once you get divorced, we tell you that you should never have gotten married in the first place, and here we are saying that maybe you should get married again. What gives? Did we go to the chick school of logic and consistency? Unfortunately, in the world that we live in, no matter how solid your credentials, there are always a couple of factors militating for you to get married (as we discussed ad nauseam in the previous section).

In light of that reality, you sucked it up and popped the question to the least objectionable chick you could find. Unfortunately, after a couple of years it was inevitable that you were going to break up, and here you are: broke, alone, and not nearly the physical specimen you once were. Do not fear, we are going to come to your rescue once again. Divorce is not a death sentence; rather, it's a rebirth of your cool (apologies to Miles Davis). You're now back in the saddle again, you're probably well along in your career, and even though you just gave up half your net worth, you should still have enough earning years left to impress a couple more twenty-five-year-olds before you're done. What do you do now? You're now at another one of those life-altering events that is going to require a little modification to the basic rules of assholedom. Let's move on to a few critical topics.

DON'T GIVE HER A CENT

Divorces are brutal.[10] Even divorce lawyers get freaked out by them, and lawyers are the lowest form of human dreck—so, if they have a problem

---

[10] The most ingenious divorce settlement in history: A friend of ours got divorced a couple of years ago and he was getting the sense that it was not going to be a calm, easy procedure. He didn't want to pay a ton of attorney's fees, but he wanted to make sure he didn't get screwed too badly. His idea? He told his soon-to-be-ex-wife to make a list containing all of their existing property. He then told her she had complete discretion to split the list in two, one representing 50 percent of the community property, the second representing the other 50 percent. He stressed to her that she could include whatever she wanted on either list, and any valuation that she provided for a particular item would be accepted, as long as it was on the list. The catch? *He* got to choose which of the two 50 percent lists he wanted to take, not she. They never even called a lawyer. Pure, unadulterated genius.

with something you know it's bad. Why are they such a nightmare? Because she's trying to get your stuff, and you're trying to keep it—that's pretty serious.

Our advice? Fight her for every goddamn nickel. It doesn't matter how insignificant the piece of property, if you know she's enjoying it with her new boyfriend, it's going to keep you up nights. You think that thirty-five-cent cigar lighter meant anything to you before? How about now that her car-wash-attendant boyfriend is using it to light up a Macanudo after he just banged the piss out of your ex-wife? Seems a little more valuable, huh? For that reason, you've got to fight tooth and nail to keep everything you can. Another bonus is that, during the negotiation, if you practically become violent over a worthless piece of junk, like a TV that can be replaced for two hundred dollars, when you ultimately give it to her you can demand something big in exchange.

UNLOAD THE KIDS

If you're reading this book and you don't have kids, it seems pretty obvious that you'd want to unload your children in the event of the divorce. If you do have kids, though, you know it ain't that easy. Watching your kids grow up—as difficult as it is for us to admit—is a pretty tremendous experience. Seeing them hit a home run, looking at their bright faces when they get an "A" on their report card, these things are damn near magical to a parent, and when you get a divorce it's brutally hard to let them go.

Whatever, dads—send 'em packing. Kids are great and all, but they're even better when you only have to deal with them once in a while. How about if you only heard from them after they hit a home run or got an "A," rather than the times that they're arrested for public drunkenness, come home bloody after getting their ass kicked, or are diagnosed with ADHD? Wouldn't that be a lot better? Of course it would.

Plus, you're single now. You need to go out and scare up some tail.

No matter what type of chick you're going to go after—old, young, hot, ugly, rich, poor—they'll all love the fact that you have kids, provided that they don't have to actually deal with the little monsters. If she knows that you're a caring parent with a sense of commitment to your family, she'll think you're great. If she can't scream her lungs out while you're screwing the bejesus out of her because the kids are in the next room, she's eventually going to get annoyed. Send the kids to live with their mom, buy a house around the corner, and everything will turn out just fine.

FAT, BALD, BROKE, AND SINGLE—WHAT IN GOD'S NAME ARE YOU GOING TO DO *NOW?*

The predicament you find yourself in now is not much different from the one you were in when you started hitting your late twenties and early thirties. The advice we'd give you is pretty much the same, but we have to make allowances for your advancing age and the fact that your responsibilities have likely increased, due to the presence of your hateful ex-wife and your disrespectful, maniac children. Add to this your inevitable march towards retirement and uselessness, and, boy, you've got a lot on your mind. Here are the major hurdles you've got to get over.

a. *Fat*—Get your lazy, fat ass back in the gym. All of the ridiculousness you hear about how your metabolism slows down, and how middle age will inevitably give you a big-ass gut is just that—ridiculous. If you're eating Domino's six nights a week because you can't cook, and you're crying about all of the work you have to do that keeps you from going to the gym, guess what? You'll be fat. If you take some responsibility for yourself, hit the gym three times a week and cut back on McDonald's, you'll be fine. One other thing to consider: plastic surgery—because sit-ups just might take too long. Young chicks don't like fat guys. Don't ever forget that.

b. *Bald*—Tough one. In all likelihood, you're screwed. The good thing about it is that, at this age, you're expected not to have hair, and you might want to wear it as a badge of honor. You might even step up to the plate and shave it all off. It worked for Andre Agassi, and he bagged a supermodel and one of the greatest female athletes of all time.

c. *Broke*—Half. Let's think about that again—*half*. Wow, that's a tough concept. If you can give up half and not be broke, you're in pretty damn good shape. Most of us can't, so you'd better get ready to go back to work. Our advice to you on this one is pretty similar to the "fat" argument above. Stop whining, stop making excuses, just get your lazy ass into the office an hour earlier and leave an hour later. Make 10 percent more calls and you'll get 10 percent more sales. This is not rocket science.

d. *Single*—On this score, you should just thank God. The nattering shrew is out of your life, the kids probably live with her, and you can start peeing with the bathroom door open again. As long as you listened to us regarding the fat, bald, and broke part of your life, single life shouldn't be that bad. A skinny, hairy, rich guy shouldn't have much of a problem scoring some new tail relatively quickly. Good luck.

DON'T SCREW UP AGAIN—MARRY THE RICH CHICK THIS TIME

TIP #46: MARRY MONEY THE SECOND TIME AROUND.

As we've said throughout this book, asshole nirvana and reality can't always coexist. Even though your essential asshole-ness may guide you down one path, the world may not be too accommodating, and you might have to compromise your bankrupt morals. For example, in a perfect world, even when you're an old, fat, bald divorced guy, your bedroom would have a drive-thru window, and there'd always be another hot, twenty-seven-year-old marketing executive on the speaker ordering a Love Value-Pak. Chances are pretty good, though, that that's not happening to you now or ever.

We can accept the fact that some of you will want to get married again. That's cool. We'd still like you to be single and banging chicks, but we understand. The only thing we've got to tell you about this particular decision is not to screw it up this time, *marry the rich chick!* When you were young there were reasons not to marry a rich girl: she's high-maintenance, you'll never be as good as Daddy, yadda, yadda, yadda. All of those reasons are completely irrelevant now. You're both old, and you're getting married out of convenience, not the kind of puppy-dog love you remember when you were young, so other practical considerations will apply.

You think we're wrong? Take a look at this real-life example: there are currently two owners of professional hockey teams who have a persistent feud and spend an inordinate amount of their time fighting each other, both personally and in the press. Every quote that has ever been attributed to either guy reveals two different characteristics—(1) they are convinced that their shit smells like daffodils, and (2) they truly believe that they are the most supremely capable individuals who have ever walked the earth. Are they captains of industry? Real estate titans who made a fortune with smart buys? Hell no, they both married daughters of Sam Walton, the guy who created Wal-Mart, and now they have nothing to do but blow their wives' billions on ridiculous pettiness, like who gets to sign the star right wing out of Boston College. Do you think those guys are bummed that they married the biggest cash depositories since Fort Knox? Again, hell no—they're probably laughing their asses off in a luxury box while the beer chick blows them between periods.

Marry money! Marry money! Marry money! You don't have much time left anyway, so you might as well enjoy it to the fullest. Find yourself some dunce heiress to a sausage fortune and spend the rest of your days drinking froufrou margaritas on an island off Martinique. You'll be a whole lot happier than if you marry the broke chick with the good sense of humor.

OLD AGE—FINALLY, YOU CAN GET BLOWN BY A WOMAN WITH NO TEETH

Everything in life comes full circle. Whether it's the popularity of *The Brady Bunch* or hip-huggers, eventually all things that were cool before will be cool again. So it is with being an asshole. Remember about two hundred pages ago, when we talked about how great it is to be an infant asshole? Remember? You shit all the time and nobody cared, you puked on people and nobody cared. Well, guess what? When you're old, it's déjà vu all over again, because you can do damn near anything and get away with it.

When you're a twenty-year-old asshole, you're obnoxious. When you're a thirty-year-old asshole, you're overbearing. When you're a forty-year-old asshole, you're an asshole. But when you're a seventy-year-old asshole, you're lovable. You don't understand what people are saying, so you have your own conversation with the voices in your head and people think you're cute. You bitch constantly about the food, and everybody rushes around trying to get you the right flavor Pablum. Hell, you can even take a dump in your shorts and instead of taking you to a psychiatrist, your daughter will just run out to the supermarket for a couple of boxes of Depends.

And regarding chicks? Oh my God, can you have yourself a field day! Talk dirty to a twenty-year-old and she'll rub your jowls. Make some rude remark in the gym and the aerobics instructor will sit down with you for a cup of coffee. Although your plumbing probably stopped working long ago, and your chances of getting a young girl are about as good as you actually controlling your bowels, as an old man you finally get a chance to do all the nasty shit you always thought about. For example, if some young punk honks at you for driving too slow, just get out of your car and piss on his hood.

> TIP #47: ASSHOLES NEVER DIE, THEY JUST LEARN HOW TO COP A QUICK FEEL AND FART IN PUBLIC.

a. *You Can Still Have Sex*—You can get laid until the day you die! Let's start with Viagra. For senior citizens, Viagra is the greatest invention since the early-bird special. You can be locked down in an iron lung, or spend twenty-three hours a day in a wheelchair, but swallow a couple of the blue pills and you'll be sporting more wood than an Oregon lumber camp. Twenty minutes after your Viagra break, Long Dong Silver will no longer be just a description of the flatware you use to eat your porridge. After you've rediscovered the two-by-four in your pants for the first time in fifteen years, your real concern will no longer be whether or not you can get it up, but how you're going to revive your wife.

   That's actually another thing we should tell you—chicks continue to have a sex drive after their fifties, sixties, and seventies. Sure, you can't have them hanging from the chandelier anymore (unless you've got time to deal with another broken hip) but, amazingly, a majority of men and women who have passed the mandatory retirement age are still interested in having sex, and would indulge that interest more often if their partners didn't sleep so goddamn much. There are tons of places you can now go to pick up a little senior citizen trim. Bingo tournaments, funerals, all-you-can-eat buffets, and emergency rooms are great places to start. Grab some seventy-five-year-old chick's ass or pinch a grandma's boob. Who the hell cares? You've only got a couple of years left, and what else are you going to do, sit around and listen to your arteries harden?

b. *All Your Asshole Buddies Are Gone*—As you enter the twilight years, you run into the same problem that you had when you were about thirty—all of your asshole buddies are gone. Most of them went to that great fraternity in the sky. This, more than your advancing age, will bring about the demise of many of your asshole skills. It is very difficult to treat people with complete contempt when you've got no base camp of operations to work from and nobody to back you up. But, luckily, by now you're probably senile so after getting turned down by a woman you can go back to the corner and have a conversation with yourself to get motivated for the next one.

c. *Old Chicks Don't Listen to Your Shit*—Even as an old asshole, some things never change—chicks are still stupid. However, after decades of experience, they do learn a few things. One of the lessons is that when they're old they don't have to listen to your shit anymore. Think about it—how much pull do you think you'll have when you can count your teeth on one hand, when you need to take pills in order to get a hard-on, and when a night on the town means that you have a cup of tea in the living room after you've finished eating dinner at 4:30?

Face it, it's tough to be an asshole when you need her help to put on your hat, go to the bathroom, or find your false teeth. The good part about it is that she really doesn't have much to offer you anymore either, so it's a fair trade. Her boobs sag, she's in love with Pat Sajak, and every time she kisses you her beard scrapes your face raw. Yet, with all of these infirmities she still maintains her ability to speak.

You're just going to have to deal with the fact that, once you hit a certain age—say, around seventy—you and your wife are partners—*equal partners*—because you're both too pathetic to assert any dominance. We hope you listened to us when you were about thirty-five and got a wife who loves you, so she doesn't mind cleaning up after you and reminding your Alzheimer's-inflicted ass where you live. If you were cocky and waited till you were fifty to marry a Playboy Playmate, she left you ten years ago to go on tour with a rock band. Karma, baby. It always comes back around in the end.

TIP #48: RELISH YOUR ASSHOLE LIFESTYLE.

d. *Take Stock of Your Life, You Asshole*—We hate to tell you, but even the greatest assholes must die, and it's time to look back and see what you've accomplished. Wasn't it great being an asshole? You got to bang tons of hot chicks who would've laughed in your face if you were nice to them. You saved most of your money, because you refused to spend it on a bunch of whiny, spoiled bitches. Your friends stood up and applauded when you landed a woman who was twenty years your junior. You laughed at rejection, you scoffed at contempt.

How could you not love being an asshole? Now that it's all said and done, you can look back on your life and realize that you owned the entire fucking world. And you didn't have to kiss a lot of ass to do it. What more could a true asshole ask for?

EVERYTHING PORNOS WERE
AFRAID TO TEACH YOU
ABOUT SEX

If you're like most assholes, you probably flipped to this section immediately. We're proud of you, boy! Just keep in mind that, to use any of the knowledge gained in this section, you're going to have to read the rest of the book first. After all, unless your aunt is Heidi Fleiss, you need to learn how to talk to chicks before you can give them Arabian Goggles (don't ask, you'll find out soon enough).

Please understand that you need to take this section with a grain of salt. It is important to remember that every sexual encounter you have during your illustrious career *must be consensual.* That means you have to ask the girl if it's okay, and she has to say "yes." And she has to be conscious. There is never an excuse for taking a woman by force, or using any sort of violence.

That being said, don't get too discouraged. There are plenty of freaks out there who will beg you to slap their ass, pull their hair, or even take a nice healthy dump all over them. Once they give you the green light, it's your job to use and abuse them until they pass out from exhaustion.

But, before we get into the really hard-core action, you're going to need to learn the basics. So, here you go—everything you need to know, from setting the mood to the Crazy Fireman (again, don't ask). Enjoy, this is what you were born to do!

a. *Mood*—The environment that you set up for sex is nearly as important as the physical act itself. If you're about to make out with your girl and the sound of death metal or gangsta rap starts blaring out of your speakers, you're probably going to end up watching *SportsCenter* by yourself this evening. Women need to be seduced; in the twenty-first century, hitting them over the head with a stick or jumping them in the foyer of their sorority house is not going to get the job done. You've got to be an expert in creating an environment in which the woman can't help but sleep with you. This is not a difficult task, if you just follow a couple of simple rules:

1. *Music*—As mentioned above, songs like *Fuck tha' Police* won't do much for your woman's eagerness to jump in the sack. If she's older, you need soft, soothing, mellifluous music that makes your woman think you are a sensitive and caring man. Pop in some Luther Vandross and try not to puke. For younger chicks, the really slow stuff doesn't cut it. They want music that is going to make them feel sexy, and they want to hear it from men. Dave Matthews has been responsible for more men getting laid than the invention of alcohol. Bruce Springsteen is another favorite. Don't worry, when you're finished banging the piss out of her you can always go back to Metallica.

2. *Lighting*—If you leave the lights blazing, your woman thinks you're secretly videotaping her, which you probably are. More importantly, no matter how skinny she is, it's guaranteed that she thinks she's a fat pig. Accordingly, she will be leery of taking her clothes off if she believes you'll see the nine ounces she's gained since the last time you saw her. Turn the lights off and keep your hands away from the rolls on her stomach.

3. *Calm*—Guys can screw anywhere. You'd have sex in the middle of a two-hundred-person party provided that your penis is at least one-and-a-half inches longer than normal. Women can't deal with chaos—it reminds them of their brains. They like a calming atmosphere. They want to hear a babbling brook, the sound of birds chirping. They want to make sure nobody bursts in on them and sees how small their boobs are. That's really not too much to ask.

4. *Food*—Food is highly sexual. The way to a man's heart is through his stomach. It's pretty much the same for a woman, but, right on top of her heart are her boobs, so you can take a quick detour and end up there, too. With women, you just need to remember the two c's: *chocolate* and *cheese*. All women love cheese; but there's something even more special about chocolate. It's often been said that women prefer chocolate to sex. Given that men care about little else than a quick pull and spill, this could be entirely true. Eating chocolate actually releases endorphins that make woman feel more sexual. Plus, while she's eating she can't talk. Need we say more?

5. *Booze*—Who are we kidding? You wanna get laid? Get her drunk. You can skip all of the things we've listed above, provided that your woman has drained six to eight shots in the last hour.

b. *Foreplay*—Foreplay is eerily similar to the Pink Floyd song that says "*how can you have your pudding if you don't eat your meat?*" Unfortunately, foreplay is something that you are going to have to deal with. Chicks are going to absolutely demand it, and this is one of many times that you'll have to give in. Sure, we know that you're entirely satisfied with a quick pump and dump, but very few women can achieve orgasm through pure intercourse. Men are physical beasts, and anything that results in discharge satisfies their primal urges. Women are much more emotional, and need to be touched, rubbed, licked, caressed, and lied to before they can really get off. However, you should remember that, while you are going to have to engage in extensive foreplay at the beginning of the relationship, as it wears on, you will slowly digress into little more than rhesus monkeys who see each other, shove it in a couple of times, scream themselves silly, and then go back to eating bananas. That state is generally known as marriage.

c. *Oral*—Should oral sex be included in the sex section? Is it sex? Former President Bill Clinton certainly didn't think so, but he's been disbarred by half the states in the Union, so you have to question his logic. In our book (and this is our book), if you get your rocks off due to another person touching you, it's sex, case closed. Therefore, we need to have a little discussion about oral sex, so you don't end up gagging, choking, or otherwise pissing off the woman you're with.

1. *Swallowing*—The most fundamentally important step in oral sex. If your chick doesn't swallow, dump her. She could be a supermodel, Ph.D., stand-up comic with $500,000,000 in the bank, but if she doesn't swallow you must immediately send her packing. Being an asshole requires you to exert a certain dominion over your woman. If she thinks without your permission, makes up her own mind, or otherwise disregards what you say, you've got about two months before you're wearing her panties. When a woman swallows, it is the clearest indication that you are in charge and that, under normal circumstances, she must follow your rules. Refusing to do so indicates that, at some point in the relationship, she's going to try to turn the tables on you by telling you how fast to drive, where your kids can go to school, or if she will allow your friends to come over and watch football. Any of these statements is cause for divorce, and, accordingly, you should save yourself the hassle by ending it all right now.

2. *Giving her oral*—The jury is really split on giving her oral sex. On the one hand, many assholes truly enjoy going down on a woman, and just because you're in charge of the process with your tongue, as opposed to your penis, it does not automatically become wrong. Of course, you would only go down there if the *pussy is nearly tasteless, odorless, and clean*. On the other hand, the various and sundry characteristics of the vagina (e.g., the smell, the taste, the texture, etc.) make the thought of munching a little rug a terrifying experience for a lot of men. We really see the positives and negatives for both arguments, and for that type of situation we're going to give you our standard advice: we don't know what the hell to do, so figure it out on your own. If you want to treat her genitalia as if it's the sarcophagus at Chernobyl, we can't tell you that you're wrong. Conversely, should you desire to get your face sticky, that's great. Either way, we've included a checklist to ensure that you make it back alive:

   i. *The lawn is mowed*—An unkempt pussy is an unlicked pussy. Every asshole worth his salt should have his bitch shaved like the day she was born. Some might prefer a little runway, but if you're going down, it needs to be trimmed.

   ii. *The belly button test*—This is designed for smell. A perfectly clean pussy smells like nothing and tastes like nothing. Most have a little bit of flavor, but it shouldn't be overpowering. If you kiss down to her belly button and can smell it from there, kiss your way back up and bite off one of her nipples. She deserves it for hooking up with a guy when she stinks like that.[11]

   iii. *The first finger test*—As we said, the belly button test will only separate the truly rank women. If your girl passes that

[11] It's important to note that some chicks just do not have clean pussies, and there really isn't anything they can do about it. The only solution to this problem is to invoke a shower rule. Unless she's fresh out of the shower, she's shit out of luck.

test, then slide a finger into her flesh taco and take a few laps. After the floodgates have opened, secretly pull your finger up and inspect it. Number one is to make sure there is no blood on it. We're assholes, not vampires. And number two is to sniff it and see if the pussy is truly clean. Make sure you do this without her noticing; otherwise it can really piss a chick off. They are extremely sensitive about this subject.

iv. *The second finger test*—The second finger test is designed for texture. There is an extremely distinguishable difference between a clean, wet pussy, and a dirty, pasty pussy. You'll know when you feel it. Wet pussy is fine, it goes down smooth like a nice Coors Light. Pasty pussy is disgusting. It's like giving your dog a mouthful of peanut butter. It sticks to the roof and puddles up on the sides of your mouth. You'll taste it for a week, and every time you swallow, you'll start to gag. No amount of brushing or toothpaste will ever get rid of it.

d. *How to Eat Pussy*—Now that you know what to look for, it's important that you learn what to do. Now, you may think you already know, but unless a chick has specifically taught you, then you don't have a fucking clue, and you probably eat pussy like a high school kid. Once you find the clit, just start slapping that thing around with your tongue. Avoid the hole, every first-timer sticks his tongue in there, and it does nothing for the chick. Concentrate on the clit. That is the only guarantee with eating pussy, because, after that, every chick has her own weird little fetishes. Some of them like to be fingered while you eat, some want a fist up their ass, some want you to pinch their nipples and bite their ankles while kicking them in the kidney during orgasm. The point is, you're going to have to figure out all that stuff on an individual basis. All we know is that if you do nothing other than lick the clit, she will start twitching like you just shoved an electric rod up her ass. This is a good thing.

e. *Use Condoms*—It's the twenty-first century, and if you're not using them you probably won't live long enough to enjoy using all of the knowledge gained from this book. In addition to not dying, there are a couple other distinct advantages to the old rubber.

TIP #49: USE CONDOMS.

1. *You won't get anybody pregnant*—This is not brain surgery. Pregnant women have ruined the lives of every great asshole in history. Don't let it happen to you.

2. *It decreases your sensitivity, so you can last longer*—Skin on skin is a tough proposition for any man. Putting that layer in between you and her should increase your stamina at least two-fold.

f. *Fake an Orgasm*—Women have been using this ploy for years to trick us into thinking that we are sex gods, even when we can't make their legs shake. Well, now it's time to turn the tables with the help of Mr. Condom.

1. *The first go-around*—Don't *ever* fake the first orgasm. It's the best one, and it's really for you, and not for her anyway. Unless you've been dating for a while, women have grown to expect a pretty quick trigger on the first go-around. Besides, even if you did fake it, it would just make it that much faster, which would come off as truly pathetic.

2. *The second time*—This is where the magic happens. With your second hard-on, you can do some serious fucking. Flip

her around, tag it from different angles, and make sure that she at least fakes an orgasm. Right before you're going to launch your soldiers, fake a massive orgasm. Let out a roar and collapse on top of her. Then peel your fat ass out of bed and go flush the condom. Toss a little cold water on your hog to calm it down. By this point, 90 percent of men are done. Most women never expect a third round, so they are ready for sleep. Imagine her surprise when you cuddle up next to her and she feels your purple-headed warrior preparing for a third battle.

3. *Round three*—If you've given it enough time, this one will last even longer than second one. And the best part is, you can fake it again.

4. *The fourth and beyond*—By the time you've nailed her a third time, she already thinks that you are a sexual god. If you want to really drive the point home, you can fake number three and go for four, but you need to let her be your guide. Most women will dry up by then, and it will become painful. If you're not careful, she may never again want to be tormented by your insatiable cock. However, if you've got yourself a really horny slut you can fake orgasms until the sun comes up, because you won't be through pummeling her until you finally release that second shot.

g. *Deviance*—Once you've been having sex for a number of years, vanilla just isn't going to cut it anymore. And let us tell you, once you've been around the block a couple of times, oh my God, there is an entire Pandora's Box of deviance and sickness that will be thrust into your face . . . if you're lucky. The sexual insanity and perversion that you will find as you move about society is shocking, grotesque, disgusting, and a hell of a lot of fun if you do it right.

TIP #50: SEXUAL DEVIANCE IS ENTIRELY ACCEPTABLE.

Many of the things that happen far from the public eye are morally offensive and entirely degrading to women. Because you are an asshole, these are two qualities that you highly advocate, and therefore, you must become skilled in the arts of sexual misconduct. Here are the major topics you need to know about:

1. *Toys*—Dildos, cat-o'-nine-tails, fur handcuffs, vibrators, two-liter Coke bottles—there are so many toys available on the street these days, you'd almost have to be the Unabomber not to have stumbled across a sex store in the last month. And, regardless of what your chick says, she loves using them. Why? If you put a seven-inch black dildo in her hand she's going to work that thing so expertly that, in less than five minutes, she'll be doing backflips off of the bed.

2. *Threesomes*—Threesomes only count if it's two chicks and one guy. Any idiot can get his chick to agree to poke him and his good-looking buddy. Shoot, she's probably been waiting to blow your friend for as long as you've been dating her. But getting her to agree to mow some other chick's box—well now, that's a whole different story. You should find out a girl's willingness on this topic relatively early in the relationship—like the first date. If she is dead-set against hooking up with chicks, it is perfectly acceptable for you to leave her at the restaurant with twenty dollars in cab fare. If, on the other hand, she exhibits some semblance of intrigue, then you should immediately start pouring drinks down her throat and hit the nearest strip joint.

3. *Video*—Videotaping you and your chick can be an eye-opening experience, since you can, for the first time, really take a look at

what the two of you are doing in bed. There is probably nothing more sexually enticing than watching yourselves screw. Plus, you'll find out if either of you are getting fat.

h. *Positions*—There are three basic sexual positions: missionary, doggy-style, and her on top. These are kind of like the Moe, Larry, and Curly of sexual adventure: you know them, you feel comfortable with them, you could spend pretty much all day dealing with them. Anything after that falls into the category of "other," which we'll show you later on. But first, here are the basics:

1. *Missionary*—Missionary is the sexual status quo. It's the position espoused by all religious organizations, it's the one you most often see in less-than-X-rated movies, and it requires you to look at the woman you're in bed with. For all of these reasons, the asshole is staunchly anti-missionary. Sex should be used as an extreme expression of everything that is you—you're exposed, you're not constrained by what society tells you, and you're about to experience the height of human passion: the orgasm. Why in God's name would you want run-of-the-mill? Isn't it enough that you wear the same clothes as everybody else, and restrain your desire to punch people in the mouth because of societal mores? The missionary position should be considered nothing more than a four-second pit-stop on the way to some out-of-control, death-defying, weird positions. Run by it accordingly.

2. *Doggy-style*—Now, doggy-style is much more like it. You are in complete control, you don't have to look at her, so you're less likely to hold back during some particularly aggressive moves, and your woman is entirely, utterly helpless—just like you want her. Doggy-style also allows you to engage in some pretty strenuous ass-smacking and hair-pulling, two favorites in the

asshole's sexual bag of tricks. Most interesting about this particular position is that it is the favorite of the majority of women. This seems somewhat counterintuitive, because women have been screaming for years that they actually want to be in control. Well, guess what? Again, they're lying to you. Women want to be dominated—it's an evolutionary demand, and the only reason they would buck that trend is because tight-ass Gloria Allred,[12] the biggest bitch to ever strap on pumps, tells them they shouldn't. So, go ahead, have her get on her hands and knees; and if you're worried about leaving hand prints on her ass, don't stress about it—she'll be showing them off to her friends first thing tomorrow morning.

3. *Her on top*—Many assholes would think that getting her on top is a no-no because it allows her to be in semi-control. Wrong. This is actually the perfect position, because she thinks she's in control when, in reality, you are in charge of the entire process. Think about it: when she's on top, she's either on her knees or squatting, both of which are extremely unstable. By grabbing her ass or thrusting your hips just so, you can knock her off to the side, or damn near over the headboard. Plus, because she's in an awkward position she has to move gingerly, while you, lying on your back, can be drilling up and down like a jackhammer. This is just another situation where you can pretend as if you're letting the woman have some semblance of authority, when in the back of your mind you know that a quick smack on her ass, or a tug on her boobs, and you're right back on top.

4. *Everything else*—The range of other positions and activities in bed is so vast, if we tried to describe them in detail this little book would turn into a three-volume set. So, we've compiled a

---

[12] In case you don't know, Gloria Allred is probably the most famous women's rights attorney in the world and Satan's purported fuck toy.

list of sixty-nine (get it? *Sixty-nine?* Huh, huh? Sorry, sometimes we're dorks, too) of the most demented, deviant, dangerous, and degrading sexual acts of all time. It's everything an asshole could want, and more. Just continue reading and get ready to be shocked, disgusted, morally outraged, and altogether prepared for your next conquest.

SIXTY-NINE INSANELY DEVIANT SEX ACTS

Disclaimer: The following sexual positions are not real; they are just something we made up when we couldn't figure out how to finish the book. You should not try them at home as they may cause injury, disease, or even death. Then again, they may also cause your woman to worship you like a god, drop to her knees at the mere sight of your bulging penis, or spend the rest of her existence begging you to give her just five more minutes of sexual euphoria. The choice is yours.

1. THE ALTAR BOY: While standing up, have a chick get down on her knees and try to swallow your hog. While she's sucking away, use your fingers to part her hair down the middle and start reciting scripture.

2. ANGRY DRAGON: Immediately after dropping your load inside a girl's mouth, smack the back of her head until the "stuff" comes out of her nose. With a vicious look in her eyes and dribble out of her nostrils, she'll look like an angry dragon.

3. ARABIAN GOGGLES: While she's got her tongue in your ass, you place your testicles over her eye sockets. This is difficult logistically, but can be accomplished if you practice a bit.

4. **BLOCKING THE BOX:** If you and a buddy are tag-teaming some sorority chick, get her from behind while he's up front. In an entirely selfish move, release your seed so that he is prevented from using that input after you're done. (Aka: Access Denied Error, Road Closed Due to Bad Conditions.)

5. **BOHEMIAN SNAP:** Once you've got her in the "six pack" (fingers in her box and your thumb in her butt) try to snap your fingers together while quickly pulling them out of her. The pressure will torture the thin membrane in between her two holes, forcing her to scream out like an angry Bohemian.

6. **THE BOOMERANG:** After letting go in a girl's mouth, she will act as if she's going to tongue your ass but, to your surprise, she spits it right inside you.

7. **BLUMPKIN:** This requires the services of a truly classless whore. The blumpkin consists of her blowing you while you're taking a heinous dump.

8. **BROWN NECKTIE:** While going backside on some girl, rather than letting go of your load, you pull it out and throw it between her boobs, leaving a disgusting brown streak.

9. **THE BRUSH-BACK PITCH:** When some chick is blowing you, scream "*batter up!*" and then quickly pull out your pickle and dump it in her ear.

10. **BUCKING BRONCO:** While going doggy-style, you grab her tits or hips as tightly as possible and call her a "no-good whore." She will jump up and start running around the room, giving you the feeling of riding a bronco, as she tries to buck you off.

11. **CHEESE GRATER:** A blowjob from a girl with braces.

12. **CRAZY FIREMAN:** Seconds before you erupt, light her pubes on fire and put it out with your ejaculate. Also known as the "flaming amazon."

13. DAISY CHAIN: Partner A is giving oral to partner B who is giving oral to partner C, and so on, until the final person is giving oral right back to partner A.

14. DEAD-HORSING: Wait until your girlfriend has passed out drunk, and then ravage her like a prison inmate.

15. THE DOUBLE-TAKE: When you are having anal sex, but it's so easy that you keep looking down because you can't believe it's not the other orifice. Also known as the "are you kidding me?"

16. DIRTY SANCHEZ: While having sex, you throw your finger in a girl's butt, pull it out, and wipe it across her upper lip, giving her a shit mustache.

17. DOGS-IN-A-BATHTUB: Putting both of your testicles into a girls butt. It is more difficult than trying to keep dogs in a bathtub.

18. DONKEY PUNCH: While in the doggy-style position, right before you cum, pull out and insert it in her butt while punching her in the back of the head. If she passes out, the anal constriction can be absolutely heavenly.

19. DUTCH OVEN: When a chick is going down on you, rip a truly hideous fart and pull the covers over her head.

20. FLYING CAMEL: While in a standard missionary position, balance yourself on her body without using your arms to prop you up. Then, flap your arms and let out a long, banshee-like howl.

21. FISH EYE: Put a finger in her butt and wait for her to turn around to see what the hell is going on.

22. FISHHOOK: Once you put your finger in her butt, you pull it back towards her vagina.

23. FOUNTAIN OF YOU: While sitting on her chest, masturbate like a madman, building up pressure to let it go all over her torso.

24. **FUR BALL**: When giving a girl oral, you get enough hair caught in your throat that you think it's a fur ball.

25. **THE GAME OF SMILES**: Several guys sit around a table while a woman gives random blowjobs underneath. Anyone who smiles must buy beers.

26. **GAYLORD PERRY**: Putting a minimum of three knuckles in your woman's love spot.

27. **GLASS-BOTTOM BOAT**: Wrapping your partner in Saran Wrap and taking a dump all over her.

28. **THE HIGH DIVE**: Pulling your pickle all the way out of her and then, in one motion, bringing it back home.

29. **THE HINDENBURG**: If a girl is so bad at oral sex that you're forced to cry "Oh! The humanity!"

30. **THE HOOVER**: While in the doggy-style position, tie her arms, lift her up at the hips, and run around the room with her face pushing across the carpet.

31. **HOTDOG IN A HALLWAY**: If your woman's thing is so wide that you can barely feel your penis going in there. Also knows as "fucking an open window."

32. **HOT LUNCH, OR CLEVELAND STEAMER**: While getting a blowjob, you drop a load on your partner's chest.

33. **HOUDINI**: While in the doggy-style position, pretend you just let go, then pull out and, as she turns around, unload on her front side instead.

34. **THE INDIAN COCK BURN**: When a girl grabs your boy and twists it as if she were trying to start a fire without a match.

35. **THE JEDI MIND TRICK**: When having sex, you repeatedly shout "I'm *not* fucking you, I'm *not* fucking you."

36. **JELLY DOUGHNUT**: When a woman is giving you head, right before you blow your load you punch her in the nose and cum on her face.

37. JUMPING THE CURB: While throwing it to your lady doggy-style, get going with long, fast strokes, and pull all the way out during a stroke and replant yourself in her ass instead of her box. If she complains, you can say it was an accident! (Also known as "The Sneaky Pete.")

38. THE LOST SOLDIER: After unloading, carefully slide your dick out of the condom, while still leaving it inside her.

39. MANGINA: The act of tucking your limp penis behind and in between your legs, thus imitating a woman's genitalia. Also know as the "dussy" or the "tuck." When you turn around and bend over, your cock and balls will resemble a fruit basket.

40. MANHATTAN CHILI-DOG: Take a dump on her chest and then shove your pickle between her boobs.

41. THE MENTHOLATUM: The act of getting head from a woman who, just moments earlier, ate numerous cough drops. This will ensure a pleasurable, tingly feeling on your penis.

42. NEW YORK-STYLE TACO: When you go down on a girl, you boot on her box. Happy trails.

43. ON THE ROCKS: A great party favorite accomplished by dunking your ball sac into someone's drink after he's left the room. When the person returns, enjoy the sight of him drinking your scrotal sweat. Enjoy extra laughs if you leave a nice pube in there sticking up like a tacky drink umbrella.

44. PEARL NECKLACE: Well known. Whenever you cum on the neck or cleavage area of a girl, it takes on the look of beautiful jewelry.

45. PINK GLOVE: This frequently happens during sex when a girl is not wet enough. When you pull out to give her the money shot, the inside of her twat sticks to your hog. Thus, the pink glove.

46. STINKY PINKY: When banging her from behind, stick your pinky in her ass, then reach around and hook it into her nose.

47. **RAM:** When you're attacking from behind, start ramming her head against the wall in a rhythmic motion. The resistance of the wall should allow for deeper penetration. Very handy for those lulls in penile sensitivity.

48. **RAY-BANS:** Put your testicles over her eye sockets while getting head. (Picture it: ass on forehead.) It may be anatomically impossible, but it is definitely worth a try.

49. **REAR ADMIRAL:** An absolute blast. When getting a chick from behind (with both partners standing), bend her over and don't let her grab onto anything for support. Then, drive your hips into her backside so that you end up pushing her forward. The goal is to push her into a wall or table. It's almost as much fun to have her trip and hit the floor face-first. You become an admiral when you can push her around the room without crashing into anything.

50. **RIM JOB:** Another name for Tossing Salad (see #60). The chick tries to lick your heart by entering through your pucker.

51. **ROAD RAGE:** While getting a blowjob in the car, take a hard left, open the passenger door, and laugh as she falls out the other side.

52. **SCREWNICORN:** When a dyke puts a dildo on her forehead and goes at her partner.

53. **70, 71, OR 72:** A 69 with one, two, or three fingers inserted into the anus.

54. **SHOP-VAC:** When a talented trollop stuffs your entire package (balls and all) into her mouth and blows you with amazing suction power.

55. **THE SIX-PACK:** Using the same hand, slide a finger or two in both of her holes. Once you've got a good grip, try to lift her up like you're holding a six-pack.

56. **68:** Just like the 69, except she blows you and you owe her one.

57. SKIING: While facing in the same direction, a girl gets between two guys and jerks them both off, thus imitating some hardcore cross-country action.

58. SNOWMOBILE: Always a blast. When nailing a girl on all fours, sweep out her arms so she falls on her face.

59. THE STRANGER: Sit on your hand until it falls asleep, and then jerk off. It elicits the feeling of a hand job from someone else.

60. TOSSING SALAD: Another prison act, where one person is forced to basically chow asshole with the help of whatever condiments are available, i.e., Jell-O, olive oil, syrup, etc.

61. THE TRIFECTA: Screwing three women in the same night, without any of them knowing about the others. Showering in between is strictly forbidden.

62. TROMBONE: When a girl jerks you off while simultaneously giving you a rim job. It looks like she's playing a trombone.

63. TUNA MELT: You're down on a chick and discover that it happens to be that time of the month. By no means do you stop. Also known as "getting your red wings," because the blood will leave trails on your face.

64. THE TUPPERWARE PARTY: You and two of your buddies triple-team your favorite whore. One puts his penis in her mouth, another in her vagina, and the third in her anus. So named because she is sealed air-tight.

65. WAKE-UP CALL: Waking up in the middle of the night with the hard-on of your life. You then turn to your fast-asleep partner and dry hump her ass into oblivion. The clincher to performing a wake-up call is to act like nothing of the sort happened in the morning. "Sweetheart, what's that on your back?"

66. THE WALRUS: After cumming inside a girl's mouth, you pinch the center of her two lips together and hold her nose. This

will force the cum to dribble out of the sides of her mouth, resembling the tusks of a walrus.

67. WESTERN GRIP: When jerking off, turn your hand around, so that your thumb is facing towards you. It is the same grip that rodeo folks use.

68. THE WOODY WOODPECKER: When a girl is sucking on your balls (teabagging), tap the head of your cock on her forehead and ask, "Who's your daddy?"

69. ZOMBIE MASK: While getting head, wait until you're about to erupt and then ask your chick to look up so you can see her pretty face. Then pull out and shoot your load in her eyes. She'll be temporarily blinded and will stumble around the room like a zombie.

Karl Marks was born and raised in Olney, Maryland. When he was 18 years old, he left for Los Angeles seeking a better life, a suntan, and a little wife to call his own. All he found was unemployment, smog, and hundreds of starving actresses who will put out for a five-course meal. He is now a regular on the West Coast comedy circuit, headlining clubs such as the Improv, the Icehouse, and the Friars Club. Using the stage as his soapbox, he successfully offends thousands of bitter women to the raucous applause of drunken men. His mother and three sisters should be proud.

Dan Indante is a bitter, vindictive attorney. Living in Los Angeles, California, he has talked to virtually every dim-witted, silicone-implanted blonde bimbo who has ever lived, despite the fact that not one of them could complete a sentence without hurting themselves. Rather than climb into a tower and take out every person unlucky enough to be born with breasts, Dan channeled his rage and fury into writing this book. He continues to practice law under an assumed name in the hopes that no feminist organization will ever find out his home address.